OUTDOORLIFE
THE ULTIMATE
SHOOTING SKILLS
MANUAL

OUTDOOR LIFE

THE ULTIMATE SHOOTING SKILLS MANUAL

JOHN B. SNOW
WITH CHRIS CHRISTIAN

weldon**owen**

CONTENTS

AR RIFLE

SHOTGUN

A NOTE FROM THE EDITOR: LEARN FROM THE EXPERTS

Shooting is magic. Thumb an enchanted metal capsule in a special tube, close the action, aim downrange, and pull the trigger. The smoke and fire—call it brimstone, if you will—and loud boom promote this idea of sorcery, but surely the most compelling detail of all is the tiny hole in your distant target, exactly where you said it would be. Bewitching.

Shooting is fun. There are few things as satisfying as consistently busting clay targets with a shotgun or punching tight groups of bullet holes in a distant bullseye target. It's even more fun to shoot with a friend, challenging and encouraging each other with each volley, and surprising each other with your skills and the capabilities of your gear.

Shooting is sport. The top competitive shooters are world-class athletes, with the hand-eye coordination of fighter pilots and bodies that are honed for both endurance and strength. Top-flight Olympic trap shooters make breaking 100 straight targets look easy. Try it yourself, and you'll be humbled by the levels of concentration and physical strength required.

Shooting is intricate. Even simple firearms are marvels of engineering, innovation, and evolution. In order to safely and consistently deliver a payload downrange, a gun must contain a violent detonation, channel the bullet or shotshell pellets to a precise aiming point, and then repeat the action, sometimes in very short order.

Shooting is complicated. Despite what you may hear on the news or read in a paper, shooters are overwhelmingly safe, responsible, and respectful, Still, guns are awesome machines, capable of intense destruction—but also immaculate protection. They should be used wisely, discretely, and with utmost restraint and respect.

All these perspectives are contained in this book, and there are no better guides to the world of shooting than its authors, John B. Snow and Chris Christian. A competitive shooter and instructor in shotgun and handgun skills, Chris is one of the most respected gun writers in the country, and he has written for most of the leading firearms publications. John is the Shooting Editor of *Outdoor Life* magazine, a job that requires him to be as conversant in the latest trends in high-performance shotguns as in concealable semiautomatic pistols and historic bolt-action rifles—plus long-range precision rifles, MSRs (modern sporting rifles), and hunting firearms of every type.

John's knowledge of guns is amplified and informed by his field skills. He's a frequent competitor at 3-Gun and precision-shooting events, teaches at various firearms facilities, and is a sought-after advisor on gear from suppressors to precision optics to sporting-clays shotguns.

John is also a hunter. He knows firsthand how elk rifles should perform in subzero conditions, how waterfowl shotguns should swing in a duck blind, how the perfect hog gun should be configured, and how to score a double on crossing doves.

In short, John is a real-world expert, a shooter who has poured into this book his years of experience in the field, the gun range, and the laboratory. Read it and learn. But also enjoy, because the greatest gift of guns is an enduring sense of magic. And fun.

—Andrew McKean
Editor-in-Chief
Outdoor Life magazine

A NOTE FROM THE AUTHOR: THE ART & SCIENCE OF SHOOTING

The art and allure of shooting is simple. The idea is that by doing something *here* (aiming and pulling a trigger), a person controls what happens out *there* (hitting a target). The ability to have an instant and tangible effect on the environment beyond our immediate reach must have thrilled our prehistoric ancestors who first hurled a stick or stone at something and connected. That same jolt of satisfaction courses through us today when we bust clay targets with a shotgun or ring steel plates with a pistol.

Though the thrill of shooting is encoded in our DNA, the act of shooting and the gear we use is ever evolving. And that is the point of this book. Firearms technology and shooting techniques that were on the leading edge 10 years ago, and in some cases just 5 years ago, have in many instances been refined, modified significantly, or scrapped altogether.

The chapters that follow serve as a showcase for the most current shooting equipment and shooting methods in use today. Chris Christian, a frequent contributor to *Outdoor Life,* did most of the work on the handgun and shotgun chapters, while I took the lead on chapters covering precision rifle and carbines. The emphasis here on what's new in shooting isn't to imply that traditional technique is obsolete. The fundamentals of marksmanship—sight alignment, breath control, trigger press and follow-through—are as relevant today as ever. What we've done is present the best of the old techniques and gear, and provide some useful context concerning the history of firearms, while also highlighting state-of-the-art skills and technology.

This was a pretty broad task to try to accomplish. The world of shooting covers a lot of ground but I think that anyone who is interested in firearms, their development, and how to wield them correctly will find much here to motivate them to get out and pull some triggers. To this end, every chapter includes practical, well-illustrated drills and lists the top instructional schools in the country in different shooting disciplines.

This is a good time to be a shooter. For one thing, we are entering a golden age of ballistic performance that our forefathers couldn't have imagined. Our rifles are better, our bullets fly truer, our powder is more accurate, our shot shells hit harder, our optics are more precise. Thanks to advances in manufacturing, every shooter can experience these benefits—even those on a tight budget.

The other reason to be bullish on the future of the shooting sports has nothing to do with the quality of our equipment, impressive though it may be. The essential, underlying enjoyment that people experience while shooting remains undiminished, and that right there the reason that shooting will continue to flourish.

Show someone who has never used a firearm before the proper way to handle it and have them knock a target off a fence post with a BB gun and they will instantly get it. Don't believe me? Try it yourself. And prepare to welcome a new shooter to the club.

—John B. Snow
Shooting Editor
Outdoor Life magazine

THE EVOLUTION OF THE MODERN SHOOTER

THE START OF RECREATIONAL SHOOTING

The moment that two people took turns trying to hit a target downrange with a firearm marked the beginning of recreational shooting. From that most basic start, which probably happened in the 1400s before the principal of rifling was even discovered, the shooting sports evolved.

Today's sportsmen enjoy a breadth of shooting activities that would have been unimaginable to those who first wielded those ancient hand cannons.

Our traditional target sports are formal affairs. Riflemen placed at fixed shooting positions attempt to hit targets from standing, sitting, kneeling and prone positions. Competitive air gun shooters do this at 5 meters, while Palma and F-Class shooters go out to 1,000 yards.

Shotgunners, looking to mimic bird hunting, developed the sports of skeet and trap. The first targets used in England as early as 1750 were live birds. In the 1860s, glass balls were substituted for live birds. Then, in the 1880s, clay targets, similar to what are used today, were invented.

Like our oldest rifle sports, these shotgunning disciplines take place according to rigid rules that dictate the exact dimensions of the field, the size and speed of the targets, and the number of targets. Modern trap dates to the early 1900s and skeet from the 1920s.

This same formality can be found in the handgun target sports like bullseye and Olympic pistol.

THE RISE OF ACTION SHOOTING

Recreational shooting has taken an interesting turn in the last few decades. Action shooting sports that are scored based on the time it takes a shooter to complete a stage, with penalties added for poor shooting, have grown in popularity. The winners in these events are the shooters with the lowest total time for the match—quite different from the original shooting sports, which were judged purely on marksmanship.

Pistol shooters led the way with this trend. The International Practical Shooting Confederation was founded in 1976 and was itself an offshoot of sports like the quick-draw competitions that dated back to the 1950s.

This concept took hold and blossomed into several organizations that host matches today. The emphasis on "practical" shooting as a way to hone self-defense skills has guided the structure of many of these sports, though many of the stages one sees are all about having

fun pulling the trigger and have only the loosest relevance to any possible defensive scenario. There are no formal course layouts for these sports, with the exception of the Steel Challenge. The layouts are limited only by the imagination of the people running the match and the physical constraints of the shooting area.

Shotgunners have also let their hair down. Like action handgunning, sporting clays is a sport where course designers have fun mixing up traps, targets and presentations, creating a much more fluid experience than skeet or trap offer.

The equivalent to this on the rifle side is the advent of sniper competitions, which require shooters to make precision shots under challenging and dynamic conditions. It's one thing to hit a target at 600 yards. It's another to do it while balancing on a swaying piece of plywood or from a moving vehicle or after completing a 3-mile run—but that's what makes sniper competition unique.

THE CHALLENGE OF 3-GUN

Looking back, the sport of 3-gun seems inevitable. It takes the run-and-gun spirit of action pistol shooting and adds shotgun and AR-style rifles into the mix. A typical stage requires shooters to transition among the three types of firearms while engaging multiple targets with each along the way. The sport is fast, fun, sometimes chaotic, and is a great test of the shooter's gear and of that person's ability to problem solve under pressure while maintaining their focus.

3-gun is sport where Murphy's rule reigns supreme. If something can go wrong, it will. And the best shooters learn how to cope with those SNAFUs while taking out targets at blazing speed.

A BRIEF HISTORY OF FIREARMS

The story of how firearms developed traces its roots to the Han dynasty in the second century AD when a man known as Wei Boyang wrote about the mixture of three elements that form the basis of gunpowder. The rest, as they say, is history.

12TH–13TH CENTURY Examples of "fire lances," made first of bamboo and later of steel, appear in accounts of battles during 1132 and on silk prints from 1260. These contraptions were used to shoot shrapnel toward enemies in times of war and must have been nearly as terrifying to the men employing them as for the men they were shooting at.

1300S The development of cannons and firearms accelerates rapidly around the world as enterprising tinkerers learned to build stronger devices to contain and direct the explosive force of gunpowder and, in turn, concoct more potent mixtures of gunpowder. The hand cannons of this time were crude—merely a metal tube with a small jutting handle.

1400S Matchlock rifles are invented during this time and become the dominant firearm for the next 200 years. The history of firearms of this period focuses on their use in warfare, but these were doubtless used in hunting and competition; thus, the recreational shooter and gun hunter were born.

1500S Rifling is introduced, which dramatically increases projectile accuracy by imparting spin to stabilize it in flight. Ornate wheellocks are also created, but due to their expense do not replace matchlock firearms. Examples of beautifully crafted firearms belonging to royalty, who no doubt shot them for pleasure, abound.

1600S With the invention of the flintlock rifle, guns become more common and effective. By the late 1600s, flintlocks are the dominant arm of European and American armies, and remain so until the 1840s when new technologies, such as self-contained cartridges and breech loading mechanisms, started to appear.

1700S One of the most elegant arms of all time—the Kentucky long rifle—is developed. This gun, also known as the Pennsylvania long rifle, fired a small caliber lead ball that was ideal for harvesting small game on the American Frontier, and was a formidable form of personal protection as well.

1800S This era sees an explosion in firearms technology and applications: the first sporting shotguns, Samuel Colt's first mass-produced revolvers, the lever action Spencer repeating rifle, the first self-contained cartridges, and more. John Browning gave us many of his enduring designs. Firearms become more

Wheellock Pistol

Colt Navy 1851 Revolver

Mauser M98

Steyr AUG

specialized based on their purpose. Long range target rifles, small pocket pistols, hunting shotguns, and the machine gun were all products of the 1800s.

LATE 1800S The dual developments of smokeless powder and Paul Mauser's bolt-action rifle have a profound impact on both warfare and the future of hunting. Using lighter kicking cartridges that deliver small projectiles at previously unimaginable speeds, shooters of all stripes become more deadly and effective.

EARLY 1900S Improved manufacturing processes, and an increased emphasis on volume instead of individual craftsmanship, change the nature of the industry.

 Costs drop and a flood of surplus military rifles ushers in the era of cheap, affordable firearms. Coupled with the invention of the car and an expanding road system, the number of hunters and sportsmen in America flourishes.

MID TO LATE 1900S Guns formerly made exclusively of wood and steel incorporate synthetic materials like plastic and fiberglass into their construction. Designs like the M16, Steyr AUG and Glock 17 become mainstream. The specialization of firearms during this

period continues to the point where every shooting discipline and type of hunting has a preferred— sometimes required—gun to go with it.

2000 Laser rangefinders and ballistic calculators that factor in real world environmental conditions help shooters make previously impossible shots.
The rise in action shooting sports has been the most notable trend, where dynamic competitions that involve moving, shooting, and problem solving on the fly have grown in popularity. Hunting arms are tougher and more durable thanks to finishes that resist harsh abuse and corrosive environments.

WHAT'S NEXT? Despite these advances, shooters tend to be a very traditional group. Just take a look at Cowboy Action shooters who are happy to wield the guns of the Old West. Some advances, like replacing mechanical triggers with electronic ones, make sense from an engineering standpoint, but have been rejected by the shooting public. We will doubtless see more electronics incorporated into our shooting disciplines, however. Optics will become more advanced and capable, new generations of ammunition delivering more speed and accuracy will be rolled out, and firearms that work better under ever harsher conditions will be invented.

M1 Garand

XS1 Precision Guided
Firearm

RIFLE

SHOOTING AT LONG RANGE HAS A MAGIC TO IT.

You pull the trigger, initiating a violent explosion contained within the steel between your hands, and somehow guide a small piece of pointed copper and lead to a target that is barely visible to the naked eye.

For a rifleman, the splash and shockwave of the impact seen through the scope and the sound of the metallic "thwock" that rolls back toward the shooting line is nirvana.

But those hits don't happen by accident. They require an ability to judge the wind, correct for range and atmospheric conditions, settle your breath, acquire a perfect sight picture, and press the trigger just right. These skills come only through practice.

Honing them is well worth it, whether you're a competitive shooter, a hunter, or a casual plinker. The information in this chapter will get your started.

On the pages that follow, we go over what equipment to get, how to set it up the right way, how to squeeze the most accuracy from it, and how to put it to use in practical field settings. We cover everything from how to run a rifle fast at point-blank range to shooting accurately beyond 1,000 yards.

The goal here is to get off the bench and into the field. The measure of a true rifleman is not how he performs shooting off sandbags under picture-perfect conditions, but rather his ability to make a good shot when the wind is howling, the rifle is braced against an improvised rest, and the crosshairs are dancing around the target. Getting a hit under those circumstances is what the magic of a precision rifle is all about.

001 TURN TO THE VERSATILE RIFLE

Given the choice of one type of firearm to carry, I'll opt for a rifle without hesitation. In the hands of a properly trained marksman, there is no firearms-related task—other than shooting targets on the wing—that a rifle cannot handle. For personal protection, hunting, competition, general recreation, and introducing people to the shooting sports, rifles have no peer.

HUNTING For any huntable creature on earth, from the smallest ground squirrel to the nastiest charging Cape buffalo, there is a rifle for the job. Hunting rifles come in a dizzying array of configurations. There are the petite and delicate .17-caliber rimfires at one end of the spectrum and the heavy, intimidating safari rifles at the other. In between these are all of the bolt-actions, semiautos, lever guns, and single-shots that are used to bring elk, deer, antelope, and other game to the table.

COMPETITION The rifles that are used in competition are specialized tools with many features and modifications designed to perfect them for their particular sport. Biathlon rifles are light, accurate, and have covers that flip out of the way to protect them from snow. Benchrest rifles have heavy barrels, feather-light stocks, and triggers that trip at the lightest touch. Whether the target is up close or out past 1,000 yards, all are designed to cluster bullets in tiny holes downrange.

PERSONAL PROTECTION Carbine-size rifles are ideal for personal protection. These rifles will usually measure around 36 inches or so from one end to the other and come in semiauto, bolt, and lever actions. The cartridges they use are generally mild, somewhere between a .223 and a .308. With sights that allow for rapid, up-close shooting, these formidable tools are an excellent option for defending your home and loved ones.

LAW ENFORCEMENT Long guns aren't as commonly seen in the hands of police officers as are handguns, shotguns, and AR-style rifles, but they still serve a vital role in law enforcement circles. Police snipers, usually attached to SWAT units, are called in on hostage-taking incidents and other scenarios where a precision shot might be needed in a split-second to save a life. Police marksmen specialize in pinpoint bullet placement at distances within 100 yards.

SURVIVAL Any rifle that helps someone out in a jam is by definition a "survival" gun, but there are certain rifles built specifically for this purpose. These can be a big-bore lever gun that a woodsman carries in bear country, the takedown .22 that a bush pilot stores in the cockpit of his plane, or a general-purpose bolt-action scout rifle, typically chambered in .308, that is meant to handle any contingency that might come up.

MILITARY A well-trained soldier with an accurate rifle is a potent weapon in any conflict. A sniper can target high-value individual targets, stop the advance of a large fighting force in its tracks, and provide covering fire and security to ground troops maneuvering through hostile environments. Sniper rifles must be able to withstand abuse and hardship, be portable enough to transport over difficult terrain, and deliver excellent accuracy in the chaos of combat.

002 GET TO KNOW THE PRECISION RIFLE

The defining characteristic of a precision rifles is the premium that it places on accuracy. Compare them to the regular sporter rifles commonly used for hunting or casual shooting, and you'll find that precision rifles are built to higher standards, using different components that are usually beefier and of better quality. They are engineered to be shot from solid rests, using either bipods that can be attached to the stock or some type of fixed support.

The optics mounted on them are also more advanced, with higher levels of magnification, specialized reticles, and more types of external adjustments. Some precision rifles are for military and law enforcement use, while others are for various types of target games. Another recent trend is the growing use of these rifles for hunting.

Here are a few things to look for when assessing a precision rifle.

Ⓐ BARREL Heavy barrels are stiffer and take longer to heat up, both of which can improve accuracy.

B MUZZLE BRAKE Compensators help mitigate recoil and allow the shooter to spot hits and misses downrange.

C BIPOD A good bipod gives the rifle support, even on uneven ground. Some bipods swivel and pivot for shots on moving targets.

D SCOPE High-magnification scopes with external elevation and windage controls are used to fine-tune the point of impact for difficult shots.

E STOCK Stocks on precision rifles tend to be heavier and stiffer than on regular rifles. Special techniques are used to make a strong and secure fit between the stock and the action.

F GRIP The vertical grip gives the shooter better trigger control.

G CHEEK PIECE Adjustable components on stocks allow the shooter to fit the rifle to his or her precise dimensions.

003 UNDERSTAND MAXIMUM EFFECTIVE RANGE

Frank Galli, a former United States Marine Corps sniper who has extensive experience with long-range shooting, emphasizes that every cartridge has its own maximum effective range, which can be thought of as the point at which a bullet slows down from supersonic to subsonic velocities. During this transition, when the bullet is going transonic, it will destabilize, losing its accuracy and making hits a matter of luck rather than skill.

004 CHOOSE YOUR BULLETS

Selecting the correct bullet for your caliber can be daunting. Fortunately, anyone with Internet can use the JBM Ballistic Calculator to figure out which bullet is best. The rule of thumb is to use the heaviest bullet at the fastest speed possible. Remember that the maker's listed ballistic coefficient (BC) for a specific bullet is tied to the highest possible muzzle velocity that the bullet

CALIBER	BULLET	RANGE (YD)	0	200	400
		MV (FPS)			
.223 Rem.	Berger 62-gr.	3,020	-2/0	-2.8/4.4	-28.4/19.8
.223 Rem.	Berger 77-gr.	2,720	-2/0	-3.6/3.7	-32.5/16.2
.243 Win.	Hrn. 105-Amax	3,000	-2/0	-2.4/2.5	-23.2/10.7
6mm Creedmoor	Ber. 105-gr. Hybrid	3,130	-2/0	-2.0/2.0	-19.9/8.7
6.5 Creedmoor	Hornady 120-gr. A-Max	3,020	-2/0	-2.4/2.7	-23.4/11.5
6.5 Creedmoor	Hornady 140-gr. A-Max	2,820	-2/0	-2.9/2.3	-26.1/9.8
7mm WSM	Sierra 175-gr. Matchking	2,900	-2/0	-2.6/2.1	-24.0/9.0
7mm WSM	Berger 180-gr. Match VLD	3,050	-2/0	-2.1/1.8	-20.5/7.5
.308 Win.	Sierra 168-gr. BTHP	2,750	-2/0	-3.3/3.1	-30.0/13.7
.308 Win.	Sierra 175-gr. BTHP	2,650	-2/0	-3.7/3.0	-32.0/13.0
.300 Win. Mag	Berger 185-gr. Match	2,700	-2/0	-3.4/2.5	-29.2/10.5
.338 Lapua Mag.	Scenar 250-gr.	2,950	-2/0	-2.4/1.9	-22.5/8.1
.338 Lapua Mag.	Hrn. 285-gr. A-Max	2,850	-2/0	-2.7/1.8	-24.2/7.7
.338 Lapua Mag.	Scenar 300-gr.	2,800	-2/0	-2.9/1.8	-25.1/7.6

can be pushed. If you cannot push a particular bullet with enough speed from the very start, you will not be able to take advantage of the high BC being advertised. When that happens, you are better off stepping down in bullet weight to bring up the muzzle velocity. A great example of this would be with .30 caliber bullets. While a 230-grain Berger has a super BC, you cannot push it fast enough out of your 24-inch .308 Winchester to take advantage of that number. Put that same bullet in a .300 Norma Magnum and watch the magic happen.

005 GO BEYOND THE BULLET

Another great thing about modern precision-rifle shooting is that we have better barrels and powders, which can help you take advantage of newest bullets out there. It used to be that Galli would recommend a 175-grain SMK out of a .308, but with a powder like Alliant's 2000MR, you can push the 185-grain Berger Juggernaut at speeds to take advantage of the added weight and higher BC.

006 CHART YOUR RANGE

The moment your bullet leaves the barrel, gravity, air friction, and even its own spin affect how far it will go and how it will deviate from true. This chart gives a sense of what the maximum effective range is for a number of calibers and long-range bullets, assuming a calm environment. The goal should be for the bullet to be going faster than 1,200 fps at the desired target range. If the transition to subsonic is around 1,120 fps, you'll see the max effective ranges for each.

MAXIMUM EFFECTIVE RANGE TABLE

The table below is calculated to correspond to a rifle with a 100-yard zero with the sights positioned 2 inches above the bore. The atmospheric conditions were set shooting at sea level at 59 degrees Fahrenheit. The drift values are for a 10 mph crosswind 90 degrees to the target. Under **Drop/Drift,** the yardages in bold indicate the maximum effective range of the load.

600	800	1000	1200	1400	1600	1800
DROP/DRIFT						
-96.1/51/1	-237.1/102.9	**(800 yd.)**				
-101.9/40.5	-232.9/79.4	**(925 yd.)**				
-71.3/26.0	-156.7/50	-294.0/84.7	-503.5/131.9	**(1,300 yd.)**		
-61.0/20.9	-132.3/39.8	-243.5/67.0	-409.1/104.6	-650.4/155.7	**(1,425 yd.)**	
-72.5/28.1	-161.2/54.5	-306.3/92.9	-531.8/145.0	**(1,225 yd.)**		
-77.9/23.5	-167.2/44.8	-306.1/75.0	-511.0/115.6	-803.0/167.1	**(1,425 yd.)**	
-71.8/21.6	-153.8/41.1	-280.9/69.2	-468.4/107.8	-738.1/158.8	**(1,425 yd.)**	
-61.6/17.9	-130.8/33.5	-235.5/55.6	-385.5/85.0	-593.6/123	-876.1/170.4	**(1,775 yd.)**
-92.8/34.3	-208.7/67/9	-404.3/117.1	**(1,000 yd.)**			
-96.7/31.6	-212.2/61.2	-399.3/103.6	-684.8/158.8	**(1,100 yds)**		
-86.7/25.3	-186.0/48.4	-341.0/01.9	575.1/128.8	**(1,225 yds)**		
-67.2/19.3	-142.9/36.4	-258.1/60.5	-424.6/93.3	-659.1/136.9	**(1,550 yd.)**	
-71.0/18.2	-149.2/34	-266.5/56.2	-433.0/85.6	-661.4/123.3	-968.0/169.8	**(1,775 yd.)**
-73.4/17.9	-153.5/33.5	-273.3/55/3	-442.6/84.5	-675.2/122.5	-989.7/171.4	**(1,650 yd.)**

007 SCOPE OUT SCOPE ANATOMY

Rifle scopes don't get nearly enough respect from shooters. A standard piece of advice when setting up a new rifle is that the shooter should spend as much on the optic as was spent on the rifle. This is a good rule of thumb. It is also regularly ignored.

Externally, scopes might look like simple tubes with a couple of knobs, but that belies the complexity of their internal works and the sophisticated engineering that goes into their construction. Consider the various demands placed on scopes: they have to have superb optical clarity, be able to keep our bullets clustered in tiny groups far downrange, survive the elements and rough handling, and withstand the repeated jarring of recoil with every shot. Given that they accomplish all this, it is a minor miracle they cost as little as they do.

Premium optics deliver more performance for the money, but moderately priced scopes, those costing a $1,000 or less, represent some amazing values. This is a peek inside what those "simple" tubes consist of.

OBJECTIVE
This is the end of the scope that faces downrange. It includes a lens assembly that consists of several lenses working in conjunction. Higher-end scopes will have lens elements with more (and better) coatings that improve light transmission.

WINDAGE AND ELEVATION TURRETS
The turrets work in conjunction with a spring located in the scope tube to move the erector tube up and down and side to side to physically adjust the position of the reticle and to bring the firearm's point of impact in line with what the shooter desires. The gearing in the turrets, which creates the "clicks" heard and felt when the knobs are moved, needs to be precise and durable, particularly on target and tactical scopes that are manipulated frequently.

PARALLAX FOCUS KNOB
Adjusting parallax on a scope is done to put the image of the reticle in the same focal plane as the target. This prevents the reticle from shifting around if the shooter's eye moves off from dead center in the scope and helps with precision placement of shots, especially at longer ranges. Some scopes come with the parallax preset and fixed. On big-game scopes, parallax is usually set to 100 yards, while on rimfire models, 50 yards is the typical distance. On some scopes, parallax is adjusted by twisting the objective bell rather than by a side knob.

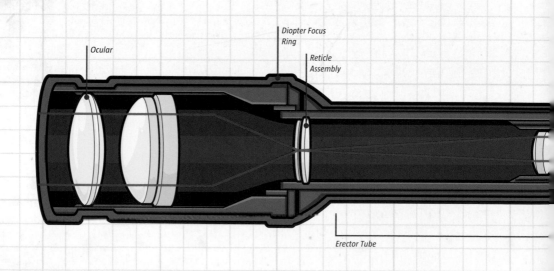

Ocular

Diopter Focus Ring

Reticle Assembly

Erector Tube

FOCUS LENS ASSEMBLY

This is moved back and forth within the scope as the parallax is adjusted to place the reticle in the same focal plane as the target.

DIOPTER FOCUS RING

This is a simple adjustment, but one that many shooters don't do or do incorrectly. This focuses the reticle to the eye, nothing more. Look at a bland background (an overcast sky or blank wall works great) and adjust this ring until the reticle is sharp. Some scopes allow the user to lock down this setting. Do that if the scope allows. If not, make a mark on the ring so that you can tell at a glance whether the ring has moved out of focus at all.

ERECTOR TUBE

This contains the reticle assembly and is physically moved by the windage and elevation turrets in the horizontal and vertical planes, respectively, to adjust the firearm's point of impact. The position of the reticle assembly depends on whether the reticle is in the first or second focal plane. On first focal plane (FFP) scopes, the assembly at the end of the tube facing the objective. On second focal plane (SFP) scopes, the assembly is at the rear of the tube, facing the ocular. The tube also contains the lenses that allow for a variable-power scope to change its magnification. Those lenses ride in precisely made tracks that move them closer together or farther apart as the power ring is manipulated. At high power, the lenses are closer together; at lower magnification, they are farther apart.

RETICLE ASSEMBLY

The first reticles were made from spider silk, which was much stronger than any wire available at the time. Later, scope makers switched to metal crosshairs, some of which would be flattened in a press, giving us the classic "duplex" configuration, with crosshairs that are thicker at the edges and a finer aiming point in the middle. Many scope makers today offer etched glass reticles with blackened aiming points, giving us the more complex reticles that are common on tactical scopes and hunting scopes with marks that help to compensate for bullet drop and wind hold-off.

OCULAR

This portion of the scope contains the lenses where the light that forms the image exits the tube. The job of these lenses is to focus the image in space behind the scope where the shooter's eye will be positioned.

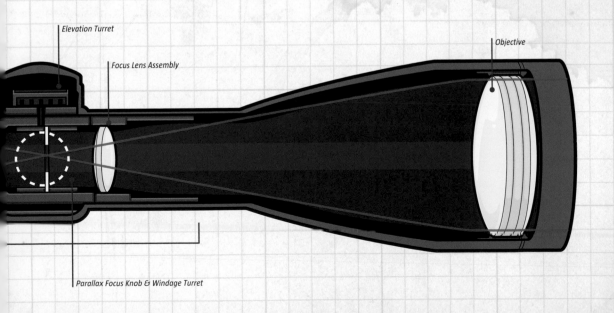

Elevation Turret

Focus Lens Assembly

Objective

Parallax Focus Knob & Windage Turret

008 FOCUS ON PRECISION OPTICS

Describing a scope as a "precision" optic is, ironically, rather imprecise. A scope that is ideal for one shooter's precision work might utterly fail for a different sort of application that requires accurate shooting. The things an F-Class or benchrest shooter needs from a scope, where the shots are taken at static targets placed at fixed ranges, is very different from what a sniper requires, who will be engaging targets at unknown distances, multiple targets in quick succession, or moving targets. But precision scopes do have some common features. They typically offer higher levels of magnification, use more expensive types of optical glass and coatings, have finer aiming points in their reticles, let the shooter adjust for parallax, employ large windage and elevation turrets, and are typically built on 30mm, or larger, scope tubes.

Zooming with a First Focal Plane Reticle

Zooming with a Second Focal Plane Reticle

009 GET THE PLANE TRUTH

Telescopic scopes have two planes of focus at which a reticle can be placed: the first focal plane (FFP), which is between the objective and the image erector lens system, and the second focal plane (SFP), which is set between the scope image erector lens system and the eyepiece. Each has its merits and preferred usages.

FIRST FOCAL PLANE Reticles in FFP scopes remain the same size with respect to the target no matter what power the scope is set on. So as the shooter cranks up the magnification of a scope and the image of the target appears larger, the size of the reticle increases at an identical rate.

In other words, the reticle in your FFP scope remains in proportion with the shooter's field of view. This is especially useful on scopes with holdover marks for elevation and hold-off marks for wind. There's no need with an FFP scope to have the power at a specific setting in order to use the reticle to compensate for bullet drop or drift. For this reason, FFP scopes are favored by tactical shooters and by hunters who plan to take animals at extended ranges.

SECOND FOCAL PLANE Most of the scopes built have SFP reticles, including many for target shooting. They cost less to produce than an FFP scope of similar quality, but for some shooters, the fact that the reticle always appears the same in the field of view, at any power setting, is a boon.

On high-power target scopes for benchrest and other sports where the targets are at known distances, an SFP scope offers everything these competitors need. These reticles often have very fine lines and a small central aiming point at the juncture of the crosshairs. These lines can be centered easily on the target, making for excellent consistency from one shot to the next. SFP scopes often have reticles with holdover marks, too. The only caveat is that the scope needs to be dialed to a specific power setting (usually the maximum) in order for the holdover marks to work.

010 DO THE MATH

When calculating range, your scope will use either mils (milliradians) or MOA (minute of angle), which are both angular units of measure. Picture an MOA or a mil as an ice-cream cone with the tip originating at the shooter's eye and an open end that gets ever wider the farther out it goes, and you've got the idea. Despite this fundamental similarity, shooters tend to fall into one camp or the other and will break into a cold sweat if you hand them a scope with the "wrong" type of clicks.

The MOA system is by a wide margin the most popular among shooters in the United States. A single minute roughly equates to 1 inch at 100 yards, so shooters get used to thinking of MOA in terms of inches. Thus, 2 MOA at 100 yards is 2 inches, 1 MOA at 300 yards is 3 inches, and so on. As long as the shooter

sticks with 100-yard increments, the math is pretty easy when corrections need to be made.

The value of a mil is 1/1,000th in terms of size to distance. This sounds more confusing than it actually is in practice. So 1 mil equals 1 yard at 1,000 yards and 1 meter at 1,000 meters. At 100 yards, a .1 mil click is .36 inch.

When using a reticle with mil increments, the mil system is fast and effective. A 3.6 mil holdover at 550 yards requires no math—just dial or hold for that value and send the shot. The idea of "inches" of drop, which is how most MOA shooters think, disappears completely.

Of course, MOA shooters can use this psychology as well, but it helps to stop thinking in terms of inches, which is contrary to how MOAs were introduced to most shooters.

011 JOIN THE CLICK

The most common values used for scope windage and elevation adjustments are either .25 MOA per click or .1 mil per click. A single .25 MOA click will move the reticle approximately .25 inch at 100 yards. A single .1 mil click will move the reticle 1 centimeter at 100 meters, or .36 inch at 100 yards.

Some target scopes offer clicks in finer increments. Adjustment values of .125 MOA per click (.125 inch at 100 yards) are not unusual.

The opposite is also true, however, with scopes like the Nightforce B.E.A.S.T. configured with click values of .5 MOA and .2 mil. This coarser type of adjustment gives the shooter more elevation per turn of the knob. To fine-tune the point of impact, this scope comes with a throw lever that can include an additional .25 MOA or .1 mil to the scope's elevation.

⊙ SNOW SAYS

Use a flashlight to identify the quality of the coatings in an optic. Peer down the objective lens into the inside of the optic. Where coatings are present, the reflections back will have a tinted cast, usually green, blue, or purple. A bright, harsh reflection indicates an uncoated lens surface.

012 ASSEMBLE YOUR PRECISION RIFLE KIT

It may or may not take a village to raise a child, but I know for sure that it takes a pile of gear to make accurate long-range shots. Here's a look at the stuff beyond the rifle, ammo, and scope that shooters use to hit targets in the next area code.

SLING IT A good sling not only helps a shooter tote a rifle but it provides extra support and stability from different shooting positions, particularly the sitting and kneeling positions. When gripped, the stiff butt section on this sling even doubles as a squeeze bag if needed, steadying the stock between the shooter's hand and whatever the hand is resting on.

GIVE IT LEGS The legs on a rifle's bipod form a triangle between the ground and the front of the stock, bracing the rifle solidly. The legs on the bipod should adjust in height for different shooting situations. Some bipods have feet that can be changed out to adapt to different shooting surfaces. The legs on any bipod need to be strong enough to handle the pressure of "loading," which is when the shooter's shoulder presses forward

on the butt of the rifle, bracing the bipod against whatever it is resting on.

ADD IT UP One essential piece of gear for a long-range shooter is an electronic ballistics calculator that can factor in environmental conditions. Air temperature, relative humidity, altitude, and air pressure can each affect a bullet's flight path, and these units have the ability to provide corrected drop tables that take all of this into account.

KEEP A DIARY A written record of the shots put through a rifle, as well as data on how it shoots from a cold bore, after cleaning, with a new type of ammo, and so on, is invaluable. After a while, the shooter gets a living history of a rifle and will know exactly when it will deliver peak performance.

GET A SPOTTER A shooting partner behind a good spotting scope will increase first-round hits and help with subsequent shot correction by giving an assessment of wind conditions and calling out windage

and elevation adjustments. If the spotting scope and the shooter's rifle scope have similar reticles, the corrections become even easier, since the spotter and shooter are seeing the same thing downrange.

FIND YOUR RANGE The best rifle and ammo in the world won't do a shooter much good if that person doesn't know how far away the target is. With long-range targets, a rangefinder that can be mounted on a tripod and that is effective out past 1,000 yards under actual conditions is worth its weight in gold. Rangefinders that automatically correct for shot angle are even better.

LAZE YOUR TARGET A mil-dot master helps shooters estimate the range to targets that are at unknown distances. Provided that the shooter knows at least one dimension of the target's size and can measure it on a mil-dot scale in his rifle scope or spotting scope, this calculator will give the range. Be fore-warned, it takes a fair amount of experience to get good at estimating the size of distant targets in mils. Be prepared to practice.

CHECK YOUR SPEED To get accurate drop tables for a given load, precise measurements of the bullet's muzzle velocity are required. The specs on the side of the ammo box just won't cut it. With the use of optical chronographs, the shooter threads the bullet through screens, which sense the passing shadow of the bullet and start and stop timers based on that. There is also an excellent barrel-mounted chronograph that uses magnets to start and stop the timers used to calculate muzzle velocity. Each type works very well.

BAG IT A squeeze bag can be as simple as a sock with some dirt in it or a crumpled-up hand towel. Better are the rectangular bags with hand straps. Either way, the job of the squeeze bag is to sit between the stock of the rifle and the ground or bench. The bag steadies the rear of the rifle and, depending on how much pressure the shooter applies, is used to make fine adjustments to the rifle's elevation and windage.

013 HUSH UP

Sound suppressors—also known as silencers, though they don't actually silence gunfire—are legal to own in all but a handful of states. And in most of the states where ownership is legal, hunting with them is also allowed, though you'd be hard-pressed to uncover that fact in the state's game regulations. This is a shame, because silencers are great additions to any firearm, whether for hunting, target practice, or competition. In other countries the use of silencers is encouraged, and in some cases, required. It is perhaps the only example where gun rights in the United States lag behind those in Europe.

If you haven't shot with a suppressor yet, do so. Experiencing one firsthand is the best way to see its benefits, but in case you don't have one handy, the following entries explain what makes

suppressors worth owning. And speaking of which, the process to purchase them is not nearly as onerous as some make it out to be. An excellent resource is the website silencersarelegal.com, which contains a wealth of information about suppressors and how to go about buying one.

014 UNDERSTAND THE BENEFITS OF A SILENCER

There are multiple benefits to using a suppressor, both in terms of personal safety and improving your own hunting and shooting experience.

SAVE YOUR EARS Suppressors significantly reduce the sound of the shot at the muzzle, though rarely muffle the noise to the point where it is technically ear-safe. Wearing hearing protection is still a smart move, of course, unless the firearm is shooting subsonic ammo. But the softer blast is much safer for the shooter's hearing, and that of anyone else in the vicinity. For this reason alone—protecting everyone's hearing—silencers should be more widely used.

IMPROVE YOUR AIM There are two reasons shooters flinch. One is the force of the gun's recoil and the other is the shock of the muzzle blast. Guns that use muzzle brakes to reduce felt recoil have significantly greater muzzle blast and increase one cause of flinching while reducing another. Suppressors actually reduce both.

The lessened kick of the gun and the softer report at the muzzle make guns with silencers very shooter-friendly and are ideal for those who are prone to flinching and for new shooters. But even experienced shooters will see their marksmanship improve when using suppressors.

SPEAK UP Because silenced guns require reduced levels of hearing protection, they make it easier for shooters to speak with each other. Range commands are easier to hear, and in hunting situations (where the use of ear protection is often difficult), they allow for better communication.

BE AWARE With a suppressed firearm, shooters have the option to go without earplugs while in the field. Being able to take full advantage of natural hearing allows shooters to be more aware of what's going on around them, which is critical in both hunting and tactical situations.

015 STUDY THE SCIENCE BEHIND SOUND SUPPRESSORS

The sound of a gunshot is composed of three individual sounds that all happen at once when the gun is fired: The mechanical sound of the gun's action working, the muzzle blast of expanding gases from the propellant that fires the bullet, and the actual sound of the bullet breaking the sound barrier. A suppressor is designed to mitigate some of all this racket.

Using a series of chambers and baffles, suppressors slow down and diffuse the expanding gasses that are leaving the muzzle, much like a muffler does to engine exhaust. The resulting sound is comparable to that of a loud air rifle, which is well below what OSHA considers harmful to a person's hearing. (Pain and injury to the human ear can result from sounds over 140 decibels, and even the sound of a .22 rimfire pistol being fired comes in at 155 dB).

MUZZLE BLAST Without a suppressor, a typical .30/06 muzzle blast would register 162 dB, or about 10 times that of safe hearing levels.

CAPTURED GAS Gas expanding behind the bullet moves into the chambers that are formed by the baffles in the suppressor.

HEAT Energy that would express itself as sound is then transformed into heat.

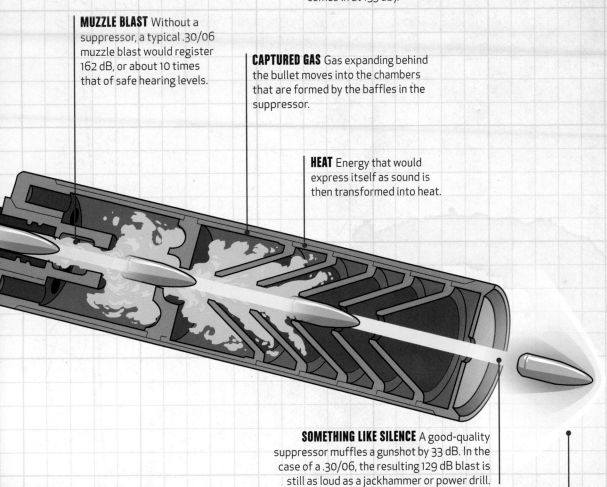

SOMETHING LIKE SILENCE A good-quality suppressor muffles a gunshot by 33 dB. In the case of a .30/06, the resulting 129 dB blast is still as loud as a jackhammer or power drill.

SHOCK WAVE A bullet traveling faster than sound (about 1,140 fps) still throws off a sonic boom that remains unaffected by the suppressor.

016 SHOOT WITH PRECISION

Sniper rifles are the rock stars of the gun world. They are used under the worst conditions to make the toughest shots when it matters most. They come in various profiles and sizes and many are able to adapt to different missions by quickly switching calibers.

REMINGTON MSR

Called the MSR for Modular Sniper Rifle, this multicaliber rifle was recently chosen by the Special Operations Command as its next-generation sniper system. It can fire .308 Win., .300 Winchester Magnum, and .338 Lapua ammunition by swapping barrels and bolt heads and is easily convertible in the field to quickly adapt to different missions. The rifle is built around an aluminum chassis stock that folds to the side for easier transport and adjusts in all critical dimensions to fit the shooter's needs. It comes with an AAC sound suppressor, Harris bipod, and detachable 5- and 10-round magazines.

ACCURACY INTERNATIONAL AX308

This company was a pioneer with its chassis-style stock design, where the stock is machined from solid metal to fit precisely and directly with the action, creating a connection that is stiff, secure, and accurate. The new AX system has a folding stock that fully adjusts for the shooter, a configurable pistol grip, side cuts in the magazine well to allow for better management of the detachable box magazines, a six-lug 60-degree bolt, and a keyhole accessory mounting system that goes along the forend. The company also makes another model, the AXMC, which is a multicaliber rifle with a quick-release barrel change system.

ASHBURY PRECISION ORDNANCE ASW 338LM

ASW stands for Asymmetric Warrior, and that's the goal of APO, as the company that makes its promises to "give the shooter an unfair advantage." The rifle has a side-folding stock and is the one of most customizable, in terms of shooter fit, on the market. The rifle's scope mounting rail extends forward of the action and has 30 MOA of declination built in for long-range shooting, and can also accommodate many other sighting and targeting devices. It is built on a Surgeon action and is fed by detachable box magazines. This particular model is chambered in the potent .338 Lapua, but the ASW line is available in multiple other calibers as well.

BARRETT M107A1

Yes, it weighs more than 27 pounds, but this beast of a sniper rifle is actually lightweight for a .50-caliber semiauto. With its 10-round magazine, the M107A1 hits like Thor's hammer downrange and can take out targets through thick concrete walls, automobiles, and lightly armored military vehicles. It comes equipped with a bipod and a flash suppressor that is built for Barrett's QDL suppressor. One reason to use a suppressor on this rifle is to protect helicopter crews from the shockwave thrown off by the muzzle brake during airborne operations.

SIG SAUER SSG 3000

This bolt-action rifle is chambered in .308 and is one of the most accurate production rifles on the market. It also, amazingly, happens to be a really good value given that most precision rifles are well north of $2,000. (The SSG 3000 cost about $1,400 as this book went to press.) The stock has an adjustable cheek piece, flush mounted cups to attach slings, a vertical pistol grip, and a "sniper hook" cutaway to secure the stock in the shoulder. The action is silky smooth, the two-stage trigger is crisp, and it feeds with either 5- or 10-round single-stack magazines.

PROOF RESEARCH TAC II

Located in northwestern Montana, Proof Research is a company that specializes in lightweight rifles built with carbon fiber–wrapped barrels. Carbon fiber barrels have a reputation for being finicky, but based on the numerous Proof rifles I've shot, it seems these folks have cracked the code. The accuracy and shot-to-shot consistency of these barrels is exceptional. The stocks and actions are built to the same exacting degrees of performance. They feed, cycle, and shoot flawlessly and are built to withstand hard use, while weighing much less than typical sniper rifles.

017 READ THE WIND

If there is an art to long-range shooting, it's reading the wind. There are some helpful rules of thumb to use when observing the effect of wind on the environment around us. By looking at how much surrounding vegetation is being moved, we can make an educated guess about the speed and, under many circumstances, the direction of the wind. A wind lightly felt upon your face is 3–5 mph; a 5–8 mph breeze agitates leaves on trees; an 8–12 mph wind raises dust; a 12–15 mph wind sways small trees; and open water begins to whitecap at 17 mph.

Another useful tool is to observe mirage, which occurs when reflected heat bends light rays, creating visual distortion. When looking through a scope or binoculars, mirage can be used to estimate wind speeds up to about 15 mph. Wind faster than that flattens mirage.

You will need to know both the speed and direction of the wind to make an accurate adjustment for your point of impact. Wind drift figures are based on what is known as a "full-value" condition, which is found when the wind is blowing at 90 degrees to the target. The more the wind blows in parallel to the shooter's line of sight, the less the wind will affect bullet flight. (Wind that is coming in at a 45-degree angle from any direction is roughly a ¾-value wind, meaning a full-value drift of 10 inches would translate to 7½ inches of actual wind drift.) Only time spent shooting under field conditions will hone these skills, but developing them is essential to shooting mastery.

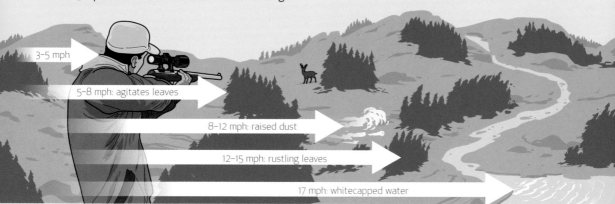

3–5 mph

5–8 mph: agitates leaves

8–12 mph: raised dust

12–15 mph: rustling leaves

17 mph: whitecapped water

018 CALL THE SHOT

A spotter can accurately call his partner's shots by looking for the vapor trail left by the bullet as it travels toward the target. To do this, the spotter should get a crisp image of the target while looking through his optic and then dial back so that the target is slightly blurry and the foreground—which is the space the bullet will traverse—is in focus. Also watch for any telltale dust in the event of a miss.

019 LEARN PUSH-PULL DIALING

When the time comes to adjust the crosshairs on your rifle, seconds count, so it pays to learn to dial in windage or elevation corrections quickly without lifting your head from the stock and losing view of the target. For a right-handed shooter, pushing forward with the thumb on the knobs and rotating them clockwise will move the point of impact down or to the left, while pulling on the turrets moves it up or to the right. Memorize this "push-pull" method to dial in faster.

020 CONTROL YOUR BREATHING

What's the most difficult shot to make? I'd say it is when your heart is pounding and you're out of breath. Hunters and competitive shooters both know this feeling. It occurs when you have to sprint to your next shooting position in a match or when you need to make the final push to the ridge of the mountain at last light. With your lungs working like a bellows and your heart pounding for all it's worth, do what biathletes do to settle down before shooting.

STEP 1 Take three deep, controlled breaths, in through the nose and out through the mouth. This will lower your heart rate and steady your aim.

STEP 2 As you get ready to shoot, let the air out of your lungs, pausing at the bottom of your breathing cycle. In this relaxed state, you have about 7 seconds to fire before the lack of oxygen affects your vision and induces muscle tremors.

STEP 3 If you can't manage the shot in this time, don't force it—you'll only miss. Take three more deep breaths to reset and try again.

021 GET THE RIGHT GRIP

One of the most fundamental parts of using a rifle is knowing how to hold it and thereby maintain proper control for accuracy and safety. With the butt of the rifle firmly in the pocket of your shoulder, grip the rifle with your trigger hand as follows:

The middle and ring finger should wrap lightly around the stock, high enough on the grip so that your trigger finger extends naturally toward the trigger. The thumb should exert no pressure at all on the stock. You can either drape it lightly over the back of the stock or lay it alongside the grip so that it isn't in contact with the rifle.

022 CONTROL YOUR TRIGGER

When setting up behind the rifle, take time to build a proper trigger position. Get the pad of your finger square against the trigger so it can move directly toward the rear of the rifle with even pressure. Also, ensure that no part of your trigger finger is brushing against the bolt handle in any way. If it is, release your grip and start over.

The trigger finger needs to be able to operate independently from the rest of the hand, going through the trigger pull (or "press" as some call it) without any other part of the hand moving. This can, and should, be practiced through dry-firing and even without a gun. The goal is to keep your sights steady and on target during that deliberate motion, and the only way that will happen is if your finger comes straight back with even pressure across the face of the trigger blade. Follow-through is essential—keep your finger pressed on that trigger until the gun stops moving after recoil.

023 USE A BIPOD RIGHT

You never want any part of a rifle in contact with a hard surface when shooting. Hard-on-hard always diminishes accuracy. This goes for shooting off a bipod as well—you don't want the feet resting on an unyielding surface if you can avoid it. (This includes your shooting mat.) If necessary, use a knife to scrape a shallow trench 1 to 2 inches deep in the ground to set the bipod in. The loosened soil will cushion the feet and help brace the legs at the same time. When shooting prone, position your body so that it pushes forward on the stock as you lay down with enough pressure to "lock" the bipod into the same position with each shot. This gives the consistency needed to make long-range hits.

024 CHANGE YOUR BIPOD'S FOOTING

The most stable use of a bipod is with both legs securely locked down and the rifle braced by the shooter. But bipods are surprisingly adaptable.

BIPOD OFF BARRICADES When shooting from over a wall or through a doorway, a bipod can be used to support the shot by deploying one leg. With just one leg down while shooting over a wall, the rifle can easily pivot to engage moving targets or multiple targets in succession. With both legs down, the rifle is more awkward to maneuver. Leaning into the rifle with enough pressure to lock the rifle in place is necessary then.

SWAP YOUR FEET Most bipods come equipped with rubber feet, which are the best choice for all-around use, particularly if the rifle might be rested on a surface the shooter doesn't want to mar. However, replacement feet are available for many types of bipods, some of which are metal and constructed with claws or dull spikes that bite into hard surfaces like concrete, asphalt, and packed dirt, and will perform better than rubber tips.

SHOOT AFTER DARK

A sniper rifle that has been paired with night vision technology is a formidable weapon. Giving soldiers the ability to make precision shots in the dark can tip the balance of power on the battlefield. Even if a shot isn't fired, a scout and sniper team, like the one pictured here during a combat operation in Iraq, can provide critical intelligence.

The first night vision devices (NVDs) that were used on rifles were fielded during World War II. Those first units were large, bulky and offered poor resolution. They also had to make use of a sizeable infrared lamp, whose light is invisible to the human eye, illuminating the area that the shooter behind the scope wanted to see.

These days, NVDs are much more sophisticated. Instead of using an external power source for any

illumination, they are able to amplify the ambient light to produce an image. Currently, NVDs are able to augment the ambient light by a factor of 30,000 to 50,000.

Though NVDs are expensive, civilian shooters also use them. They are particularly helpful for controlling agricultural pests like coyotes and feral hogs that are most active at night.

Note: This photo is a night vision shot of U.S. Marine Scout Snipers, assigned to Team 4, Company G, 2nd Battalion, 24th Marine Regiment, Regimental Combat Team 1, observing a cement factory near Bahkit, Iraq, June 3, 2008. The factory was suspected of manufacturing Improvised Explosive Devices (IEDs).

026 PRACTICE PRECISION WITH A RIMFIRE RIFLE

One problem with shooting centerfire rifles is the cost of ammunition. This is no small consideration for a serious shooter. While the availability of rimfire ammo has been a challenge, and will likely be for some time to come, it is still a great option for economical practice of precision marksmanship. And combined with a good rifle, you'll dial in your accuracy in no time.

In 2010, a friend came to me with a problem. He's an avid precision rifle shooter who lives in an urban area where even 100-yard gun ranges are scarce. But every day, while commuting to and from work, he drives by a building with a 50-yard range that allows rimfire and centerfire pistol shooting only. He wanted some advice on building a rimfire rifle that he could use to hone his long-range skills while shooting at shorter distances.

His questions were straightforward: What caliber to use? Which action? Which stock? And did the project

have any merit? Yes, I told him, the project had merit and after some thought suggested he consider CZ's latest rimfire action, which has the ability to easily swap barrels and calibers, paired with a Manner's Composite Stock.

After some introductions were made at the 2011 SHOT Show, the rifle was built and the executives at CZ were so pleased with the results that they decided to roll it out in 2012 as a production model, which is called the CZ 455 Varmint Precision Trainer. This firearm has the ergonomics of a tactical rifle, allowing the shooter to practice all precision-rifle techniques and drills for a fraction of the cost of shooting .308. And because it can swap barrels, it can also be customized for use on varmints and other small game.

027 CURE CROSSHAIR JUMP

Try dry-firing with an empty rifle on a target that affords an excellent view of the reticle. As the trigger snaps, pay close attention to the crosshairs. Did they move at all? A slight jump is common and indicates the need to fine-tune the technique.

The most likely culprit in the case of crosshair jump is poor trigger control. Work on placing the first pad of the trigger finger so that it delivers even pressure across the face of the trigger and focus on moving it straight back toward the rear of the stock.

The other issue that can lead to crosshair jump is

uneven pressure on the stock. If the shooter's head is bearing down on the stock with excessive pressure, then the gun will bounce away from the shooter's face, causing the reticle to jump, particularly if the butt of the stock isn't firmly in the shooter's shoulder. Practice getting a solid, but not overbearing, cheek weld on the stock and seating the recoil pad firmly into the pocket of the shoulder.

If you fix these two issues, then the crosshair jump will disappear, and your shooting will become more accurate.

028 AIM SMALL

Calling shots is an essential shooting skill. The goal is to know exactly where the crosshairs are when the shot goes off. With practice, a shooter can diagnose poor shots before seeing the bullet's impact on the target. Calling shots also facilitates better trigger control, leading to more accurate shooting.

This dry-fire drill helps improve both shot calling and trigger control. Pick a small aiming point—one where you cannot comfortably keep your reticle centered. As the crosshairs drift around the target, relax your breathing and break the trigger. Work to make the trigger break as the crosshairs are correctly aligned on the target.

This can be done from any shooting position, provided the aiming point presents enough of a challenge, but works especially well with kneeling, sitting, and off-hand shots.

029 TAKE A CLASS IN PRECISION SHOOTING

Instruction in precision rifles comes in many flavors, because the precision rifle itself covers such a broad array of types of shooting. The thing they all have in common, though, is that they emphasize development of good fundamentals—the same skills covered in this chapter. Depending on your particular area of interest, one of these schools will be right for you.

CONCENTRATE ON RIFLES The Rifles Only school is run by Jacob Bynum, a talented firearms instructor with years of experience teaching civilian, law enforcement, and military personnel. This school is based in South Texas, not far from the Gulf shore, and if you ever wanted to learn master shooting in the wind, this is the place for it. Rifles Only emphasizes practical shooting skills from point-blank range out past 1,000 yards. Learning to shoot accurately, fast, and under stress are all part of the curriculum. The school has an array of targets: movers, static steel, and courses of fire that are done under dynamic situations.

PLAY IT AGAIN, SAAM The letters stand for Sportsman's All-Weather All-Terrain Marksmanship, and that practical orientation is the focus of this school. The goal of the instructors here is to improve students' shooting under realistic conditions out to 500 yards. While the course work includes instruction on the environmental effects on ballistics—elevation, wind, temperature, etc—the actual shooting takes place under challenging real-world scenarios where the shooters will need to identify and use the terrain and natural rests to their advantage.

GET ON THE BENCH No shooting sport is more centered around accuracy than benchrest. Every single aspect of benchrest competition is geared toward making the tiniest groups downrange possible. In truth, benchrest consists of a small fraternity of riflemen, so it doesn't have established schools like other more generalized disciplines. But a search on the Internet will uncover several clinics and top-level instruction being offered

frequently, should you wish to give it a try. There are some excellent resources you can explore, including two outstanding websites—benchrest.com and 6mmbr.com—that have a wealth of information. You can also check out the Kelbly family, the makers of record-setting benchrest rifles and the hosts of the Supershoot, the annual benchrest championship. The folks who work there are knowledgeable, friendly, and will help guide aspiring accuracy nuts in the right direction.

GO TO HOLLAND Darrell Holland is a meticulous rifle builder who is obsessed with long-range shooting. His teaching method is just like his gunsmithing—technical and precise. He is a master when it comes to conveying the subtleties of ballistics, and this is a good thing. Because when his students start pulling triggers, they will be doing so in the highly challenging terrain of the coastal mountains of Oregon. Not only do all of these students get to stretch out their

shooting—most of which is done at ranges between 300 and 800 yards—but they also get to experience high-angle shots and get to learn to compensate for that as well.

GET SERIOUS ABOUT LONG-RANGE There are numerous types of long-range rifle competition. Some of these are formal and traditional, like Palma, which uses iron sights at distances of 800, 900, and 1,000 yards. There is also F-Class, which is a newer sport that can be described as sort of a cross between benchrest and Palma and is growing in popularity. Then there are numerous sniper and tactical matches, which are much more dynamic, where the emphasis is on solving any unpredictable shooting problems. Instruction for these sports can be had through the groups that organize them. The best way to learn about them is to attend a match. Chances are, contestants will be glad to show you the ropes and even let you shoot their gear if you're so inclined.

030 LEARN BOLT-ACTION BASICS

Bolt-action rifles were originally developed for military use, but it wasn't long before the "sporterized" versions began to appear in the hands of hunters. The popularity of these versions grew to the point that they eclipsed lever-actions as the hunting arm of choice. For several decades, turn-bolts, as the platform is also called, have accounted for the majority of hunting rifles. While they share basic components with other similar rifles, here are some key characteristics to note.

STOCK The stock is the shooter's connection to the gun, providing anchor points for both hands, the shoulder, and the shooter's head. Getting the geometry correct so that all these work in conjunction is the key to the stock-maker's art. The clean lines of the "classic" American-style stock, with the flat comb, gracefully tapered forend, and gently sloping grip, accomplish this task. This versatile stock design can be shot well from static positions, like prone or off a bench, but also excels when fast shots are required from off-hand, kneeling, and sitting positions.

BARREL A hunting rifle's barrel can be any length and contour depending on the rifle's intended use; most standard rifles have a medium contour that puts the overall rifle weight somewhere around 8 pounds.

MUZZLE Most muzzles have a recess cut into them to protect the rifling in the barrel from damage. These recesses can take different shapes. Rounded crowns are traditional, but most gun makers employ target crowns that have sharper edges and are easier to make concentrically, which helps accuracy.

MAGAZINE The magazines in bolt guns come in three varieties. A blind magazine is fed and emptied through the top of the receiver, as there is no port cut into the bottom of the stock. A hinged floorplate magazine lets the shooter empty the rifle quickly through the stock. Detachable box magazines clip into place and can facilitate rapid reloads when the rifle runs dry.

TRIGGER On a good hunting rifle, the trigger should break somewhere between 2 ½ to 5 pounds. A heavier trigger pull is advantageous with dangerous game guns or when shooting in cold conditions, to minimize the likelihood of the shooter firing before she is ready.

031 KEEP IT SAFE

Quite simply, the function of a safety is to mechanically prevent the rifle from firing while engaged. Two-position safeties are common—they have a switch that toggles between "safe" and "fire" settings. Three-position safeties, by comparison, also have an intermediate position that enables the shooter to open the bolt and unload the rifle while it is still in "safe" mode.

A good safety should be positioned so that it can be manipulated automatically as the rifle is shouldered. Safeties are positioned next to the bolt handle, on the bolt shroud, on the tang of the grip or, less commonly, within the trigger guard.

032 KNOW YOUR BOLT

Bolt-action rifles have manually operated actions. As the handle connected to the bolt is rotated up and then pulled back, several things occur. First, the bolt lugs are rotated out of the recesses in the rifle chamber that lock the bolt and barrel together when the cartridge is fired. When the bolt is rotated, the firing pin is cocked in preparation for the next shot. As the bolt is moved to the rear, the spent cartridge is extracted from the chamber and then ejected free of the rifle. Pushing the bolt forward strips a new round from the magazine and guides it into the chamber. Rotating the bolt down repositions the lugs within their recesses so that the rifle can be fired once more.

There are numerous styles of bolt actions, but two configurations dominate: two-lug bolts and three-lug bolts. Bolts with two lugs are the most common and traditional. The original Mausers were based on a two-lug design. They require the bolt handle to be moved through a 90-degree arc in order to get them out of battery.

Three-lug bolts, found on rifles made by Cooper, Sako, Browning and others, have shorter bolt throws of about 60 degrees, but can be a bit more difficult to run because the force required to cock the firing pin needs to be exerted over a shorter arc.

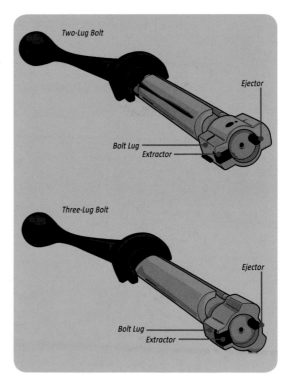

Two-Lug Bolt

Ejector

Bolt Lug

Extractor

Three-Lug Bolt

Ejector

Bolt Lug

Extractor

033 KNOW YOUR ACTION TYPES

Though bolt-actions dominate the hunting world, they are far from the only option for taking on big game. There are numerous other types of actions to choose from, each with its own virtues.

A

B

C

D

TAKE ONE SHOT For many hunters, the use of a single-shot rifle (A) is the measure of a marksman. Without an easy way to get a second shot quickly downrange, single-shots put a premium on accurate bullet placement. Falling-block rifles are an old design but are one of the strongest actions out there. A lever under the trigger is used to open and close the action; the empty shell is either kicked clear of the breech by an ejector or gently levered out of the chamber by an extractor.

GET LEVERAGE A uniquely American rifle, the romance associated with lever-actions will forever be linked to their use in the Old West. But these aren't just museum pieces: Lever guns (B) are still common in deer and elk camps across the country. They are light, handy, and pack a lot of firepower into a compact package. They're ideal for handling in dense brush, carry easily in the scabbards on horseback, and, with some of the new lever-gun ammo available, are more accurate and flatter-shooting than ever.

GET PUMPED UP Rifles that operate by manually racking the forend back and forth (C) have become increasingly rare in hunt camps. The best known of this fading breed is the Remington 7600, which for decades was a mainstay in the northeastern U.S., in areas where semiauto rifles were not allowed. Although the number of users of these rifles is small, the fan base is devout. Pump-action rifles are dependable and quick handling and come chambered in classic deer-hunting calibers like the .270 Win. and the .30/06.

BREAK IT DOWN Break-action rifles (D) open in the middle like double-barreled shotguns and are loaded manually with one, two, or in the case of drillings, three or—rarely—more shells. Rifles of this type represent some of the least (and most) expensive rifles made. At the high end, bespoke double guns from British and continental European gun makers cost as much as a house. At the other end, gun makers like CVA and Thompson-Center make affordable break-actions, many of which can change calibers by swapping barrels.

GO SEMIAUTO Ever since the introduction of the Remington Model 8 back in 1906, hunters have been using semiauto rifles (E) to take game. Most semis have gas-operated systems, where ports drilled into the barrel vent some of the gas expelled from the cartridge to a mechanism that harnesses that energy to cycle the action. They recoil more softly than other types of rifles and also offer quick follow-up shots since there is no need to manually work the action.

E

034 TRY AN UNCONVENTIONAL HUNTING CARTRIDGE

Ah, the .30/06. So useful, versatile, practical, and—dare we say it?—boring. And what of the .308, the .243, and the .30/30? They don't offer much to quicken the blood either, capable though they all are. If you desire a gun that not only gets the job done, but does so with a bit of flair and panache, then you should have these essential cartridges in your gun safe.

.17 HMR

The .22 LR might be the most popular varmint round in existence, but this rimfire rocket kicks its backside by every ballistic measure. It is speedy—2,500 fps with a 17-grain bullet—flat-shooting and almost universally accurate in the guns it is chambered for. For varmints within 150 yards, it is seriously bad news. For the shooter on the trigger, it is habit-forming fun.

.204 RUGER

This varmint vaporizer breaks the 4,000 fps barrier and has so little recoil that it is easy to spot your hits—and these two qualities can lead to uncontrolled and inappropriate laughter when shooting over a prairie dog town. The light bullets it uses also buck the wind surprisingly well. It is a sexy little number, and you can count on explosive performance out to 500 yards.

.220 SWIFT

The Swift is as old as your grandfather and burns barrels like they were made of dried pine, but don't let that stop you from acquiring the ultimate varmint round. The stubby .223 WSSM made a brief claim for the title of fastest commercially loaded cartridge, but not enough folks took a shine to it with 40-grain bullets—and eight decades after its introduction, the .220 Swift is still the king of the hill.

.257 WEATHERBY

This high plains hunter .257 was Roy Weatherby's favorite of his eponymous magnums, and if it was good enough for him, it should be good enough for you, too. It is a quintessential open-country deer and antelope round. It scoffs at long shots and high winds and burns a cupful of powder every time you pull the trigger.

.257 ROBERTS

If you want Junior to blend in with the crowd, then by all means get him a .243 for his first deer rifle. But if you want him to become a ballistic aficionado, go with this little quarter-bore stylish starter instead. Its larger bullet diameter gives it an edge over the 6mms, it can be downloaded for first-time and recoil-sensitive shooters, and it has a name that befits a Scottish laird.

6.5 CREEDMOOR

The world's foremost ballistics geeks teamed up to design the 6.5 Creedmoor as an accuracy aficionado's delight—a long-range target round with mild recoil that's also easy to reload. Offered now with Hornady's 120-grain GMX bullet and propelled by Superformance powder, the 6.5 Creedmoor is making a name for itself as a deadly hunting round as well.

.280 REMINGTON

If the .270 Winchester or .30/06 strike you as too ordinary, fear not. The .280 is an excellent all-around hunting round, although it took a while for its popularity to grow. But its star-crossed beginnings are part of its charm. The "gentleman's 7mm" is also a handloader's dream.

7.82 LAZZERONI WARBIRD

The Warbird has the profile of an ICBM and delivers very nearly the same killing power. At 400 yards, this exclusive .30-caliber magnum hits with the velocity and energy that a .30/06 has at the muzzle. Its exclusivity gives it undeniable snob appeal, but it also means you'll never find a spare box of ammo on gun store shelves.

.35 REMINGTON

Show off your sophistication by opting for this round over the .30/30 for your brush gun. Improved terminal ballistics let it easily handle large whitetails and black bears—a definite northwoods master. Also chambered for the Remington Model 8, lawmen used it to bring down outlaw Clyde Barrow of Bonnie and Clyde fame.

.416 RIGBY

Professional hunting guides in Africa just love it when clients show up with a rifle caliber that starts with the number four. And when that cartridge bears the name "Rigby," they shriek and stamp their feet like tweens at a Justin Bieber concert. The four-one-six smasher generates a thunderous 5,000 foot-pounds of energy at the muzzle. This here is a consummate dangerous-game cartridge.

035 HUNT WITH THE BEST

Hunters have never had it so good. Gun makers have been delivering more value with more accuracy than at any point in history. No matter how much money you're looking to spend (or save), you can find a reliable rifle that you can count on when the animal you're pursuing steps into the clear. These are some of the best.

MONTANA RIFLE COMPANY M1999

The rifles produced by this company are a marvel. I'm not quite sure how they make such good guns for the price. I've toured their facility and have shot (and own) numerous rifles from MRC, and the level of craftsmanship is superb. The M1999 action intelligently combines features from the Mauser M98 and Winchester M70, delivering bomb-proof reliability, elegant looks, and excellent accuracy. The trigger is an old-style M70 design, beloved among shooters for its robust engineering, and the workers at MRC take the time to hone them by hand to give them a crisp, perfect break.

WEATHERBY VANGUARD SERIES 2

The Series 2 line of rifles is an upgrade to the original Weatherby Vanguard series, and makes an already excellent rifle nearly perfect. These rifles feature better stocks, better triggers, and even better levels of accuracy and performance than the originals—and at a good price. Weatherby makes the Series 2 in a wide variety of configurations, from heavy-barreled varmint rifles to the lightweight "Backcountry." For a bit more money, you can pick up a "Range Certified" Vanguard that comes with proof of accuracy.

RUGER AMERICAN

The Ruger American is a budget-hunter's dream. Ruger pulled off an impressive trick in the design of these guns by incorporating several innovative elements while keeping the cost at bargain-basement levels. The way the action mates to the stock and the engineering of the three-lug bolt are both particularly clever and contribute to the American's outstanding accuracy. Its trigger adjusts for a clean let-off and the barrels are very well made, too.

WINCHESTER M70

For the traditionalist, the Winchester M70 is in a class by itself. The svelte lines of the "Featherweight" define the concept of the American sporter. The flat comb, gracefully curved forend, and overall slender profile contribute both to the aesthetics and the handling characteristics of the rifle. The new generation of the M70 retains the claw extractor and fixed-blade ejector of the original pre-'64 (though slightly modified) but has a new trigger system that delivers more consistent accuracy than the older models.

REMINGTON M700

The round profile of the M700 receiver is instantly recognizable among shooters. Round is both easy to produce, which keeps costs down, and lends itself to concentricity, which is a prerequisite for accuracy. The M700 has built up its legions of followers by delivering both performance and value. The 700 has been the basis for most of our military's sniper rifles and has been the rifle of choice for countless hunters for generations. Newer versions have superior triggers and there are models for every hunting and shooting application.

SAKO 85

Finns are avid shooters and hunters and, understandably, their homegrown Sakos are a really big deal there. But Sakos have had a devout fanbase in the United States as well, and for good reason. The Sako 85 action is one of the smoothest three-lug designs ever made and the barrel, trigger, and overall craftsmanship are likewise excellent. I've hunted with numerous Sakos over the years and they deliver reliable performance under the worst conditions and just don't quit.

CZ 557 SPORTER

This rifle is one of CZ's newer offerings and is one of the best hunting rifles the company has ever produced. Like all excellent rifles, this one balances well in hand and is easy to run from all practical field positions. The metalwork on the rifle is excellent, in keeping with CZ's reputation for fine craftsmanship, and the overall design, with its classic lines, will appeal to American shooters. The rifle performs great as well. The trigger and barrel are both terrific and the rifle delivers top-notch accuracy.

SAVAGE M12

Savage Arms led the revolution in affordable accuracy that's taken place over the last 25 years, and plenty of gun companies still haven't caught up. In part that's because Savage hasn't sat still and has continued to upgrade their products while delivering more gun for the money. That ethos of constant improvement is manifest in the M12 series of rifles. They come with very good adjustable triggers, excellent stocks, and what are arguably the best mass-produced barrels out there. In my experience, all these rifles shoot bug-hole groups in smaller calibers and are great for prairie dogs, coyotes, and other predators and varmints.

036 TRY OUT A TRAVELING RIFLE

None of these rifles are cheap, but you get what you pay for. In the case of this lineup, a hunter gets a rifle that will not fail, whether he is hiking along a mountain ridge in Central Asia, stomping through a mopane thicket in Africa, or stalking bear in a willow thicket in the Yukon.

CHARGE STOPPER: HEYM 88B PH

Double rifles have been a mainstay for hunters and guides facing down dangerous game for more than 100 years. The best handle like a good shotgun and offer two quick shots in a proven charge-stopping caliber. The other nonnegotiable feature of these rifles is their utter reliability. The Heym 88B PH is a basic, but still excellent, working double that does all this. What it lacks in fancy engraving, it makes up for with touches such as an articulated front trigger that protects the trigger finger as the rear trigger is tripped. The action locks up solidly with the incorporation of a Greener-style crossbolt, and the rifle operates with automatic ejectors, which cut down on the time it takes to reload.

WORLD HUNTER: WESTLEY RICHARDS M98 TAKEDOWN

If a hunter's goal is to own only one rifle, a takedown M98 from Westley Richards is the way to go. Just like all of the rifles that come from this venerable British gunmaker, the M98s are each built and assembled by hand, starting with modern CNC machined parts and putting them together with old-world craftsmanship. The M98 is legendary for its reliability and is equal to any hunting challenge. In its takedown configuration, the rifle will transport easily to wherever the hunter needs to go and, when chambered in a caliber such as the .338 Winchester Magnum, it will be able to take any game animal on earth.

SWITCH-HITTER: BLASER R8

This bolt-action rifle has a couple of notably clever features. First, it operates with a straight-pull system, meaning there is no need to rotate the bolt handle upward to cycle the action. Pulling straight toward the rear on the bolt extracts and ejects a round and pushing it forward reloads the chamber. The action is simple, intuitive, and fast. Next, the R8 can change calibers quickly, adapting to different hunting scenarios as needed. With a couple of extra barrels and scopes, the R8 is ready for most everything. The detachable box magazine lends itself to easy reloads and the platform has a well-earned reputation for good accuracy.

LAST FRONTIER: REMINGTON 700 AWR II (.375 H&H)

Alaska is rugged and unforgiving country. The gunmakers in Remington's Custom Shop built the AWR II (for Alaska Wilderness Rifle) to handle whatever a hunter traveling to the Last Frontier might encounter. The Bell & Carlson stock is durable and provides excellent grip, and the TriNyte coating on the metal can take on salt, moisture, and harsh abrasion. The 700 action has been trued and accurized by the Custom Shop gunsmiths, and the rifling in the barrels is hand cut prior to being lapped to a smooth mirror finish. Coupled with an X-Mark Pro trigger set to 3 ½ pounds, these rifles shoot very well. Get one in .375 H&H if you're going for bear.

SKY WALKER: FORBES M20

Melvin Forbes is the undisputed Godfather of lightweight bolt guns. His custom-built rifles are engineering marvels with weight trimmed from every possible component while maintaining dependability, accuracy, and safety. His carbon-fiber stocks are all reinforced with Kevlar and even though they are light as a feather, you could beat a moose to death with one, they are so strong. The "20" in the rifle's model name corresponds to the weight of the action in ounces and, with a thin contour barrel, a complete .308-size rifle weighs a wispy 5 pounds. It is the perfect companion for mountainous terrain where the hunt hinges on making a single perfect shot.

OPEN RANGE: GA PRECISION XTREME HUNTER

Rifle maker George Gardner is as avid about hunting as he is about long-range shooting competitions, and the Xtreme Hunter is born of those dual passions. The "tactical" pedigree can be seen in the Templar action, in the detachable box magazines, and the almost vertical hand position on the grip of the stock. The rifle is chambered in a 6.5 SAUM, a well-balanced cartridge that is effective at long range yet is easy to shoot from a light rifle. With an appropriate scope on top, and a skilled shooter on the trigger, this rifle will take game effectively at several hundred yards.

Z6i
1-6x24 EE

50 | YARDS

037 TAKE A TOUR OF HUNTING OPTICS

A basic variable-power scope that zooms from 3X to 9X and that has an uncluttered duplex crosshair is ideal for the majority of hunting situations. Shooters who feel they need more magnification can step up to a 4–12X scope, though a scope that goes from 2.5–8X is actually a better choice.

This applies to the "general" big-game rifle, but we live in an era of specialization and there are optics for every application, whether the quarry is a distant antelope on a windswept sage flat or a hulking black bear picking its way through a forest at twilight.

LEUPOLD VX-3 2.5–8X36

This is a perfect little scope. The magnification range covers just about any need for big game, the optical quality is outstanding, and the scope is compact and light. This scope is best suited to a zero with the point of impact at 100 yards about 2 inches high, depending on the caliber. Set up this way, the shooter just needs to hold at the center of the vitals for any big-game animal out to 250 yards or so. For the price, you won't find anything better out there. Several of my favorite rifles wear this glass.

ZEISS CONQUEST HD 5–25X50

Shooting prairie dogs, ground squirrels, and other varmints is one of the most challenging types of shooting a hunter will encounter. Skittish targets at unknown (and long) distances in usually windy terrain will test the skills of any marksman.

This scope equipped with the Rapid-Z Varmint reticle allows for quick and precise shot placement. This particular reticle is geared toward speedy varmint calibers like the .22-250 Remington, .220 Swift, and .204 Ruger.

SWAROVSKI Z6I 1–6X24 EE

If I were to pick just one scope for all my hunting, it would be this Swarovski. The reticle is simple and fast and has an easy-to-use and effective illumination, which is useful for hunting dark creatures in the timber at low light. At 1X, this robust scope is ready for any dangerous game, and cranked up to 6X, it can place accurate shots on target at long ranges thanks to the reticle's reference marks. Expensive, yes. But that doesn't detract from this scope's impressive utility.

NIKON MONARCH BDC 2.5-10X42

Almost every scope maker has some sort of bullet drop reticle in their lineup, but few work better than Nikon's BDC for hunting. The open circles make it easy work to center targets, and even the tops and bottoms of the circles can be used for reference points, thus giving the shooter a large number of holdover points for different yardages. The heavy weight of the reticle is a real benefit in low light as well. It will remain visible long after the finer stadia in target scopes have winked out in the penumbra.

VORTEX VIPER PST 4-16X50 FFP

This scope has a solid tactical configuration that would work well for a hunter who is willing to devote time and practice to mastering it. The FFP scope has large adjustment knobs and comes with FFP reticles in either mil or MOA configurations with hash marks for wind and elevation. The power range is best suited to shots in big country, though would work over large food plots as well, where long shots at relaxed animals are the norm.

BUSHNELL LRHS 3-12X44

Bushnell worked with George Gardner of GA Precision to develop this scope. The reticle is a modified version of the one Gardner uses for long-range competition. One of the biggest additions is the central aiming circle that provides a bold reference point when the scope is dialed to low magnification. The exposed elevation turret, which is oversize and has bold reference numbers, lets the shooter quickly dial for longer shots. The turret's zero-stop is another useful feature.

038 TAKE A KNEELING POSITION

You crest the hill and there, standing broadside 200 yards away, is the trophy elk you've been seeking. Just one problem: Your frantic climb has left your lungs heaving for oxygen and your legs quaking. You have seconds before the elk dashes over the next ridge. How do you pull off the toughest shot in hunting?

Follow the advice of Ben Maki, an accomplished big-game hunter who was once a top-ranked biathlete: "You can't control your heart rate, but you can control how quickly you relax." Good form is essential, which is why you need to practice first at your resting heart rate before trying to shoot well with a hammering ticker.

KNEEL TO SHOOT When speed counts, the kneeling position is often the best choice. You can get into it quickly, and it offers good support.

SLOW YOUR HEART Don't rush the shot. Take a few extra breaths to settle down. Don't hold your breath for more than a couple of seconds to steady your shot, or the oxygen in your system decreases, causing your eyes to lose focus. Stay calm; the more mentally relaxed you are, the sooner your heart rate will slow down.

ELBOW IN FRONT Get your elbow positioned forward on your knee.

SLING IT Tip the odds in your favor by using a shooting sling that's quick to deploy.

WATCH YOUR FEET Point your front foot at your target and set your butt on the heel of your back foot. With your rear knee on the ground, you'll have a solid base.

KEEP IT IN LINE With good form in any shooting position, your crosshairs should rise and fall in a vertical line as you breathe. If your crosshairs move, say, from 2 o'clock to 8 o'clock, you need to address your technique.

MASTER YOUR TRIGGER Practice dry-firing while relaxed to master your rifle's trigger. Your barrel will always move in something of an arc, more so if your heart rate is up. Your goal is to get your trigger to break consistently when you are right on target.

PUMP IT UP Exercise to elevate your heart rate and dry-fire some more. Analyze what happens with your sight picture when you're breathing hard. Once you become comfortable with your control, you can do this drill with live ammo at the shooting range.

039 SIT DOWN TO MAKE YOUR SHOT

This stable, easy-to-assume position is one of the most accurate shooting techniques. The quickest way to get into a solid position is to simply sit down and prop your knees up at a 45-degree angle relative to the target. While holding your rifle, place your elbows just in front of your knees when you rest your arms; if you place your elbows on top of or to the side of your knees, the position won't be nearly as steady.

Now, thrust your arm through the rifle's strap so it is resting on your triceps a few inches above your elbow. Sweep your hand and forearm in a circle around the sling and grip the forend of the stock. As you shoulder your rifle, the tension on the sling will lock the butt of the gun in place, giving you a steady shooting platform. If the gun isn't locked tight to your shoulder, then your sling is too long.

040 SLING YOUR RIFLE FOR MORE ACCURACY

The use of a shooting sling, practically a forgotten art among today's hunters, results in greater accuracy. A loop at the end of the properly adjusted sling cinches around the upper arm and pulls the stock tight against the shoulder when the rifle is raised.

Whether you use a proper shooting sling or a hasty sling (as shown in item 39), looping your hand on the forend controls the amount of rearward tension the sling puts on the rifle. Sliding the hand backward on the forend increases the tension; sliding forward reduces it instead. The tension should be strong enough so that you can work the bolt of the rifle with your trigger hand without having the stock slip out of position or the rifle come off target.

041 USE A REST

A backpack makes for an excellent rest, giving you the "hard-on-soft" mating between rifle and rest that's critical for accurate shooting. You want to have a soft shooting bag supporting the rear of the stock, which is used to fine-tune the elevation of a shot by squeezing it with your off hand. You can make a rear bag for next to nothing out of a heavy wool or synthetic sock that is partially filled with small plastic pellets. It weighs mere ounces. Just tie off the end, adjusting the amount of fill as needed, and carry it in a pocket.

042 SPOT GAME BETTER WITH SNIPER TALK

"See that deer?" "Where?" "Behind the bush." "The green bush?" And so starts the verbal tango (perhaps I should say "tangle") when hunting partners attempt to point out a spotted animal. A simpler method is the one used by sniper/spotter teams: Start off with an unmistakable landmark, in this case a lone tree up at the peak of the mountain. Ask whether your partner sees it. Once he says "yes," walk him to the next landmark, with directions and distances, leading his eyes to the hidden buck.

IN THIS CASE, IT WOULD PROGRESS AS FOLLOWS:

1. "See the lone tree at the top of the mountain?"

"Yes."

2. "See the tree 50 yards to the left? Go to the midpoint between the trees."

"Got it."

3. "Drop straight down the mountain 100 yards to the large boulder."

"Alright."

4. "Go 60 yards from five o'clock to the last small boulder in the field."

"Okay."

5. "The deer is 25 yards away at three o'clock, just inside the edge of the brush."

"I see him."

043 LEARN THE ETHICS OF LONG-RANGE HUNTING

Even if we have the skills to make 1,000-yard shots on targets, do we have any business shooting big game at those ranges? The answer is no, for several reasons. Shooting at extended ranges is fun because each shot is a puzzle that needs to be solved, the complexity of which increases exponentially the farther out that we attempt to go. At extreme ranges we need to add in barometric pressure, relative humidity, our elevation, and other elements into the equation—to say nothing of judging the wind over that entire distance.

Then there's the unpredictably of the target. It takes a 168-grain bullet from a .300 Winchester Magnum a full second to travel 750 yards, during which time an animal can move, turning even the best-placed shot into a horrible wounding miss.

Slight errors in range estimation can also have disastrous results. Take the vaunted .338 Lapua, the darling of so many long-range shooters right now. From 800 to 900 yards, a 250-grain bullet from the .338 plunges 56 inches, offering little leeway when you're attempting to strike the vitals of a deer. As the trajectory of a bullet drops at long ranges, so does its killing power, making even well-placed hits dicey. Bullets don't expand well after shedding so much velocity, and can pencil through their target without the tissue destruction we seek.

As hunters, it is our sacred obligation to kill game swiftly and surely, and if we cannot manage this, to pass on the opportunity. As much as I enjoy shooting at long range, the measure of a hunter isn't over-the-horizon marksmanship but rather the ability to stalk close, and then closer still, to get in range for an ethical kill.

So what is the outer limit? There is no pat answer, but once you get to 400 yards and beyond, you have to start asking yourself some tough questions about your shot. At the very least, you need to account for bullet drop, and soon thereafter an ever-growing list of variables. The bottom line is that big game should never be used for target practice.

044 BORE-SIGHT A RIFLE

To get a rifle on paper before firing a shot, pull the bolt from the action and secure the rifle in place with a good rifle rest and some sandbags. Position the crosshairs on something large downrange that you'll be able to see with your eye as you peer down the barrel. The edge of the target stand, a large metal gong, or even a good-size rock will all work. Without touching the rifle, move your head from the scope to the bore. Make sure your eye is centered when looking down the barrel. By using this technique, you should be able to see just how close the crosshairs are to where the bore is pointing. Adjust the scope until the reticle and what you see down the barrel line up. Do this at 50 yards, but with a bit of practice, you will be able to get your first shot within a few inches of the crosshairs even at 100 yards.

There are two types of bore sighters I recommend, both of which can help get a rifle on paper with the first shot. A magnetic bore sighter attaches to the rifle's muzzle and places an optical grid in front of the scope. When looking through the scope, the shooter can make elevation and windage corrections to align the scope's crosshairs with the bore sighter's grid. The advantage of this system is that it can be used anywhere. A second type of sighter goes into the chamber of the gun or is inserted into the barrel and projects a laser beam downrange. With the dot on a target downrange, the shooter fiddles with the scope until the crosshairs are on it.

045 SHOOT BETTER OFF A BENCH

Bench shooting is about getting all the accuracy you can out of a rifle. The shooter's goal is to minimize the amount of human input into the system when pulling the trigger. This is most notable in heavy barreled rifles that often shoot the best when allowed to recoil freely off the rest without the shooter gripping or putting any pressure on the stock. But sporter-weight hunting rifles usually do better when they are firmly grasped around the grip and pulled securely into the pocket of the shoulder. The trick is to keep this pressure isolated to the biceps while the rest of the body stays relaxed.

046 TRY DIFFERENT AMMO

One of the simplest ways to improve a hunting rifle's accuracy is to run a variety of ammo and bullet types through it. It is not unusual at all for a rifle to prefer one type of load (or loads). And of course, ammo isn't cheap. So what should you do with the rounds that don't give the best accuracy? Use them for practice and for fouling your rifle after cleaning. You can also split several boxes with a buddy, each of you taking the rounds that work best.

047 UNDERSTAND POINT-BLANK ZERO

The concept behind point-blank zero (PBZ) is pretty simple. The idea is that a shooter can hold dead center on a target of a given size, say about 8 inches for argument's sake, and will hit as long as the bullet rises no more than 4 inches above the line of sight (LOS) and drops no more than 4 inches below the LOS. It is like shooting down a tube. With the rifle zeroed correctly, the PBZ is the distance the bullet can travel down the tube before it drops more than 4 inches below the crosshairs.

For example, a .30/06 firing a 165-grain bullet at 2,800 fps that has been sighted 2.7 inches high at 100 yards will be 3 inches high at 135 yards and will be 3 inches low at about 270 yards. In this instance, any deer within 270 yards requires no adjustment on the part of the shooter for elevation. The same hunter can put the crosshairs in the middle of the chest and squeeze off a shot with confidence.

To determine the PBZ for a given load, use one of the numerous free ballistic calculators that can be found online.

048 GLASS FOR GAME

Scouting for game is no easy feat, even with a good set of binoculars. The trick to glassing is to do it in a deliberate, unrushed manner. When you settle on a spot, keep your binoculars still and then look all around the area in view. Once your scan is complete, shift your binoculars upward (or over) to glass the adjoining ground. Since the extreme edges in the binoculars will often be out of focus, you should make your circles overlap. This way you'll be less likely to overlook that bedded buck. You should make a habit of looking for bits of an animal—the symmetrical spread of ears or the head, the white patch from a mule deer's rump, the glint off an antler—rather than the whole body. You'll spot more game this way.

When picking the spot to place your bullet on an animal, visualize where the bullet will exit and take careful note of the position of the animal's front leg and shoulder on the off side. This helps account for quartering shots and ensures that the bullet's path goes clearly through the animal's heart and lungs.

If the shooter only focuses on the near side of the target, he runs the risk of making a poor shot if the animal isn't perfectly broadside.

049 UNDERSTAND RANGEFINDERS

Rangefinders emit pulses of laser light, which are invisible to the naked eye, that reflect off of objects downrange. Distance is determined by measuring the time it takes for the reflected photons to return to the unit. The lasers in rangefinders all have to be eye-safe, meaning they cannot exceed a certain power threshold. The attributes that make for a better rangefinder are its optical quality and its software.

A rangefinder with a small objective lens made of plastic cannot hope to perform as well as a premium rangefinding binocular. Clearer optics with large objective lenses will do a much better job transmitting the beam and receiving the reflected photons. Those secret algorithms that are employed by manufacturers to run the emitting and sensing diodes are guarded like nuclear launch codes. Better algorithms yield faster and more accurate results and do so under more challenging environmental conditions.

050 TREAT YOUR RANGEFINDER RIGHT

Rangefinders are great devices, but they can be sensitive. Watch out for these environmental factors that will degrade a rangefinder's performance.

Smoke, snow, haze, rain, fog, smog, and dust all hinder rangefinders. As the laser travels through the air, it will bounce off these elements and scatter, leaving less energy for the unit to detect. Rangefinders also won't work as well at high noon in the middle of a desert as they will when the light is lower. The radiation floods the sensing diode with light, thus making the rangefinder's task more difficult.

The degree to which a target reflects infrared energy determines how friendly it is for your rangefinder. Ice and snow, for example, are terrible IR reflectors, even though they can easily blind you with reflected light.

Rangefinders emit their beams in a slight cone shape so that the farther they travel, the more dispersed the beam becomes. Bigger targets, therefore, reflect better.

051 GET BETTER READINGS

As useful as a rangefinder can be, it's not a perfect tool, and you have to know how to use it well. Here are a few steps you can take to improve your rangefinding.

STAY STEADY Rest the unit on a pack, against a tree, or, best of all, mount it on a tripod.

CHOOSE LIGHT OVER DARK Generally speaking, lighter areas of a target, such as a light patch of dirt on a hillside, will reflect better than darker areas.

CONTROL THE TRIGGER Put the same care into ranging a target as you would if you were shooting at it. Breath control, a clean press on the "trigger," and good follow-through are key.

CHOOSE YOUR TARGET Various objects are better or worse for rangefinding. The best are leafy green plants, game animals and rocks are somewhere in the middle, and ice and snow are the poorest objects.

EYEBALL IT If you don't have a rangefinder handy, or if it isn't working for some reason, you can also make an educated guess at an animal's range by visualizing the number of football fields between you and it.

052 BECOME A BETTER HUNTER

Most hunters fancy themselves crack shots. But anyone who has spent significant time afield, and is honest about it, will admit that not every shot they've taken has been perfectly placed. At some point, we've all misjudged distance, misread the wind, yanked the trigger, or otherwise caused a bullet to hit something other than the spot we intended. Practicing on our own, while beneficial, isn't always enough to remedy poor technique. This is where instruction comes in.

053 TRAIN WITH OUTDOOR LIFE

A growing number of schools are catering to hunters who want to improve their skills with a rifle. Along with Jacob Bynam at Rifles Only, I have developed one such course: the Outdoor Life Shooting School. This school and other similar courses seek to train sportsmen to become better shots with the equipment they actually use under realistic field conditions.

By the end of the class, not only will students walk away better shooters, but they will also have a more accurate yardstick by which to gauge their own ability when considering a potential shooting situation while hunting. The ability to know one's limits—and when to turn down a shot—will not only lead to more success in the long run, but helps fulfill one of the core ethical responsibilities that all hunters have, which is to take game in a humane manner.

The course starts by building a solid foundation of essential shooting skills, encompassing topics such as breath control, trigger control, recoil management, and rifle manipulation. From there, students learn how to engage targets from prone, kneeling, sitting, off-hand, and other improvised positions.

Gear selection and preparation are also covered. The instructors go over various methods of zeroing in a rifle and the correct ways to mount optics and accessories. The various factors that go into selecting the right type of ammunition, with respect to accuracy and terminal ballistics, are discussed as well. Once the basics are mastered, the difficulty of the drills is increased by placing the targets at longer ranges.

Over the course of three days, the class covers technical knowledge about ammo selection, how to use hunting optics more effectively, and information on engaging more challenging targets. By the end of the class, students will be shooting out to 600 yards and will learn how to cope with stress as they shoot, through the use of timed drills that require hits on multiple targets and rapid reloading.

Courses are conducted at the Rifles Only facility in Texas and at select shooting facilities across the United States.

054 HUNT WITH PRECISION

Magpul Dynamics offers an excellent class, called Precision Hunter, that covers many of the same elements as the Outdoor Life Shooting School. The class, held in Yakima, Washington, consists of courses on:

- Rifle setup and accessories
- Telescopic sight theory and operation
- Basic angular units of measure (minutes of angle and milliradians)
- Basic external ballistics and ballistic solvers
- Understanding ballistic drop compensated turrets and reticles
- Reading atmospheric conditions and wind
- Unconventional and field shooting positions
- Establishing ranges to targets
- Terminal ballistics and bullet composition
- How to know your limitations

This is as good an outline as any for assembling a comprehensive course curriculum when it comes to hunting-rifle skills. Use this as a guideline for any class that you consider taking. Many of the schools that are mentioned elsewhere in this chapter have hunting-specific courses as well that are worth taking.

055 JOIN THE BLACKPOWDER REVOLUTION

The earliest firearms were muzzleloaders. Way back in 13th century China, it occurred to somebody that he could scare the silk robes off of his enemy by stuffing gunpowder down a bamboo tube and topping it with bits of metal, porcelain, or, better yet, an arrow or two, pointing it in his enemy's direction, and putting a match to the works.

For hundreds of years, muzzleloaders were the long gun of choice for military and hunting applications and were improved through a series of refinements that continue to this day. At this juncture, muzzleloaders are divided into two camps: those that pay homage to the original smoothbores and rifles that predate the 20th century, and their ultramodern offspring.

056 CAST YOUR OWN BULLETS

Kentucky rifles, like their musket predecessors, fired round lead balls, which were easy to make, provided you had the metal, a heat source, and a mold to cast from. Simple bullet molds, essentially a metal block with handles and a set of spherical cavities, were used to make projectiles anywhere the lead could be heated up and melted.

Modern devices follow pretty much the same idea: melt your lead in a pan or crucible, pour it into the mold, let it cool, crack open your mold, and voilà!—instant ammunition. While not as accurate as modern rifled bullets, they can be easily made in your garage with a blowtorch, at a hunting cabin's stove, or—just like the originals—over a campfire in the wilderness.

057 HUNT WITH A CLASSIC FLINTLOCK

For those of us who were born 200 years too late to travel alongside Davy Crockett or Lewis and Clark, there is still plenty of opportunity to use the same kinds of guns as those heroes and their contemporaries. The Kentucky rifle from Pedersoli is one such, an authentic replica of the type of rifle that hunters carried when the Appalachian Mountains were the frontier.

Just like its forebears, the ignition is provided by a small piece of flint gripped in the jaws on the hammer.

The .32 caliber model was popular because the smaller bore diameter meant that less lead was required to mold each bullet. Simple open sights put a premium on having excellent trigger control and marksmanship fundamentals. The steep drop-off at the comb was desirable to help keep the shooter's face away from sparks when the gun was fired, and a trap door in the stock provided a storage area for small items.

058 TRY OUT A NEW OLD-STYLE GUN

Rather than stay bound to the old traditional designs, no shortage of companies have decided to improve upon the traditional muzzleloading design with modern innovations that enhance reliability and accuracy, while still hearkening back to the originals.

Other than the telltale ramrod beneath the barrel, the Ultimate Muzzleloader looks just like a regular Remington 700. But this is one with new technology incorporated into it. The ignition system uses modified pre-primed, reusable .308 brass, can handle higher pressures, and is built to deliver more consistency for better accuracy. It's designed to use 200 grains of black powder for higher velocities and more flattened trajectory; with a 250-grain bullet, it achieves muzzle velocities over 2,400 fps. The bottom of the stock has a trapdoor (where the magazine sits on a regular Remington 700) that holds additional pre-primed brass

for faster reloads. The adjustable X-Mark Pro Trigger can be set to break anywhere from 2 ½ to 5 pounds and the M700 receiver easily accepts scope bases and rings to mount optics.

Another example of the modern muzzleloader, the Vortek has a sleek profile and reduced weight courtesy of a striker-fired ignition system. It also incorporates several features common to other modern muzzleloaders on the market. The striker button is pushed forward to cock the rifle—there is no external hammer to work. This sleek system has a faster lock-time for better performance, a two-stage trigger set to break at 2 pounds, and a storage compartment inside the removable butt pad. The breech plug protects the gun's interior from the elements, and can be removed quickly and easily from the rifle.

059 BITE THE (MODERN) BULLET

Muzzleloader projectiles have come a long way over the centuries. The first spherical balls were eventually replaced by the Minié ball, a conical lead bullet made with grooves in its sides and a cavity in its bottom. The hollow base of the bullet would expand when fired and engage the rifling in the barrel to spin-stabilize its flight. Using an expanding base to get the bullet in contact with the rifling was a revolutionary step, and one of the today's most recent innovations uses the same principal.

The Federal B.O.R. Lock muzzleloader bullet has a cup at its base made of polymer with a fiberglass reinforced bottom. When the rifle is fired, the cup is forced forward and slides up ramped surfaces on the bullet, which jams the cup into the rifling to spin-stabilize the bullet.

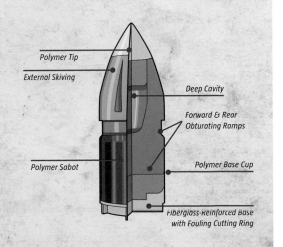

Polymer Tip

External Skiving

Deep Cavity

Forward & Rear Obturating Ramps

Polymer Sabot

Polymer Base Cup

Fiberglass-Reinforced Base with Fouling Cutting Ring

060 USE A GENERAL PURPOSE RIFLE

"One rifle for any task." That's the goal of the scout rifle, also known as the general purpose rifle. The concepts behind this rifle were articulated by Col. Jeff Cooper, who had brainstormed with some of his cohorts to come up with a rifle that was equally useful for personal defense and hunting.

The specifications they developed for the rifle were quite exact. It would be:

- A bolt-action rifle fed by a detachable box magazine.

- Chambered in .308 Win.

- Equipped with ghost ring iron sights.

- No more than one meter (39.37 inches) in overall length.

- Between 6.5 and 7.5 pounds total weight.

- Able to mount a low-magnification scope with long eye relief forward of the receiver.

- Accurate enough to group 4 inches or less at 200 yards. A competent marksman should be able to hit an 8-inch target at this range from practical field positions.

Currently only two "true" scout rifle models are in production, although some models like Springfield's M1A SOCOM series come very close. Custom gun makers will also modify a standard bolt-action into a scout rifle. For a time, Savage made a scout rifle as well, the M10 FCM. While not currently in production, it can be found online and in stores that sell used guns.

061 TAKE AIM WITH THE BIG TWO

There are two production rifles at this time that basically adhere to the scout rifle concept, each made by Steyr and Ruger.

STEYR MANNLICHER SCOUT

This is the original production scout rifle. Cooper was intimately involved in its development, working closely with Steyr to refine it before it went into production at the end of 1996. The rifle was first shown to the public early in 1998. The rifle is technically advanced with many interesting (and expensive) features: The ghost ring sights fold down flush when they are not needed; the buttstock holds an extra magazine; the rifle has many low-profile attachment points for a sling, which is another feature that Cooper deemed important; and there is an integral bipod in the forend that can be deployed when needed.

Though prohibitively expensive for most shooters, this rifle shoots and runs very well and accomplishes the task Cooper intended. The stock is well made and ergonomic and greatly enhances the rifle's handling. It is slick, handy, and capable. One drawback: the bipod does not work very well. It's too tall for many purposes and collapses if the shooter leans into it too hard.

RUGER GUNSITE SCOUT

After Steyr released their scout rifle, the instructors at Gunsite ,who keep Jeff Cooper's legacy alive, worked with Ruger to develop their own version, and it's hard to imagine that the Colonel wouldn't be pleased by what they created. I've shot many Ruger Scouts since they were introduced in 2011 and they have all been outstanding little rigs. Their accuracy is impressive. With a fixed-power 2.5X scope, I've engaged man-size targets out to 800 meters.

Cooper's dictum for 200-yard accuracy is a chip shot for these guns. As with the Steyr, the stock on Ruger's Scout is excellent. While not as refined—or as costly—as the Steyr Scout, this doesn't detract from the Ruger in any way. This rifle is rugged and built for hard use. The gun is nimble and can get on target quickly, with excellent accuracy and proven reliable action. It uses readily available magazines and has multiple mounting options for sights—but no bipod included.

062 PRACTICE SCOUT RIFLE DRILLS

Want to be the best shooter you can be with a scout rifle? Give these two precision drills a try. Figure out your average time for each and work to beat it.

SHOOT ONCE Place a paper plate downrange. With the rifle held at the low ready (muzzle facing downrange a 45-degree angle to the ground, butt of the stock in the shoulder), wait for the buzzer to go. In a smooth motion, bring the rifle up while taking the safety off. As the sights drift into the target, break the shot.

Start doing this with an empty gun, calling your shot as the trigger clicks. You'll find that you'll have less success if you jerk the rifle up in an attempt to move fast. Smooth is key. Once you've gotten the rhythm down, do the drill with a single shot. Start close, 15 yards or so, and slowly work your way back.

TAKE FIVE Place five paper plates downrange at least 1 yard apart. With the rifle at the low ready, engage targets at the go signal. Do this drill at distances from 15 to 200 yards. Employ different stances: off-hand, kneeling, sitting, and prone. Keep the rifle in your shoulder the whole time and lean into the gun to manage the recoil.

063 LEARN ABOUT LOW-MAG OPTICS

Somewhere along the line, hunters drifted away from low-magnification optics. Our shooting forefathers did very well with open sights, and the earliest telescopic sights had modest levels of magnification. A 4X scope was deemed excellent for longer shots (which it is) and 2.5X scopes were quite common. But the mentality of "more is better" took hold at some point and hunters thought that if an optic could crank up to 16X, then that must be better. Well, for big-game hunting, it isn't.

Even though high-magnification scopes continue to dominate the market, especially in light of the long-range hunting craze, there are a good number of savvy shooters who are opting for better balanced optics on their rifles. Scope makers have responded to growing demand with a number of excellent, and affordable, optics with 1X magnification at the low end.

064 KNOW WHY YOU SHOULD GO LOW

The benefits of setting a scope at a lower level of magnification are many. Here's why you should crank your power down.

GET A BROADER VIEW The shooter can see more when the scope is set to a lower power. This aids in initially locating the animal and is a huge benefit in tracking the animal after the shot. If needed, a follow-up shot is much more likely with the scope's power dialed down.

STAY ON TARGET At high magnification, every tremor, heartbeat, and breath is exaggerated when looking through a scope. This can cause the shooter to hesitate and second-guess the hold, messing up the shot as the trigger breaks. With less perceived wobble at lower magnification, the shooter can relax and let the crosshairs drift around the vital zone and make a better shot.

OPEN THE EXIT PUPIL When magnification is cranked up, the exit pupil shrinks. A smaller exit pupil makes it more difficult for the shooter's eye to locate the image, and it makes the image look more murky in low-light conditions. Neither of these is good.

065 VIEW THESE FIVE GREAT LOW-MAG OPTICS

There are plenty of low-mag optic options out there, and many of them perform quite handily. Take a look at the following selection.

(A) LEUPOLD VX-6 1-6X24MM CDS

With a magnification range up to 6X, there's little this new optic from Leupold can't do. I mounted one on a .416 Rigby recently and it withstood all its punishing recoil without complaint. Cranked up to 6X, it delivered 1 MOA accuracy with that classic caliber at 100 yards. For even more demanding long-range work, you have the option of ordering a custom elevation turret that's calibrated to your specific load.

(B) TRIJICON TR24-3 ACCUPOINT 1-4X24MM

The AccuPoint system from Trijicon is the best reticle illumination system for scopes built today. An exposed array of fiber optics located on the ocular lens housing illuminates the center of the German No. 4 reticle, which is a simple crosshair with no holdover marks. Requiring no batteries, it naturally dims as the light gets lower (which is what you want), and there's a sleeve that can expose or cover more of the fiber optic to regulate the brightness of the amber-colored dot. It excels for shooting at ranges from point-blank to 300 yards.

(C) NIKON MONARCH AFRICAN 1-4X20

This handy little scope is one of the best values on the market. I used it to kill a Cape buffalo in Africa and mounted it on a slug gun for hunting moose in willow thickets. It's also an excellent option for an inexpensive 3-gun scope. The German No. 4 reticle gets on target fast. The scope has .5 MOA adjustments and a 1-inch main tube. It weighs only 12 ounces and has generous mounting dimensions.

(D) BURRIS 1-4X24MM MTAC

This optic was built for competitive shooters as well as for law enforcement and tactical applications. It is built on a 30mm tube and has .5 MOA click adjustments. It comes with Burris' Ballistic 5.56 Gen2 Reticle, which has holdover marks from 100 to 600 yards that are calibrated for .223 Remington bullets from 50 to 77 grains. With a bit of practice, the marks can be adapted for other calibers as well. The reticle also illuminates.

(E) WEAVER TACTICAL SUPER SLAM 1-5X24 CIRT

This 1-5X scope from Weaver is a tough little unit. I've dragged mine through some really punishing and gritty conditions, and other than some scuffs and scratches on the exterior, it's held up perfectly. The CIRT reticle on the first focal plane scope has decent milling capability for longer shots, but is uncluttered for effective close-range work. It's meant primarily for competitive and tactical applications but would also work well on a hunting rifle.

066 GET IN A FIGHTING STANCE

Every athletic activity requires good footwork, and shooting a rifle is no exception. Position your feet correctly to become a better shot. I call the stance I use a "fighting stance" because it mimics the basic position used by boxers and other martial artists. This posture gives you good balance and mobility. You can quickly shift around or pivot if necessary, and being squared up to the target gives you the best view of what's going on downrange.

Start with your feet about shoulder-width apart. If you're a right-handed shooter, cheat your left foot forward a few inches. Flex your knees slightly and keep your weight evenly distributed between your feet. This position should feel comfortable and relaxed.

When you bring the rifle up, lean forward just a touch. If you're standing straight up, or worse, leaning back, you'll have a much harder time recovering from recoil. But with your weight into the rifle, you will get back on target quickly.

Keep your elbows tucked in close to your body. There's no need to chicken-wing the rear arm by lifting the elbow up high. This is a dynamic shooting position, not a static target-shooting stance.

067 RUN A BOLT GUN RIGHT

When firing a bolt-action rifle, the shooter should automatically work the action and get another round in the chamber while the rifle is still up and shouldered. One of the worst habits a shooter can adopt is firing once and then lifting his or her head off of the stock to look at what happened downrange. To avoid this, dry-fire with an empty gun and, after pausing for about a half-second for proper follow-through, run the bolt.

The forward hand should have a firm grip on the stock, pulling it back into the pocket of the shoulder. This will keep the gun from slipping out of place as the other hand cycles the action.

068 CHANGE YOUR MAGAZINE

On rifles with detachable box magazines, performing magazine changes at the right time and in the right way will keep you in the action.

STEP 1 Start by grabbing a fresh magazine with your non-trigger hand. It should be placed on your body so that when you bring it to the rifle, the bullets are facing the correct way. Pinch the magazine between your thumb and index finger and draw it out.

STEP 2 If the magazine in the rifle has run dry, hit the release and let it fall to the ground (A). If you want to top off the rifle, and have the time and are in a safe position, grasp the magazine you're looking to replace with the last three fingers of the hand that is still holding the fresh magazine, hit the release, and keep that magazine in your hand (B).

STEP 3 Insert the fresh magazine into the rifle. Hit the bottom of the magazine with your palm and then give it a tug downward to make sure it is seated securely in place. If you have the old magazine in your hand, place it in an empty pocket or in a dump pouch. Don't get a partially empty magazine mixed in with the full ones.

F-CLASS

This relatively new style of competition is shot from the prone position (like Palma) and allows the use of scopes and front and rear rests (like benchrest). In the Target Rifle (F/TR) class, the guns are limited to .223 Remington and .308 Winchester, but the Open class guns can be chambered in anything. The rifles have weight restrictions that are determined by the class and gear used. The open-class rifles max out at 22 pounds, while the F/TR guns can weigh 18.15 pounds if a bipod is used or 16 pounds if a front rest is employed.

F-Class is a 1,000-yard sport, though matches are shot at shorter distances as well.

HIGH POWER

The High Power category covers a lot of ground, but is best thought of as a multiposition, multidistance discipline. Some shot strings are rapid fire, requiring 10 shots within 60 seconds, while the slow-fire stages allow 10 minutes for 10 shots. These matches are classically shot at distances of 200, 300, and 500 or 600 yards, though clubs without enough room will shoot at closer ranges on reduced-sized targets. The course of fire will include standing, sitting or kneeling, and prone shooting.

The rifles have metallic sights and they must be capable of holding at least five rounds and have the

ability to be reloaded quickly. (Some of the 1,000-yard matches allow the use of scopes.)

Rifles fall into two categories: Match and Service. Some Match rifles look like something out of a sci-fi movie, while the Service rifles are limited to the M16, M14, M1, and their commercial equivalents.

METALLIC SILHOUETTE SHOOTING

This interesting sport originated in Mexico in the early 1900s. At that time, live animals were staked out at different distances and shot at from the off-hand (standing) position. In the late 1940s, someone had the bright idea to switch to metal cutouts, and that's why

the sport today employs steel chickens, pigs, turkeys, and rams, all of which are placed downrange at a variety of distances.

Silhouette shooting can be done with almost any type of firearm, but matches are most commonly held with centerfire and rimfire rifles.

The centerfire rifles often look like hunting rifles topped with large, high-magnification scopes. Caliber selection varies, as the shooters want a bullet with moderate recoil that is stout enough to knock over the steel targets.

PALMA

Palma shooting traces its origin to September 13, 1876, when the first match was held at the Creedmoor Range on Long Island, New York. It is a slow-fire discipline shot from the prone position at 800, 900, and 1,000 yards. In the United States, any rifle with metallic sights that has been chambered in .223 Remington or .308 Winchester is eligible to shoot a Palma match—although the .223 has a hard time at those ranges. International Palma regs are much more restrictive. The rifles come in many shapes, sizes, and colors, but are configured to be shot with a sling because supports like bipods and rests are not allowed.

COWBOY ACTION

This game is about speed, not fine-tuned accuracy. Cowboy action shooters use old-style lever guns with slicked-up actions and low-recoil rounds in order to spit lead downrange as fast as possible. Pump-action rifles are also permissible, though not very common. The targets used include steel plates and paper cutouts, and the array is limited only by the match director's imagination. Each stage is timed and the lowest time wins. Stages are shot with rifles, shotguns, and handguns, so the lever gun is used for only a portion of the shooting.

The lever guns employ pistol cartridges—the .38 Special being most popular—that must meet certain criteria for power and speed. The rifles also must have exposed hammers, be fed by a tubular-style magazine, and be based on a style of rifle built "approximately," according to the rules, between 1860 and 1899.

070 FIRE THE MOST ACCURATE RIFLE EVER

Benchrest is a game of accuracy, pure and simple. Over the course of the competition, whoever can shoot the smallest groups—which are usually measured down to the thousandth of an inch—takes home the honors. Benchrest also has competitions based on shooting for points instead of tight groupings.

Benchrest consists of different classes of firearms that are shot at varying distances, depending on match specifics. Each class of rifle must conform to certain weight and equipment restrictions. The most common centerfire benchrest rifles are the light and heavy varmint classes, which can use any type of scope but must weigh less than 10½ and 13½ pounds, including sights, respectively.

For most matches, the targets are at 100, 200, and 300 yards, though some benchrest matches are shot as far away as 1,000 yards.

STOCK The stock is flat underneath the forend so that it sits securely on the front rest, and is stiff yet incredibly lightweight. Stocks are commonly laminated wood,

reinforced with carbon fiber, and weigh about a pound. The butt plates are usually metallic. Shooters often add or subtract weight from the stock so the rifles can be shot in both light and heavy varmint divisions. Altering the weight also changes a rifle's balance, letting shooters tweak its handing characteristics.

TRIGGER Triggers on bench rifles are set to fire at a light touch; weights of 2 ounces or less are common.

FRONT REST Top-quality front rests are impressive pieces of engineering, costing $1,000 or more. Many are controlled by a joystick that moves the forend horizontally and vertically to help the shooter carefully position the crosshairs.

REAR BAG Shooters have strong preferences when it comes to rear bags. The material used has an effect on how well it supports the stock, and the bags come with various profiles. The bags can also be squeezed to fine-tune the crosshairs' elevation.

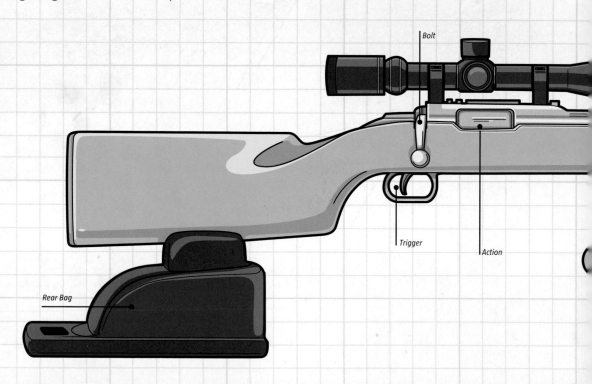

Bolt

Trigger

Action

Rear Bag

BARREL This is the heart and soul of a benchrest rifle; one that shoots exceptionally well will be babied over the course of its life. If a barrel isn't shooting well, even in the middle of a match, shooters will not hesitate to swap in a new one if they think it will perform better. Benchrest barrels are usually very heavy bull barrels with muzzle diameters over .75 inch. On unlimited guns that have no weight restrictions, the barrel diameter can be as large as 1.45 inches.

MIRAGE SHIELD This plastic strip is affixed to the top of the barrel to minimize the mirage seen through the scope created by heat coming off the barrel.

BOLT Depending on shooter preference regarding the technique used to run the action, the bolts on benchrest rifles can be positioned to either side of the action, though many operate just like standard bolt-actions.

BEDDING Unlike traditional sporter or tactical rifles, where the action and stock are screwed together, benchrest actions are glued to the stock. This method of assembly eliminates any uneven torque and stress on the action that can compromise accuracy.

SCOPE The optics used in benchrest are powerful and light. Fixed-power scopes with 40X or 45X magnification are common. The crosshairs used in benchrest are very fine and sometimes have a small center dot.

ACTION Benchrest actions come in different materials and profiles. Round steel actions—either stainless steel or Chrome-Moly—are most common, but aluminum types with steel inserts are used as well, and some have flat-bottomed profiles. Actions can be configured for left- or right-hand operation, and the loading port can be opposite of the ejection port to aid in rapid firing to take advantage of stable wind conditions.

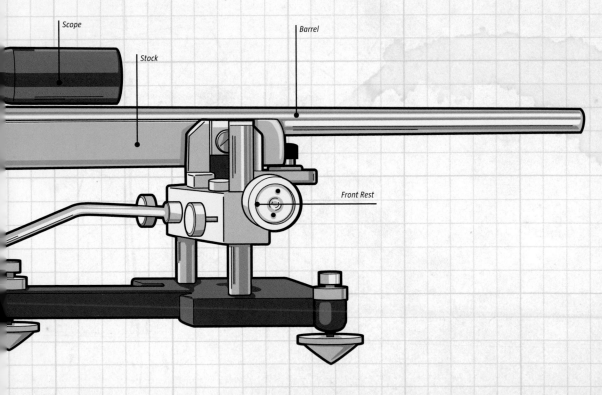

Scope

Stock

Barrel

Front Rest

071 GAIN PERFORMANCE AND SAVE MONEY

Why reload? Whenever that topic comes up, we invariably discuss the cost savings or performance gains. Both reasons are valid. Reloading in volume will save money. All you have to do is look at the cost of your favorite ammo, then price out all the needed components, and figure out how many rounds it will take to recoup the expense of the initial investment in the reloading setup.

As for performance gains, this motivates a lot of shooters as well, though perhaps less so than in the past. There are so many types of factory ammo out there that shoot well that it is no longer a given that a reloader will see better results by making his own ammo. Though for more obscure calibers—the

Ackley Improveds of the world, for instance—the accuracy gains can be significant.

The ability to customize your ammunition is a reason to reload as well. Perhaps your favorite bullet isn't available in a factory offering. Reloading solves that problem. Then, there's also the issue of ammo availability. Using progressive reloading systems, a shooter has the ability to load ammo in quantities that might be difficult to obtain through other means.

I've reloaded for all these reasons, but among these motivations, I have to confess that I do it mainly because I enjoy it. Crafting good quality ammo by hand is a pleasure in itself. Give it a try and you might find it addictive as well.

072 GET THE BASIC SETUP

Someone new to reloading can pick up a complete starter kit from companies like RCBS or Hornady for $250 to $400. These kits will include the press itself as well as a reloading manual and the accessories needed to prepare the cases and weigh and throw the powder charges. A basic die set for standard rifle calibers costs about $25 to $50. This includes a full-length resizing die and a bullet seater die.

Beginning with a two-die set makes the most sense for someone reloading for the first time. Not only are the dies cheaper, they are also easier to use. Once comfortable with making handloads this way, a shooter can then go on to more sophisticated reloading techniques and gear.

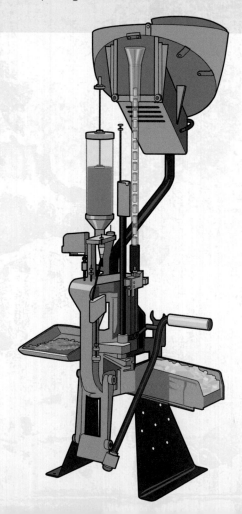

073 CHOOSE ACCURACY OR VOLUME

Loading your own ammo means making a choice between single-stage setups for more accurate work or a progressive setup for quick mass-production style reloads.

Redding makes some of the finest reloading equipment available, and for accuracy work, a shooter would be hard pressed to do better. The company's single-stage presses are excellent, but the T-7 turret press lets the user quickly switch between dies, avoiding the need to remove and replace them with each new operation.

The multiple holes for dies allow the shooter to set up and use more advanced reloading techniques (like neck sizing dies with bushings or body dies that leave the neck alone) more easily, too.

Coupled with an electronic powder dispenser, such as those made by RCBS or Lyman, a setup like this is capable of turning out high-quality ammo quickly.

A shooter graduating to this level of equipment might want to also consider some more involved case preparation. Trimming case necks so that the brass will hold the bullet with uniform tension, and using a cutter to make the primer pockets uniform as well, are two processes that, though time consuming, can yield better accuracy.

Progressive reloaders perform several operations with each pull of the handle. Once the machine is set up, this allows the user to crank out hundreds of rounds per hour. And if that isn't enough, there are reloaders that run electronically that can turn out a 1,000 rounds every hour—or more.

One of the most highly regarded progressive reloaders is the Dillion Precision XL 650. With each pull on the handle, this machine resizes and deprimes the old brass, puts in a new primer, measures and drops the powder charge into the case, seats the new bullet, adds a crimp to the cartridge, and drops a completed round into a bin. All the operator does is place a bullet onto the prepped case with the left hand while using the right hand to run the lever.

AR RIFLE

THERE ISN'T ANY TYPE OF FIREARM THAT EVOKES MORE PASSION THAN THE AR-15 AND THE OTHER MEMBERS OF SO-CALLED MODERN SPORTING RIFLE (MSR) FAMILY.

In combat, it has been our main service rifle since the mid-1960s. Its baptism by fire in Viet Nam was shaky, to put it mildly, and the servicemen who first carried it took a strong dislike to the M16 because of its poor performance. But in the five decades since then, the kinks have been worked out of the system to the point that it has become the most tactically evolved and capable battle rifle on the planet. The disgust felt by the soldiers who first wielded the rifle has been replaced by deep feelings of respect and admiration by the current generation of the military.

We see similar split reactions in the civilian world. There are those for whom the MSR is the embodiment of evil, when it comes right down to it, based solely on how it looks and its ergonomics. They don't like that it is black and that it has a pistol grip and an adjustable stock. They know that they don't like that it has a "barrel shroud," although if you ask them to define what a barrel shroud is, you'll almost certainly get a blank look. Never mind that MSRs are used in the barest minority of any crimes involving firearms—they want them banned. To hell with them, I say.

The AR has become America's most popular rifle because it is a damn fine gun. It is easy to shoot, it is accurate and, thanks to the ingenuity of American gun builders, it has been adapted to a perform a dazzling number of tasks. This chapter provides an overview of all the shooting chores that MSRs excel at, as well as the many skills and drills that a shooter needs to master the rifle.

Pick one up, spend some time shooting it and get some good instruction and you'll come to understand why MSRs are so beloved by so many of today's shooters.

074 TRY THE GUN THAT CAN DO ANYTHING

More than one person out there has made the wry comment that owning an AR is like "a Barbie doll for shooters." That is essentially the truth, in spite of the jesting quality of this statement. ARs come in a nearly endless array of calibers and configurations. And when it comes to accessories, forget it. No other firearm platform can compete. There are enough add-ons out there to customize an AR for any task. The ability to snap on grips, sights, lights, lasers and slings is part of the reason that ARs are among the most versatile rifles in history. Here's a look at some of the many uses an AR can be put to.

MILITARY The AR-15 (later designated the M16 by the military) was plagued by major shortcomings when it was first deployed, prone to jamming and other various malfunctions. But eventually the flaws were corrected and the rifle—and the tactics used to employ it—was refined to the point where its status as a preeminent infantry rifle is no longer in question. It excels in a variety of roles, everything from Close Quarters Battle (CQB) to use by snipers and designated marksmen.

LAW ENFORCEMENT In addition to military use, AR-15 and M4 rifles have taken on a growing role in law enforcement circles. Chances are, instead of a shotgun in a police vehicle's gun rack, half the time you'll see an AR parked there instead. The rifle's compact size and proven capabilities in an urban environment have made it a top choice as a patrol rifle for police use, and for SWAT teams nationwide.

SPORT SHOOTING Action shooting sports that involve ARs, such as 3-gun, are on the rise. This is hardly surprising given that running and gunning through a stage of targets with an AR is about as much fun as you can have with your pants on. These sports are an effective way to train with the platform.

COMPETITION ARs are a common sight in the Service Rifle division of High Power Competition. The rifles are typically equipped with shooting slings and have open sights. The courses of fire vary, but can reach out as far as 600 yards depending on the specific match. These rifles look stock from the exterior but usually have aftermarket barrels and triggers.

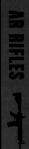

BIG-GAME HUNTING For big-game hunting that doesn't require lots of walking and where multiple targets might be present—think feral hogs or culling does—an AR-15 is a logical choice. But the relative weight and bulk of the platform can make it less than ideal for mountain hunting and scenarios where all-day walks are in the offing.

VARMINT HUNTING Shooting nirvana is being on the trigger of a heavy-barreled AR chambered in .204 Ruger, preferably proned out on the edge of a prairie dog town. Varmint shooting and ARs go together better than peanut butter and chocolate, and combining the two is the best recipe for politically incorrect laughter known to man.

PERSONAL PROTECTION Some people might look at you funny if you suggest that ARs are great for personal protection and home defense, but pay them no mind. All the attributes that make the platform ideal for boot recruits in the armed forces—ease of use, excellent ergonomics, light recoil—make it a good option for the home. Add on a light or laser and ARs are just about ideal for home defense. Polymer-tipped 55-grain .223 loads are an ideal choice for a home defense load in the AR-15. The bullets have excellent terminal ballistics but are less likely to over penetrate through walls and other barriers compared to most handgun ammo.

⊕ SNOW SAYS

The most important reason to get an AR if you don't already have one? Zombies. These rifles make short work of the undead and are ideal for precise head shots on lumbering flesheaters. Grab a handful of extra mags and throw a light and laser sight on your rifle and you're good to go. Arrow launchers are a nice touch too.

075 KNOW WHERE THE AR CAME FROM

The AR-15, today more generically known as the Modern Sporting Rifle or MSR, was born during a time of turmoil and transition in the history of the U.S. military. During the 1950s, the Cold War was in full swing and we were entering an era of nuclear deterrence when future conflicts directly involving major powers seemed less likely than smaller-scale actions in proxy states. This was a radical change from the set-piece battles of the First and Second World Wars.

THE LAY OF THE LAND In the late 1940s, the Soviets had fielded the game-changing AK-47, ushering in an era of arming infantry with assault weapons on a mass scale. Lightweight, easy to wield, reliable, and packing a great deal of firepower, the AK-47 gave the Soviet Union, and its allies, a terrific advantage over its adversaries. The United States, meanwhile,

adopted the M14 in 1957, a heavy-caliber firearm cut from the traditional "battle rifle" exemplified by the M1903 Springfield and M1 Garand—and it became obsolete the moment that it began rolling off the production line.

AMERICA STEPS UP By the early 1960s this deficit could no longer be ignored. Even though the M14 represented a step backward (at least in its role as a general issue rifle; as a specialized weapon, it is an excellent firearm) the military had been exploring the concept of high-velocity small-caliber weapons since the 1950s.

This was the context in which the AR-15—later designated the M16/XM16E1—came to the fore. On paper, it was an ideal choice. It fired a 55-grain 5.56mm bullet faster than 3,200 fps, and it also fulfilled the military's requirements for penetration downrange.

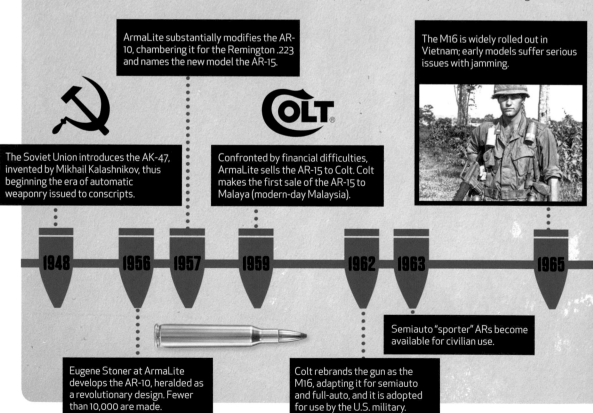

ArmaLite substantially modifies the AR-10, chambering it for the Remington .223 and names the new model the AR-15.

The M16 is widely rolled out in Vietnam; early models suffer serious issues with jamming.

The Soviet Union introduces the AK-47, invented by Mikhail Kalashnikov, thus beginning the era of automatic weaponry issued to conscripts.

Confronted by financial difficulties, ArmaLite sells the AR-15 to Colt. Colt makes the first sale of the AR-15 to Malaya (modern-day Malaysia).

1948 · 1956 · 1957 · 1959 · 1962 · 1963 · 1965

Semiauto "sporter" ARs become available for civilian use.

Eugene Stoner at ArmaLite develops the AR-10, heralded as a revolutionary design. Fewer than 10,000 are made.

Colt rebrands the gun as the M16, adapting it for semiauto and full-auto, and it is adopted for use by the U.S. military.

A BAD BEGINNING Unfortunately, this rifle, the brainchild of Eugene Stoner and his colleagues at ArmaLite, was not ready for deployment. As C. J. Chivers phrased it in *The Gun*, his excellent history of the AK-47: "The early M-16 [sic] and its ammunition formed a combination not ready for war. They were a flawed pair emerging from a flawed development history. Though prone to malfunction, they were forced into the troops' hands through a clash of wills and egos."

The results on the battlefield were catastrophic: These rifles jammed in battle and the soldiers that were carrying them died.

PATH TO SUCCESS So why are the M16, its little brother the M4, and their civilian AR-15 counterparts still part of the landscape? Because, through the course of the ensuing decades, those flaws were worked out of the system, and the platform has now lived up to its potential, both on the battlefield and as a civilian sporting arm.

Improvements were made to the ammunition. The rifle's barrel twist rates were optimized for various bullets. The chambers were properly chrome-lined. And, more recently, the incorporation of different sighting systems and accessories, along with the development of specialized uppers, barrels, stocks, and hand guards, has made the MSR America's most versatile and popular rifle.

No matter the application—hunting, personal protection, competition, plinking—the AR-15 can be configured to get the job done.

ARs become the United State's most popular rifle type, with close to four million in civilian use.

The M16 becomes the U.S. Army's standard service rifle, thus replacing the outdated M14.

Widespread restrictions on usage and modification come into being in the United States as part of the Assault Weapons Ban.

1968

1994

2004

2012

Ownership of the design of the M4 carbine , which was derived from earlier carbine M16 rifles, is taken by the U.S. Army.

076 DISSECT YOUR AR

The AR-15 was designed to be modular, giving shooters the ability to interchange parts. With the profusion of aftermarket accessories available today, it is easy to create an AR-15 with a custom configuration. But most ARs share these elements in common.

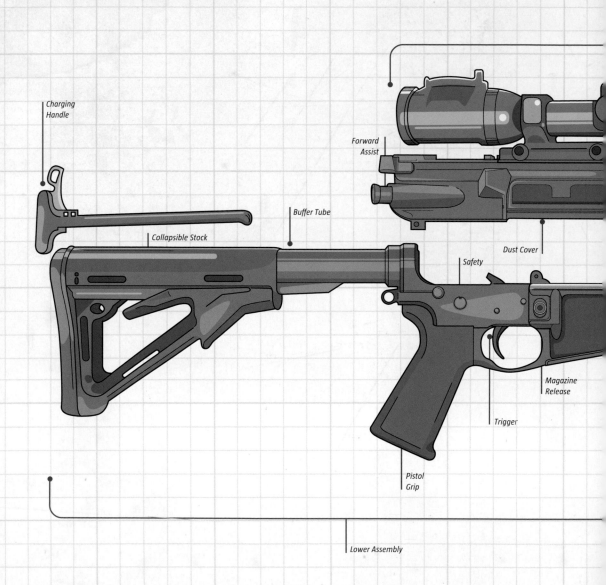

Charging Handle

Forward Assist

Buffer Tube

Collapsible Stock

Dust Cover

Safety

Magazine Release

Trigger

Pistol Grip

Lower Assembly

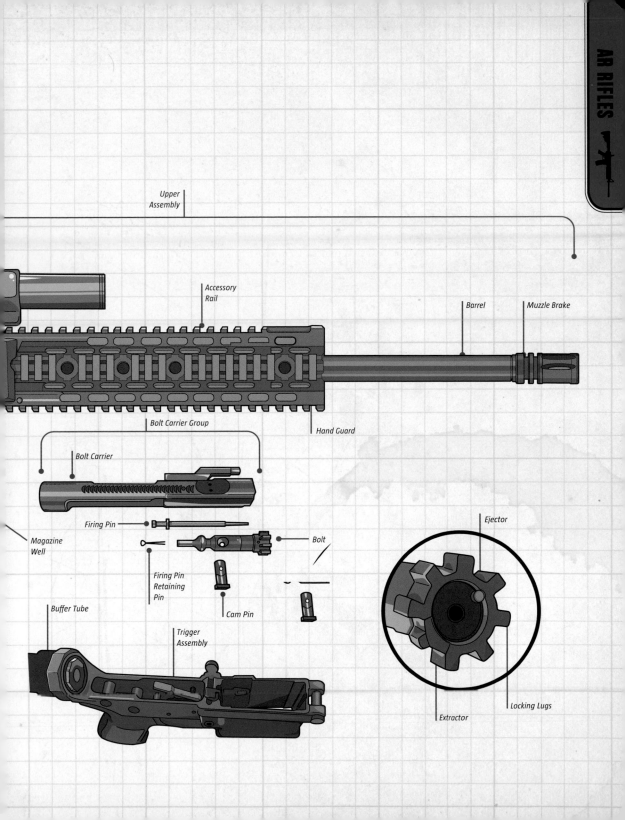

Upper
Assembly

Accessory
Rail

Barrel

Muzzle Brake

Bolt Carrier Group

Bolt Carrier

Hand Guard

Firing Pin

Magazine
Well

Firing Pin
Retaining
Pin

Cam Pin

Bolt

Ejector

Locking Lugs

Extractor

Buffer Tube

Trigger
Assembly

077 DIAL IN A 50/200 ZERO

The most useful, general-purpose zero for an AR is to put it dead-on at 50 yards. With a typical sight setup (the sight position 3 inches above the bore) this will put the bullet 1½ inches high at 100 yards and dead-on again at just beyond 200 yards, hence the 50/200 designation. At 300 yards, the bullet has only dropped 7 inches, making corrections for shots out to that distance simple.

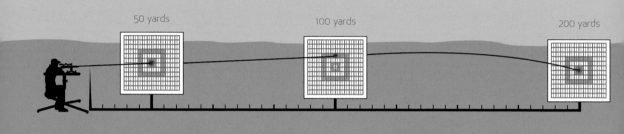

50 yards   100 yards   200 yards

078 SLING RIGHT

A single-point sling is a versatile, comfortable way to carry an AR. These slings attach near where the buffer tube joins the receiver. Slings that have some elastic in their construction provide give and keep the rifle from jarring against the shooter's body while he or she is walking or running.

To correctly wear the sling, put whichever hand is used to trigger the rifle through the loop. When it is hanging, the sling should bear down on the opposite shoulder (i.e. the left shoulder for righties). Adjust the sling so that butt of the rifle rides up at the top of the sternum. At this height, the rifle will remain held tight against the body but will be easy to maneuver into a shooting position.

When raising the rifle to take a shot, index the butt of the stock against the lower part of the shoulder. As the muzzle is lifted toward the target, the rifle will rotate naturally into place, aligning quickly with the shooter's eyes.

079 DO THE SMACK-YANK DRILL

When seating a new magazine in an AR, it is important to smack the bottom of the magazine firmly with the palm of the hand. Then grab onto the magazine and yank down to make sure it is secure in the magazine well. Fail to perform this smack-yank maneuver and sooner or later (probably sooner) you will embarrass yourself in front of all your shooting buddies because the chamber will be empty and your rifle will go "click" when you pull the trigger, and, best of all, the magazine will fall to the ground with a clang that announces to the world that you are a noob.

080 PRACTICE A SINGLE-SHOT DRILL

This drill will teach you the fundamentals of stance, posture, and trigger control. Start with your rifle held in the low ready position, with the muzzle at a 45-degree angle pointing downward at the ground between you and the target. Place the butt of the rifle near the top of your shoulder. Then, on the "up" command, raise the rifle in a smooth motion, and bring the sights up to your eyes without moving your head. As the rifle is coming in line with the target, flick the safety off and start applying pressure on the trigger, thus "loading" it. Continue to squeeze as your sights line up on target, breaking the shot as soon as the sight picture is correct. Practice this with dry fire and single live rounds at distances from 3 to 50 yards.

081 FIGHT YOUR WAY UP

When moving from a prone to standing position, or vice versa, with an AR—or any rifle for that matter—the shooter should keep the rifle in an active fighting position every step of the way. Here's how that's done.

STEP 1 When the decision is made to move out of the prone position, pull the rifle tight into the shoulder with the hand on the grip, place the lead hand on the ground and push the body into a kneeling position with both knees on the ground. Reacquire a two-handed grip on the stock and scan for targets.

STEP 2 Right-handed shooters should lift their left leg, placing the left foot just in front of the body, assuming a classic keeling shooting position. Keep scanning downrange.

STEP 3 Step forward with the rear leg, going into a standing position. Since each change in stance places the shooter's head at a different elevation, the view and perspective of the environment changes, which is why it is important to continue to look for targets downrange.

082 KNOW YOUR COME-UPS

I was once at a sniper match competing with a bunch of long-range shooting specialists, some of whom had no problem making first round hits at 1,200 yards. Then we encountered a stage where we had to shoot tennis balls hanging from strings about 15 yards downrange that some of these shooters couldn't believe they were missing.

They didn't know their come-ups. When shooters take on targets within 20 yards, bullets will start to impact low as the bullet has not yet risen to meet the line of sight of the optic. On a target at 3 yards, an AR will shoot about 3 inches low, which can miss small targets like the head box on a standard IPSC target.

Shoot at a small black dot from distances of 3, 5, 10, 15, 20, and 25 yards and make note of your come-ups. Include that data on your range cards to make sure you're ready for close-in shooting.

083 SHOOT OFF-HAND

Some shooters just love to grab onto the front of the magazine well to help steady an AR when shooting off-hand. But positioning the lead hand out along the hand guard, will yield better results. This is the reason why hand guards that extend out 15 inches or more are so popular among competitive shooters.

Grasp the rifle with the hand cupped underneath the hand guard and the thumb pointed downrange. Grip the rifle far enough forward so that the arm is straight and the elbow is locked. This creates strong rearward tension pulling the rifle back toward the pocket of the shoulder, keeping the rifle in place and allowing fast, accurate shot placement.

084 SHOOT FASTER

Set up three targets, spaced about 5 yards from each other, 15 yards downrange and then shoot them in this order—1, 2, 3, 3, 2, 1—for a total of six shots. Do this a few times and record your results with a timer. The catch is that only clean runs count—either with A-Zone hits on cardboard silhouettes or hits on 8-inch steel.

Now, if you want to drop at least 1 second from your time, do this. Instead of pausing before each press of the trigger, which shooters typically do in order to make a precise hit, learn to shoot as your sights are drifting onto the target without stopping your swing.

This takes a bit of practice to master, but once you smooth out your technique, you'll save about .2 seconds with each transition from one target to the next.

085 LEARN TO REVERSE-KNEEL

Common in 3-gun matches are barriers that competitors need to shoot from while engaging targets. Typically these barriers are positioned at an awkward height and are often flimsy, thus rendering most traditional shooting positions less effective. For barriers at waist height, a reverse kneeling position is often the way to go. Instead of stepping forward with the weak-side foot and kneeling, when employing this technique, the shooter steps forward with the foot that is on his or her strong (trigger-hand) side.

Brace the elbow of the trigger hand on the knee and use the other hand to brace the hand guard of the rifle against the barrier. Depending on the type of barrier, the shooter can often make a U-shaped cradle with the thumb and index finger to rest the hand guard in, or can trap the rifle against the barrier by gripping the barrier and hand guard together with the fingers of the weak-side hand.

086 LEARN ADVANCED PRONE POSITIONS

There are more ways to shoot lying down than just getting down on your belly. Here are a pair of more advanced techniques.

Roll over

Lie supine

ROLL OVER This position is quick to assume and is an effective way to shoot under low barriers such as cars. The shooter kneels down and then bends forward until both of his forearms are lying flat on the ground. In this position, the rifle is on its side, with the ejection port pointing directly at the ground. The shooter really needs to push his face firmly up against the stock in order to get a decent sight picture. The leading hand should be placed between the rifle's hand guard and the ground.

There are two important things to remember about this position: It will kick up a lot of dust and debris, so be sure to wear eye protection; and with the rifle on its side, the bullet's point of impact will shift significantly on longer shots. See item 87 to learn how to compensate for this issue.

LIE SUPINE This position is ideal for engaging targets from low cover, such as street-side curbs, while exposing as little of the shooter's body as possible. To get into this position, the shooter lies flat on his back and rests the rifle on his chest with the ejection port facing directly up. In order to see through the sights, the shooter needs to lift his head up off the ground. Mounting the rifle to the shoulder is impossible while in this position. Instead, the shooter can brace the butt of the stock against the biceps. Similar to the rollover, the point of impact will shift because of the rifle being held at a 90-degree angle. For larger targets at close range, this isn't a big deal, but for longer shots and shots on small targets, the shooter will need to compensate.

087 KNOW YOUR 90-DEGREE HOLD

When you turn a rifle on its side, the point of impact shifts. If the rifle is rotated counterclockwise, then the shots will impact to the left of the aiming point. The reverse is true if the rifle is rotated clockwise; shots will impact to the right.

Second, the bullets will strike low. With the rifle held in the normal attitude, the bullets will travel upward, countering gravity, to achieve whatever zero the rifle has been set up for. But if the rifle is on its side, the bullets no longer rise in the vertical plane. Instead, gravity will start pulling the bullets downward right away with respect to the shooter's line of sight.

The bottom line is this: With the rifle rotated to the left, hold high and right. With the rifle rotated to the right, hold high and left.

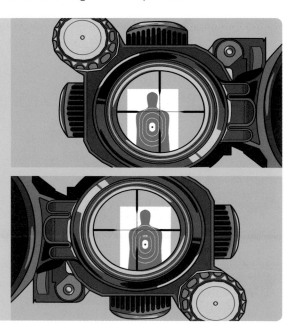

088 SHOOT AN AR ON A BUDGET

We are blessed to live in an era with such a profusion of AR-style rifles. Among the most fun to shoot are those chambered in .22 LR. They are also very useful tools to improve your AR handling skills and sharpen your marksmanship at a fraction of the cost.

The best buy in a dedicated .22 AR is the Smith & Wesson M&P 15-22. The controls on these rifles are identical to those found on a regular AR. The bolt release, magazine release, and safety are positioned the same, and they all operate in the same manner, meaning that training on the .22 platform will provide a seamless transition when it comes to handling a larger AR later on.

The throw on the charging handle is not the same (on the .22 it doesn't move very far back), but I don't consider that a serious limitation.

Best of all, these rifles run like a cat on fire. I've shot numerous M&P 15-22s over the years and own one and they all have functioned flawlessly. The only problem I have with mine is prying it from the hands of my children who have an insatiable appetite for trigger time with the S&W.

Speaking of which, they are great rifles for kids. With a collapsible stock, the ergonomics couldn't be more kid friendly. Also the weight of the rifle, which is lighter than a typical .223, makes it simpler for a smaller person to wield. The cost is difficult to beat, too. You can get them for $520 to $560, depending on the model.

089 ADD AN UPPER

Your other option for a good, cheap .22 is to purchase a rimfire upper for an existing AR lower. Companies such as CMMG, DPMS, Tactical Solutions, and many others manufacture them and, in theory, they should just snap onto your lower and shoot. That isn't always the case, however. Functionality can be spotty with some upper and lower combinations, and they can be picky about the types of ammo they like.

But don't let this scare you off. Having an upper that attaches to your lower gives an added degree of realism to your training, as the rifle will have the same trigger pull and will be closer to the weight of your centerfire AR. (You will still have to purchase and use special magazines built for .22s, though.)

And plenty of shooters have had great success adding on a .22 upper. Cost of these varies, but you can plan on spending at least $500. Most companies also offer complete rifles in .22 LR. Those start around $800.

Classic Upper

Suppressor-Ready Upper

Ultra-Light Upper

090 STAY ON TARGET

Having a .22 LR AR doesn't do you any good if you don't have targets to bang away at. The best targets for this work are those made by MGM Targets. The company's durable rimfire targets are easy to set up and will take thousands of bullet impacts without getting damaged.

MGM offers a wide variety of target styles: auto-poppers, dueling trees, plate racks, spinners, and many more choices.

To engage multiple targets more quickly, learn to master your trigger so that you are pressing it to get a clean break just as the sights of your rifle are drifting onto their mark. Set up a line of four targets and drift from one to the other, with the goal of hitting every one of your targets over the course of one smooth swing of the gun. If you're stopping the barrel to try and take a more precise aim, you're wasting time.

Start this drill in close, engaging the targets from 12 yards back. Gradually increase your distance from the targets and the distance between the targets in order to improve your trigger control.

091 DON'T SWEAT THE AMMO

Some shooters might be reluctant to invest in a rimfire AR, upper receiver, or related mods, as ammo for them has been scarce for some time—demand has rapidly outstripped supply at times, especially when the price of other ammo types goes up and shooters stock up on rimfire as an alternative. Still, manufacturers are working to catch up, and the shortage won't last forever. At some point, those who are hoarding the stuff will find their stockpiles adequate and stores shall once again be able to keep .22s on their shelves.

092 MAINTAIN YOUR AR

One of the original design goals of the AR was to make it easy for a soldier to maintain it while in the field. Disassembling an AR for field maintenance requires nothing more than the tip of a bullet to loosen the pins that hold the upper and lower receiver together and to remove the retaining pin inside the bolt carrier group (BCG), which allows the BCG to be disassembled.

But there are a host of tools specifically for ARs that are useful for cleaning and maintaining the platform. Anyone who runs an AR should consider adding these to his or her kit.

GUNNER'S MOUNT

This armorer's block is an excellent example of what to look for in a high-quality maintenance system for AR rifles. The base plate comes with trays to keep small parts organized and plenty of holes for mounting jigs that hold specific AR parts.

The jigs in this modular system adapt to different components of AR rifles and can fit into them with remarkable precision. There are jigs that snug up in the interior recesses of the upper and lower receivers, for example, and that secure them with retaining pins so that the rifle is fully supported while any maintenance work is being done.

AR BENCH BLOCK

This hockey puck-like block supports the traditional M16 front sight assembly. Holes in the puck are positioned to capture the retaining pins on the front sight as they are tapped out of place with a punch.

CLEANING BRUSHES

Several companies make cleaning brushes that are contoured such that they will clean both the bolt recesses in an AR as well as the chamber. These are

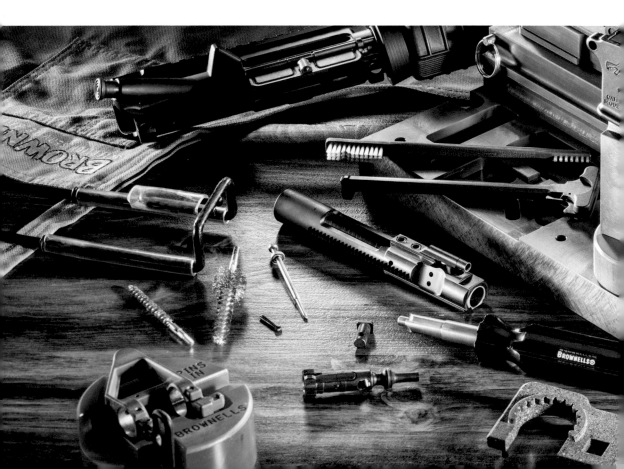

very handy for removing gunk and bits of brass that build up in recess.

BORE GUIDE

The best way to clean any rifle is from the chamber end while using a proper bore guide. A guide protects the rifling in your barrel from damage and helps prevent solvent from getting all over the interior of the firearm.

HAND GUARD REMOVER

On ARs with clamshell-style hand guards, this tool is a lifesaver. Even though it's possible to manipulate the delta ring that holds the hand guard pieces in place with bare hands, this tool makes the chore more pleasant.

AR MULTITOOL

This steel wrench is a minor miracle. It can help with the installation or removal of free-float hand guards,

barrel nuts, butt stocks, and other parts of an AR. It also has cutouts for removing or tightening down standard-sized nuts and a screwdriver tip.

FIELD CRADLE

To clean an AR in the field, a portable cradle that positions the rifle correctly with the muzzle down is a boon. With the chamber elevated, any oils or solvents in the barrel will move down toward the muzzle rather than leak back into the receiver where they can gum up the trigger and other components.

AR SCRAPER TOOL

This simple tool performs a vital task: It clears away carbon buildup from the bolt, bolt carrier, and firing pin without scratching or damaging the components.

⊙ SNOW SAYS

The first ARs, meaning the M16s that were fielded in Viet Nam, were a real disaster. They were poorly made, lacking chrome lining inside the chambers, among other things, and were prone to corrosion and malfunctions. To make matters worse, troops were given ammo that didn't work well in the rifle and they weren't supplied with cleaning kits. Many servicemen died because of these errors and the M16 ended up developing a terrible reputation—and rightfully so.

Today's ARs have evolved beyond this ill-fated start to become the world's premier battle rifle. But it is worth remembering the terrible price we paid to get to this point.

093 KEEP YOUR AR RUNNING

Given the harsh use ARs are subjected to, it's a wonder they run as well as they do. Keeping an AR-style rifle in top shape isn't hard, though. Just remember the handy acronym MEAL.

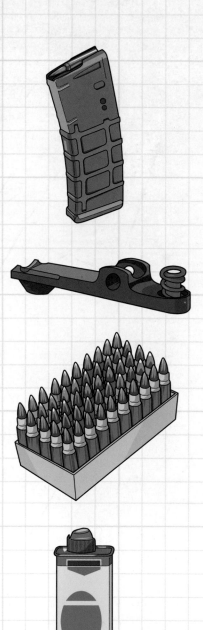

MAGAZINE The magazine is one of the weakest parts of any semiautomatic. They can get gummed up with dirt and debris. Or the feed lips can get bent when they are dropped to the ground, thus causing cycling failures. Remember, magazines are easily replaced. Test your magazines and discard them if they fail. Don't join or "marry" your magazines. They will be more prone to damage if you do.

EXTRACTOR Potential problems here include a weakened extractor that can break, weak extractor tension, or a dulling of the extractor that can lead to cycling failure. Should you experience extraction failure, most notably in the form of a stuck cartridge in the chamber, your most likely cause is the extractor. Either replace the spring or, if the extractor is no longer sharp, replace the entire unit.

AMMO Some shooters think ammo is a good place to economize. It isn't. If you buy subpar ammo, expect to have problems with misfires and other issues. It comes down to quality control. Good ammo is manufactured with accurately metered powder charges, bullets that are seated correctly, quality cases, and sealed primers. With poor ammo, these aren't a given. Stick with ammo from reputable makers.

LUBRICATION Lubrication is a must for AR rifles—but where should you put it and in what quantity? The most critical place for oil is the bolt. A generous dollop on the bolt body and a lighter coating on the firing pin is what I recommend. Conversely, keep the workings of the trigger and the interior of your magazines free of lubrication. Synthetic motor oil is great for use on ARs. One key advantage is that it doesn't contain carbon, which can lead to nasty fouling, and in a heavier weight, such as a 10W-50, the oil tends to stay in place, which is also a good thing.

094 GET UNSTUCK

To extract a case stuck inside an AR, grip the charging handle and sharply strike the butt of the rifle against the ground, a bench, or other firm surface, while pulling down hard on the handle. Most of the time this move will pop the stuck case free. If you have an adjustable buttstock, collapse it to the shortest setting to avoid damaging the stock or buffer tube before doing this.

095 CLEAR A JAM SAFELY

Push an AR hard in dirty conditions and sooner or later you're going to have to clear a jam. When you experience a failure to fire, perform the following drill automatically.

SMACK Smack the magazine on the floor plate to make sure it is seated correctly.

RACK Rack the action to clear out the old ammo that might be causing the failure.

ROLL Roll the rifle to the side as you rack the action to let the rounds that potentially caused the failure to fall out to the ground.

You should be able to do this and get back on target and pull the trigger again without looking. If the rifle still doesn't go bang, you will need to remove the magazine from the rifle, inspect the action to make sure it is clear of ammo and try again.

096 MEET AMERICA'S FAVORITE CARTRIDGE

To label the .223 Remington as America's most beloved centerfire cartridge is a terrific understatement. Its popularity outstrips that of its challengers, such as the .30/06 and .308 Win., by such a margin that if any ammo companies were brave enough to show off their sales figures, you'd realize just how lopsided the competition actually is. The legions of .223 fans out there will nod their heads in knowing agreement. A quick list of all its virtues would start with its versatility. It can be used on big and small game. It is outstanding for varmints and predators. It is excellent as a round for personal protection. Its accuracy and light recoil make it a logical choice for teaching first-time shooters the basics of marksmanship. And these same qualities make it ideally suited for competition. Even if it didn't enjoy the status that comes with being one of the longest-serving rifle rounds in U.S. military history, it strikes such a lovely balance that it still would have thrived. You just can't keep a cartridge this good down.

097 LEARN SOME HISTORY

The Remington .223 has been around for over half a century, growing ever more popular. Here are some key milestones along the way.

1957 Originally known as the .222 Remington Special, the cartridge is developed by Eugene Stoner, who was working at ArmaLite and Remington.

1959 It is renamed the .223 Remington in order to differentiate it from the many "triple deuce" .222 cartridges of the time.

1962 The U.S. Air Force makes a substantial purchase of M16 rifles chambered for the new .223 caliber.

1964 Remington Arms offers the new .223 Remington as a standard commercial load.

1965 Gen. William C. Westmoreland urges widespread adoption of the M16 (aka the XM16E1), assuring the cartridge's success.

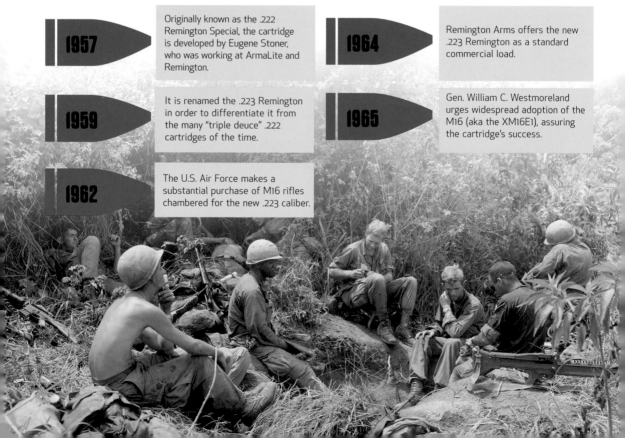

098 USE THE RIGHT LOAD

The .223 is loaded commercially with a staggering variety of bullets and, if for some reason you cannot locate the .223 in a bullet you want, reloading this cartridge is a simple matter. Here are a few standout options.

LIGHT BULLETS

Bullets weighing in between 35 and 45 grains are the speed demons of the .223 universe. Hornady's 35-grain NTX bullet, loaded with Superformance powder, steps out at 4,000 fps, while Federal's 40-grain Nosler BT has a 3,700 fps muzzle velocity. The bullets in this range are ideal for varmints. One thing to be aware of is barrel twist. Nosler's 35-grain lead-free ballistic tip, for example, requires a 1-in-14-inch twist in order to shoot accurately. If your barrel twist isn't slow enough, accuracy with these lightweights will suffer.

MIDDLE WEIGHTS

These bullets are the sweet spot for the .223. Between 45 and 60 grains, shooters will find dozens of different bullet styles to choose from. Monolithic designs, such as the Barnes Triple Shock, Hornady GMX, and Federal Fusion work well on game up to the size of deer, while 50- and 55-grain bullets with thin jackets make varmints pop like water balloons tossed off a skyscraper. For personal protection, any 55-grain polymer-tipped bullet will work well. They have excellent terminal ballistics and won't over-penetrate through walls and other structures the way pistol rounds can.

HEAVY LOADS

Heavy-for-caliber .223 loads, which range from 60 to 90 grains, are among the most interesting rounds made today. These bullets, with their higher ballistic coefficients, extend the .223's effective range quite a bit. Loads like the 77-grain OTM from Black Hills have been real game-changers. Introduced in 2002 for the military, it turned the .223/5.56 into an 800-meter sniper round and has also made its mark in competitive circles. Twist rate, again, is a big issue. Berger's 90-grain Match VLD bullet has a recommended barrel of a 1-in-7-inch twist. If your barrel doesn't have a fast enough twist, these heavy bullets won't stabilize. Provided they are designed to expand and retain their weight, these heavier bullets are excellent for whitetail-size game. Consider something like the 60-grain Nosler Partition for these types of hunting chores.

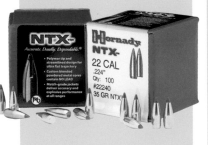

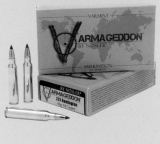

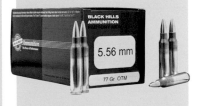

099 CHART AR CALIBERS

The rise in the popularity of AR rifles has resulted in new platforms in cartridges designed for nearly everything. Whether you're a hunter, competitive shooter, or general enthusiast, you can find an AR to specifically fit your needs.

.22 Long Rifle

The all-American .22 LR is the perfect beginner or training cartridge since it produces very low recoil and not much in the way of muzzle blast either. The mild .22 is a great way to introduce new shooters to the AR platform and works well on varmints and pests at close range.

6mm Creedmoor

The 6mm Creedmoor is relatively unknown outside of long-range shooting circles, but it is both an accurate and potent cartridge. It can propel 100-grain bullets at over 3,000 feet per second, and it benefits from a wide range of available .243/6mm bullets.

.204 Ruger

The .204 Ruger cartridge, which is based on the .222 Remington Magnum, drives a 32-grain bullet at 4,225 feet per second, making it one of the flattest-shooting varmint cartridges ever designed. It's also extremely accurate and an excellent choice for varmints and predators all the way out to 300 yards.

6x45 (6mm-223)

This .223 Remington is necked up to accept 6mm/.243-inch bullets and works well in AR rifles. It's a mild-recoil round with a boost in power over the standard .223 and is a much better deer cartridge than its parent cartridges, though the effective range for deer-size game is about 150 yards. It's an excellent varmint-hunting cartridge, pushing a 75-grain bullet in the neighborhood of 2,700 feet per second.

.223 Remington /5.56 NATO

A huge selection of .223 and 5.56 ammunition is out there for the taking, and shooters can find just the bullet they are looking for, whether for competition, marksmanship training, or hunting. In addition, this caliber is just about perfect for varmints, small predators, and 'yotes.

25-45 Sharps

The Sharps Rifle Company's 25-45 Sharps cartridge is fully compatible with .223/5.56 bolts and magazines, which means that all that is required to swap your existing .223 AR to the 25-45 is a barrel change. The new 25-45 pushes an 87-grain bullet at 3,000 feet per second, providing a significant boost in energy over the .223 for hunting deer, antelope, and hogs.

.243 Winchester

There's a good chance that you already have a .243, as it is one of the most popular and versatile hunting cartridges on the market. Loaded with bullets weighing 80 grains or less it is a fantastic varmint and predator cartridge, but with heavier, tougher bullets, it makes an excellent deer and antelope round.

6.5 Creedmoor

The Creedmoor is based on the necked-down .30 TC cartridge and has quickly become a favorite among long-range shooters and hunters. Hornady factory loads push a 120-grain bullet at over 2,900 feet per second. Using this round also means firing long, aerodynamic .264-inch bullets that do a great job bucking the wind. It's large for varmints, but it's a fantastic round for deer-size game.

.300 Winchester Magnum

There's no game in North America (and very little in the world) that you can't take with the popular and time-tested .300 Winchester Magnum. If you're looking for the ultimate long-range big-game AR cartridge, this is it, but you'll pay a premium to have an AR in this caliber.

6.5 Grendel

Bill Alexander's 6.5 Grendel, which debuted back in 2004, has gained quite a following among long-range AR shooters, thanks in large part to the fact that 6.5mm bullets possess a high ballistic coefficient for better long-range accuracy. With 123-grain Hornady SST bullets leaving the barrel at just under 2,600 feet per second, this is an effective long-range hunting round for deer, antelope, and the like.

.338 Federal

Based on a necked-up .308 Winchester, the .338 Federal will do everything that its parent cartridge will and then some. With bullets weighing from 185 to 210 grains, it packs more punch than the .308 for big game like elk and moose and will stop an angry bear in a pinch.

6.8 Remington SPC II

The 6.8 fires familiar .277-inch hunting bullets in weights from 80 to 120 grains. This is a solid varmint cartridge and works well on deer-size game at moderate ranges, but velocity and energy begin to drop sharply after a couple hundred yards.

9mm Luger

The 9mm isn't a big-game cartridge, but it's fun to shoot and will work on varmints and pests at close range. If you've got a 9mm pistol, it's nice to have an AR that shoots the same rounds. The added velocity gleaned from a longer barrel also makes this an ideal self-defense AR.

.300 Blackout

The Blackout is available in bullet weights from 110 to 220 grains, but the larger bullets are subsonic and don't perform as well on game as the 110-125 grain loads. With velocities ranging from about 2,200 to 2,400 feet per second in these weights, the Blackout makes an excellent varmint and deer cartridge within 300 yards.

.450 Bushmaster

The .450 Bushmaster fires 250- to 275-grain bullets between 2,100 and 2,200 feet per second, making it an excellent close-range round for pigs and deer-size game. The .450 is a good choice for anyone who wants to pursue big game at moderate ranges or in heavy cover. It hits with enough authority to drop even the biggest, toughest hogs, and it's an ideal cartridge for hunting black bears over bait.

.308 Winchester

The .308 Winchester is by no means a new cartridge, but it is nonetheless an effective varmint and big-game round. Because it requires a larger AR-10 platform, rifles will be heavier than those that fit AR-15 cartridges, but this is one of the most versatile cartridges on the market for anything from varmints to elk and moose.

.458 SoCom

The SoCom is available in bullet weights from 250 to 500 grains, but bullets in the 250- to 350-grain range with velocities from 1,750 to about 2,000 feet per second are the most effective for big-game hunting. The SoCom is a close-range cartridge, but it is very effective on game such as wild pigs, black bear, and deer.

100 SEE THE SIGHTS

Given the variety of ARs out there, it should not come as a surprise that there are multiple options when it comes to sighting systems. At one end of the spectrum is the traditional, basic M16-style iron sight; at the other, variable power rifle scopes with high upper-end levels of magnification. All have their place.

Most ARs today come with a Picatinny rail on the upper based on the correct assumption that the owner will likely want to put some type of optic on it. That wasn't always the case. Not so long ago, the default sights on ARs were aperture-style iron sights. Don't overlook the utility of this traditional hardware. With a protected front post and two different-size peeps that the shooter can toggle between—a larger peep for more rapid target acquisition and close-in shooting and a smaller, finer peep for precise shots at longer ranges—these sights are nearly indestructible and, with a bit of training, very effective.

SNOW SAYS

I still use iron sights on all my competition ARs, specifically the offset sights that allow the shooter to switch from the scope on top to the iron sights by simply rotating the rifle 45 degrees. These sights let the shooter transition to close-in targets in an instant and also serve as a great backup in case the main optic breaks.

101 SCOPE IT OUT

A standard 3-9x40mm variable power scope can accomplish a lot of tasks on an AR. But the best scopes for everything but extreme-range shooting are 1-6X optics, or, if you can afford them, scopes with a 1-8X magnification range. These will handle everything from targets at powder-burn distances out to 500 yards.

Many scope manufacturers make reticles with holdover and windage marks that are calibrated for ARs. These reticles are most commonly etched to match the trajectory of a 55-grain bullet travelling at 3,100 fps, though reticles for other popular .223 loads are also offered. I have shot a number of these scopes and they work very well.

The best reticles are those that have clean designs where the holdover marks are easy to distinguish from each other so that the shooter doesn't need to count down from the center to figure out which mark is the right one for a distant target.

102 MOUNT IT RIGHT

To properly position a rifle scope on top of an AR, offset mounts are usually required. These will place the scope far enough forward to achieve two critical goals. As with all rifles, the main concern when mounting a scope on an AR is achieving the correct eye relief. The second goal, unique to ARs, is to make sure there is enough clearance between the ocular lens housing on the scope and the charging handle so the shooter can easily grasp the handle and charge the rifle.

Offset mounts make it easy to position the rear of the scope so that it is just forward of the charging handle. So positioned, the eye relief on the scope is also usually correct, though ARs with stocks that adjust for length of pull make it simple to fine-tune eye relief.

103 LOOK AT NONMAGNIFYING OPTICS

Nonmagnifying optics offer a lot of configurations. In general, these sights are an improvement over iron sights because of their ability to function well in low light and, in some cases, because they have holdover marks for engaging targets at longer distances.

RELY ON REFLEXES Reflex sights project an aiming dot back to the shooter's eye. The design eliminates the effect of parallax and offers unlimited eye relief. They are lightweight but can be somewhat fragile unless encased in a protective chassis. Battery life for these is usually measured in years, as the amount of power it takes to illuminate the dot is less than what the battery loses when actually disconnected.

GO HOLOGRAPHIC Larger and beefier than reflex sights, holographic optics project a bright reticle back to the shooter. The intensity of the reticle can be dialed up and down, based on the shooter's requirements. The hardened design is meant to withstand the rigors of combat. They can be combined with magnifiers that swing into place for longer shots.

GET MORE FIBER By gathering ambient light in order to illuminate the aiming point, fiber optics eliminate the need for batteries. Some manufacturers offer these sights in conjunction with glowing tritium and battery-powered aiming points to offer the best of all worlds. Fiber optics designs are also found in fixed- and variable-power scopes as well.

TRY THE ONE TRUE OPTIC 1X optics are scopes that do not magnify and have large, bold reticles. The simplicity of their design makes them especially rugged.

104 ACCESSORIZE YOUR AR

An AR without accessories is like a Thanksgiving turkey without the stuffing, gravy, cranberry sauce, side dishes, and pumpkin pie. It just ain't right. Depending on the task at hand, you'll find add-ons that will help you shoot better, faster, and under poor conditions. This is just a small sampling of the numerous and varied options that you will find are available to add on to your AR.

MUZZLE BRAKE OR FLASH HIDER A good muzzle brake keeps your sights on target with each pull of the trigger as the exhaust ports funnel gas to counteract recoil. A flash hider minimizes the flame at the muzzle when the gun is fired, preserving the shooter's low-light vision and making it harder for others to detect the shot.

HAND STOP This helps to position the lead hand in a consistent way on the rifle and augment the shooter's grip. This is especially handy on short-barreled rifles to prevent the hand from accidentally going over the end of the rifle and in front of the muzzle.

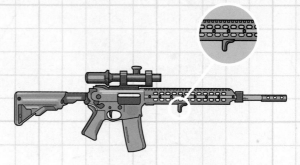

VERTICAL GRIP This increases a rifle's stability for close-quarters shooting and works well on ARs configured for personal protection. For other tasks, such as long range shooting, hunting, and competition, a grip can be cumbersome.

LASER In low-light situations a weapon-mounted laser can be a lifesaver. With a press of a button, a red or green beam dot illuminates the target. It is especially effective on targets within 50 yards.

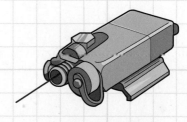

WEAPON LIGHT I consider most accessories optional, but bad things often happen in the dark, and there is nothing that tips the scales in your favor more than a quality weapon light. Get one that emits at least 600 lumens. Dual-switch models with momentary on/off and a regular on mode are best.

BIPOD For any long-range shooting, a bipod is an essential add-on. Features to look for include the ability of the rifle to pivot on the bipod, and legs that adjust quickly to accommodate various shooting positions. It's also beneficial if the bipod has a quick-release latching mechanism that locks in place so that it won't come loose until the shooter removes it.

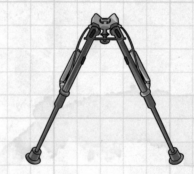

GRIPS Adding a new grip to an AR is simple: Just unscrew the bolt on the inside of the grip and swap in the new one.

OVERSIZE CHARGING HANDLE The standard spec charging handle on the M16 is not built very well. The gripping surface is small and the design is prone to breakage under hard use. A larger and more robust charging handle makes a lot of sense. You'll be able to run the rifle more effectively and you will have eliminated a potential weak link.

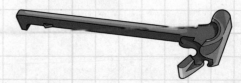

105 REACH OUT

Many ARs designed for action shooting have long hand guards so that the shooter can fully extend the lead arm when firing. With the elbow locked and with a tight grip on the hand guard, the rifle is held firmly in the pocket of the shoulder, giving additional support when shooting off-hand or from other unsupported positions.

106 VIEW THE BEST ARS

AR rifles come in all shapes, sizes, and configurations for different missions. Here's a sampling of some of the finest, and most interesting, ARs currently being produced.

DANIEL DEFENSE M4 ISR-300 BLACKOUT

This rifle takes quiet to a whole new level. A sound suppressor is permanently attached to the 10.3-inch barrel, and with subsonic 300 Blackout loads, the rifle hardly makes a sound. The buttstock is rugged and comfortable, and adjusts for length of pull. The top rail allows for multiple accessory mounting options.

JP ENTERPRISES GMR-13

ARs chambered in pistol calibers are nothing new. But what's different about the JP GMR-13 is that it works reliably. It functions on a blowback design and the lower is engineered to accept Glock 17 style magazines. Chambered in 9mm, recoil with this rifle is virtually nonexistent. It is ideal for personal protection or any type of situation where one might be shooting indoors.

PWS MK107 DIABLO

Gun nuts love to argue about piston driven versus direct impingement ARs; all I know is that the rifles from PWS don't know the word "quit." This even goes for their short-barreled rifles, like the 7¾-inch Diablo pictured here. This .223 rifle is meant for Close Quarters Battle duty, favoring maneuverability and fast handling at the cost of muzzle velocity, which clocks in around 2,350 fps, compared to the 3,200 fps that a 55-grain .223 generates from a longer barrel.

NOSLER VARMAGEDDON AR

This rifle is the result of a joint project between Nosler and Noveske, and the result is the stuff of prairie dog nightmares. Chambered in .223, it is deadly out to 400 yards on any type of varmint, especially when coupled with Nosler's 55-grain Varmageddon ammo. The rifle's narrow, free-float hand guard has the KeyMod system for adding accessories. It has an oversize ambidextrous charging handle, an outstanding trigger, and Magpul's excellent PRS stock.

COLT AR15 A4

This rifle is pure old-school. From the clamshell hand guard to the fixed, solid buttstock to the flash suppressor, all these features hearken back to the original M16s. But this model isn't just for nostalgia buffs. It's still an effective and versatile rifle for personal protection, hunting small game or varmints, duty patrol, or just recreational plinking. It comes with a 20-inch barrel; its overall length is 37 ½ inches and it weighs about 7 ¾ pounds empty.

ALEXANDER ARMS 6.5 GRENDEL GDMR

The 6.5 Grendel is a well-balanced cartridge that is able to work in AR-15-size actions while launching a much heavier bullet than a standard .223. Alexander Arms pioneered this cartridge and offers rifles ranging from lightweight hunting rifles to heavy-barreled sniper models. The GDMR is a precision rifle capable of taking on long-range targets. Alexander Arms worked to strip unnecessary weight from the GDMR while maintaining the rigidity required for precision shooting.

NEMO OMEN MATCH 2.0

AR-type rifles are no longer confined to the original AR-15 (.223 Remington/5.56 NATO) and AR-10 (.308 Winchester) size actions. This rifle is chambered in the potent .300 Winchester Magnum, significantly upping the AR platform's firepower. Between the 22-inch barrel and the extra metal that goes into the construction of the action, this rifle weighs nearly 11 pounds empty. But that weight, along with the large A-10 muzzle brake helps make the rifle more manageable under recoil.

WINDHAM WEAPONRY VARMINT EXTERMINATOR

This manufacturer is relatively new, but its employees, most of whom worked at Bushmaster before it moved out of Maine, have decades of rifle-making experience. One of the most accurate rifles in their lineup is the Varmint Exterminator model. It is chambered in .223 and has a heavy contour 20-inch barrel. The rifle has an A2 style stock, a rail along the top of the receiver to mount a scope, a vented aluminum free-float hand guard, and ships with a single 5-round magazine.

107 LEARN TO SHOOT FASTER

Mike Voight is scary fast on the trigger. And the reason for that is because he knows how to move fast the right way.

Voight puts it like this: "My eyes are very fast, my hands are okay, my body sucks, and my feet are terrible."

What he is saying is that there is a hierarchy of speed and movement that every shooter needs to factor in when approaching a series of targets. Your eyes can move, process, and react to information faster than any other part of your body. The next quickest tools in your arsenal are your hands. Working with your eyes, your hands can shift and engage targets rapidly.

You start to lose time when you need to move your body around, such as when bending at the waist to shoot targets that are obscured by cover. But moving your body is faster than repositioning yourself by moving your feet, which is the slowest way to engage targets.

108 BE FAST AND SMOOTH

Shooting with Mike Voight is both an educational and humbling experience. The fact that he's a gentleman and has a great sense of humor goes a long way when he takes a look at your shooting technique. Because I can promise you that he will deliver the bad news by the bucketload.

Here's a case in point. Voight and I were working on a drill that required us to transition between small and large targets set at different distances. Once I got into the rhythm I was doing ok—or so I thought. One key to good shooting is to be smooth, and that's what I was focused on. The saying, "slow is smooth, smooth is fast," applies to any type of dynamic

shooting. And when Voight asked me what I was doing, I told him that.

"Well, slow might be smooth, but fast is faster," he said. And he demonstrated what he meant.

Whereas I was shooting in a steady "bang . . . bang . . . bang" cadence, Voight altered his trigger speed based on the target. The close ones he mowed down in an instant, while the targets that were further away were taken with a bit more deliberation. Knowing how to introduce this dynamic judgment into your shooting technique—while not compromising on the ability to get hits—is what separates the smooth shooters from the truly fast ones.

109 CHOOSE YOUR HUNTING AR

More sportsmen are taking their ARs hunting as manufacturers have worked to create cartridges and rifles configured for big game. Sleeker, lighter, and with adequate killing power, these rifles are among the best for chasing hogs, deer, elk, and antelope.

DPMS GII HUNTER

This rifle from DPMS is a major step forward in hunting ARs. Built on an AR-10-size action and chambered in .308, this rifle only weighs 7 ¾ pounds. Engineers stripped material from the action and used a carbon fiber hand guard to shed weight. The rifle's reliability was improved by adding a second ejector in the bolt face. The Magpul MOE rifle stock has excellent ergonomics and the overall smooth lines of the rifle make it comfortable to carry.

STAG ARMS MODEL 7 HUNTER 6.8 SPC

The Model 7 Hunter uses the 6.8 Special Purpose Cartridge (SPC) round that gives 300–400 foot-pounds of energy advantage over the 5.56/.223 Remington while sharing the same action length. With premium bullets like the 85-grain Barnes TSX or the 115-grain Remington Core-Lokt Ultra Bonded, it is an ideal deer or hog gun. The matte-finished rifle features a Hogue rubberized and free-floated forend, a full-length, rifleman's buttstock, and a 5-round mag that's not overly cumbersome.

450 BUSHMASTER RIFLE

The original bacon-busting AR, the 450 Bushmaster is a complete rifle, though it features an upper barrel assembly that can be mated to standard AR-15 (.556 NATO) receivers. Its proprietary cartridge sends a .45-caliber, 260-grain slug at 2,180 fps from a 20-inch barrel for 2,743 foot-pounds of energy. It comes with a 5-round magazine, though factory 9-rounders are available. That's a lot of lead going to a good cause.

AMBUSH 300 BLACKOUT

Chambered in the interesting .300 Blackout, this rifle is a versatile hunting tool. The cartridge fits into an AR-15-size platform, which makes this rifle light and portable, and comes in both subsonic and supersonic loads. If the shooter chooses to use subsonic rounds, a suppressor is highly recommended in order to achieve the necessary back-pressure to reliably cycle the gun's action. Typical subsonic loads fire 220-grain projectiles at about 1,000 fps. An excellent all-around hunting load is the 130-grain Barnes TSX, which leaves the muzzle at 2,075 fps. The rifle features an adjustable buttstock and full-length rail along the top of the upper for mounting optics.

110 GET YOUR PIGS IN A ROW

While it's tempting for hunters to take the lead pig in a pack because it's the closest, a fast-firing AR grants the opportunity to shoot several at a time. Pigs that watch a companion fall in front of them often change direction rather than continuing the beeline. So choose a low-magnification optic like red dot or a 1-6x scope, then pick the rear pig, fire, and swing ahead to the next pig in line as they continue running.

III CHECK OUT COMPETITION ARS

Any AR-15–style rifle can work in 3-gun and action-shooting competitions. With few exceptions, the targets don't require pinpoint accuracy. The only real requirement is reliable functioning. It's no good when a rifle seizes up in a match, though that is more often the result of subgrade ammo than any issue with the rifle. Rifles designed specifically for competition do give an edge, however. They handle better, have upgraded triggers, are made with stiffer stocks and actions, and have other ergonomic touches that enable them to be shot faster. These are some of the best.

COLT COMPETITION PRO CRP-18
This one is ready for competition right out of the box. Just add an optic, a sling, top off some magazines and head to the match. The 15-inch free-float hand guard has a low profile and wraps around the 18-inch match barrel and gas block, which can be adjusted by hand with no tools. The crisp two-stage trigger helps the rifle's accuracy. The barrel comes with an 8-inch twist, making it ideal for heavier .223 bullets, from 55 to 77 grains. The oversize charging handle is more ergonomic and robust than a standard latch and the 6-position buttstock adjusts quickly for different lengths of pull.

SEEKINS PRECISION SPR03G
Glen Seekins rifles shoot as nicely as they look. He oversees a boutique shop of talented gun makers who build high-performance ARs for many applications. As the name suggests, the SPR03G is a competition rifle for 3-gun. The foundation of the rifle is Seekins' ambidextrous lower and proprietary upper, with a 15-inch hand guard and 18-inch stainless barrel. The adjustable gas block (the shooter can tune it for specific types of ammo), gas tube, and bolt carrier are all coated with Melonite to enhance the rifle's durability. The adjustable buttstock gives a solid and comfortable cheek weld.

NOVESKE SHOOTING TEAM RIFLE

The Noveske name is among the most respected in the AR world, and its Shooting Team Rifle lives up to the reputation. This top-of-the-line AR is for serious (or at least affluent) competitors. The hand guard accepts KeyMod components and is 16.7 inches long, so even long-limbed shooters can grip the hand guard with the lead arm fully extended. As with other high-end competition rifles, it has an adjustable gas block, stiff buttstock that adjusts for both cheek height and length of pull, a free-floated match-grade barrel, and an excellent trigger. A rail extends from the rear of the upper all the way down the hand guard for mounting iron sights, optics, and whatever other accessories the shooter desires.

STAG ARMS MODEL 3G

This rifle is a basic, yet fully capable 3-gun AR. It has a 5.56 NATO / .223 Remington chamber to safely function with both types of ammo. The barrel is made with an 8-inch twist, which is fast enough to stabilize the larger .223 bullets (55 grains and up) that competitors typically like to shoot. The 15-inch free-float hand guard provides plenty of room for the lead shooting hand. The rifle can be ordered with a fixed or adjustable buttstock, depending on the shooter's preference. The Geisele 3-gun trigger is set to break at 3 ½ pounds, which is perfect for competition.

112 KNOW AK ANATOMY

The AK-47 is, without question, the most successful assault rifle in history. It was designed to be a simple, rugged infantry weapon that was light to carry, easy to produce and maintain, and required minimal training. It succeeded on all counts. Unlike any rifle before it, the AK-47—and its later variants—offered a practical way to equip soldiers en masse with a full-automatic rifle that could deliver mass volleys of fire on enemy positions.

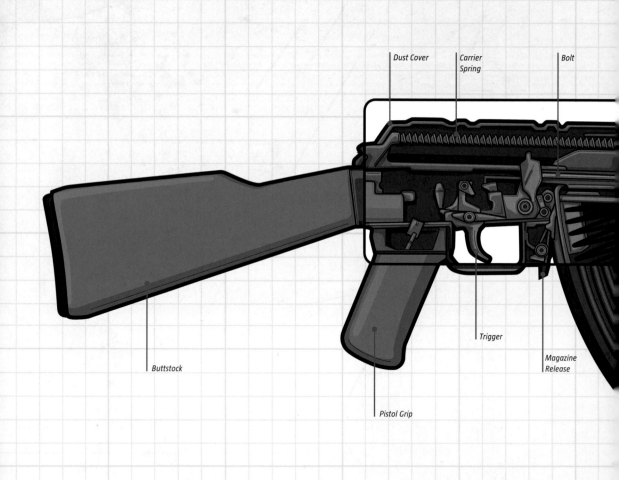

Dust Cover

Carrier Spring

Bolt

Trigger

Magazine Release

Buttstock

Pistol Grip

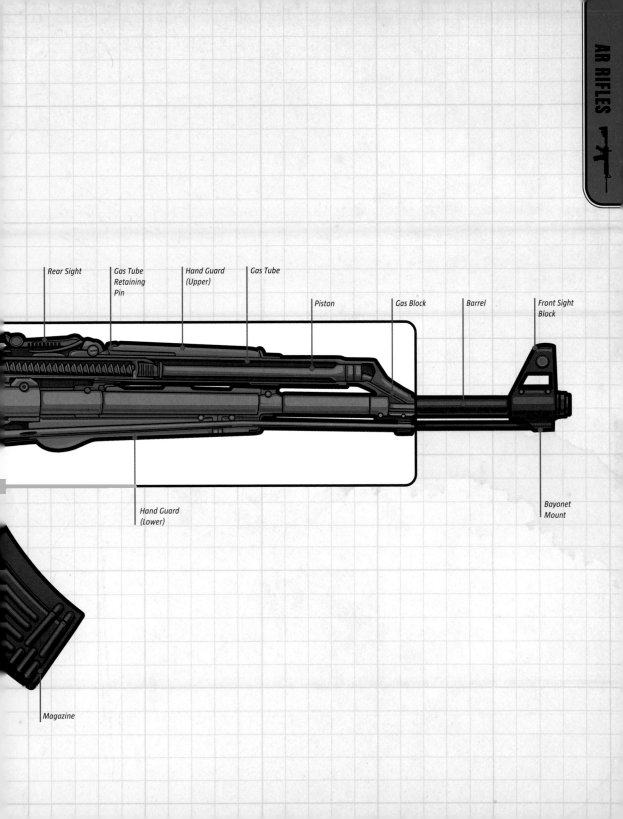

Rear Sight

Gas Tube
Retaining
Pin

Hand Guard
(Upper)

Gas Tube

Piston

Gas Block

Barrel

Front Sight
Block

Hand Guard
(Lower)

Bayonet
Mount

Magazine

113 STUDY AK HISTORY

The name AK-47 is derived from the Russian words "Avtomat Kalashnikova", in honor of its automatic firing capabilities and its principal designer, Mikhail Kalashnikov. The 47 denotes the year 1947, when the trials started on the version of the rifle that was finally approved for adoption by the Soviet armed forces soon after.

By any measure, the AK-47 is the most successful assault rifle in human history. In terms of the number of guns produced, duration of service, and worldwide deployment, it has no equal.

The genius of the rifle is not that it was original. It is actually an amalgamation of several preexisting design concepts. The trigger mechanism, safety catch, rotating bolt, and gas-driven action borrowed heavily from other firearms. But these features were combined with a platform that offered legendary durability and low manufacturing costs.

The result was a lightweight rifle with moderate recoil that was easy to wield and that still placed tremendous firepower into the hands of individual soldiers. Accuracy was a secondary consideration. The fact that it gave soldiers the ability to deliver massed fire in an effective fashion was what made it unlike any other rifle before and, some would still argue, ever since.

114 REVIEW THE AK-47 TIME LINE

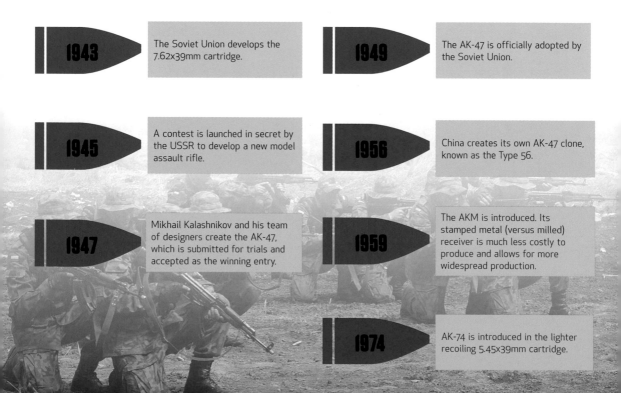

1943 The Soviet Union develops the 7.62x39mm cartridge.

1949 The AK-47 is officially adopted by the Soviet Union.

1945 A contest is launched in secret by the USSR to develop a new model assault rifle.

1956 China creates its own AK-47 clone, known as the Type 56.

1947 Mikhail Kalashnikov and his team of designers create the AK-47, which is submitted for trials and accepted as the winning entry.

1959 The AKM is introduced. Its stamped metal (versus milled) receiver is much less costly to produce and allows for more widespread production.

1974 AK-74 is introduced in the lighter recoiling 5.45x39mm cartridge.

115 MEET THE MAN

Mikhail Timofeyevich Kalashnikov was born in 1919 to peasants and went on to become a lieutenant-general in the Soviet Army, a Hero of the State, and one of the most famous firearms designers in history.

A self-taught tinkerer, Kalashnikov was conscripted into the Red Army in 1938 and because of his small stature and mechanical aptitude was made a tank mechanic. During World War II, he became a tank commander and was seriously wounded in combat. During his recuperation from late 1941 to 1942, he worked on a design for a new rifle for the Soviet military. That design was never adopted, but his ingenuity caught the eye of his superiors, who then reassigned him to a small-arms design group.

It was there that he, along with other engineers, developed the iconic AK-47. He continued to develop, expand, and improve the AK family of rifles throughout his later career. All told, he helped create about 150 different firearms designs.

He died in 2013 at the age of 94 in a Russian hospital after a prolonged illness.

The AK-47 has spawned numerous variants that are in service around the globe. Some of these appeared not long after the introduction of the originals from Russia, while others are of much more recent vintage. Common to every model is the gas-piston driven action, the basic controls for operating and manipulating the rifle, and the distinctive AK profile.

IMI GALIL AR (ISRAEL)

Based on the Finnish Valmet Rk 62, itself modeled on the Polish version of the original Russian AK, the Galil started production in 1972 to replace the Israeli FN FAL, which demonstrated spotty reliability in the sandy conditions of desert warfare. Still in production today, the Galil was chambered in 5.56x45mm and 7.62x51mm because of Israel's links with NATO and the United States.

AKM-63 (HUNGARY)

The vertical foregrip jutting from the metal fore-end on the AKM-63 is the most distinctive visual departure from the Soviet AK-47 ARM. First produced in 1963, this rifle was chambered in 7.62x39mm. The Hungarian armed forces switched to a more reliable variant, called the AK-63, in 1977 and still use the rifle to this day.

ARSENAL AR-M1 (BULGARIA)

Founded in 1878, Bulgaria's oldest and largest maker of arms started producing assault rifles in the 1950s, beginning with copies of the AK-47. Over the years, the company has produced nearly a dozen different AK styles, and their imported kit parts are among the most sought-after for AK-pattern rifles in the United States. The AR-M1 is an improved model that features the AK-74 front sight post and different furniture. It is chambered in 5.56x45mm and 7.62x39mm.

INSAS (INDIA)

The Indian Small Arms System is the standard infantry weapon of the Indian Armed Forces. While patterned after the AK, with the long-stroke gas piston, rotating bolt head, and stamped steel receiver, the INSAS is chambered in NATO 5.56mm. Transparent 20-round magazines and a diopter rear sight on the dust cover are distinctive features on the INSAS. The family of rifles includes the standard assault rifle, a carbine, and a light machine gun. It has been in service since 1998.

TYPE 56 (CHINA)

This Chinese version of the AK-47 has been in constant production since 1956. Approximately 10 to 15 million of these stamped-receiver AKs have been produced. Given China's historical support of North Vietnam, American troops encountered these in the hands of NVA and VC troops during the Vietnam War. Production continues to this day thanks to Norinco, which took over from Chinese state factories in 1973.

ARM (EGYPT)

Also known as the "Maadi" for the factory where it has been produced since the 1950s onward, this rifle is an Egyptian copy of the Soviet AK-47 ARM. This is one of the more common AKs found in the United States and has been imported in large quantities over the years. It is in service with the Egyptian armed forces and comes in different configurations. The ARM features stamped receivers and is chambered in 7.62x39mm.

MD. 86 (ROMANIA)

Manufactured by RomArm S.A. in Bucharest, this has been the standard-issue rifle for Romanian forces since 1986. American shooters are more likely to know this rifle as the AIMS-74, which is its moniker when imported into the states. Despite having been chambered 5.45x39mm like the newer AK-74s, the md. 86 has more in common with the older model 7.62x39mm AKM rifles.

TABUK CARBINE (IRAQ)

Under orders from Saddam Hussein, the Iraqi Ministry of Defense started production of this AKM clone. Under the guidance of Yugoslavian technicians, the Iraqis produced what is by most accounts a very robust and high-quality rifle. These are ubiquitous in Iraq and were fielded opposite coalition forces in the Gulf War and during Operation Iraqi Freedom.

PMK (POLAND)

While Poland was part of the Warsaw Pact its military fielded various AK-style rifles, including the pmK, a faithful clone of the Soviet pattern AK-47 and its later variants. Since joining NATO, the country has equipped its forces with 5.56mm rifles that can accept standard M-16 magazines. The Kbs wz. 1996 Beryl rifle, which was first adopted in 1997, retains elements of the AK system, and is now the standard issue rifle in Poland.

VEPR (UKRAINE)

This rifle, whose name means "wild boar," is the first domestically produced assault rifle made in Ukraine. It owes much of its DNA to the AK-74, including the basic operating system, 5.45x39mm chambering, and barrel length, but its bullpup configuration sets it apart. In spite of the desire to equip its forces widely with this rifle, production has been slow and the majority of Ukrainian military personnel still carry AK-74s.

VALMET M76 (FINLAND)

This is doubtless one of the more interesting AK-pattern firearms made. Chambered in 5.56x45mm NATO, 7.62x39mm Russian, and 7.62x51mm NATO, the M76 was the refinement of previous Finnish AK rifles such as the M62. Though it has been made in numerous configurations, the tubular style buttstock is a visual trademark. In addition, the rear sight attaches to the back portion of the dust cover.

ZASTAVA M92 (YUGOSLAVIA)

Though Yugoslavia is no more, this rifle is still often referred to as the Yugoslavian M92. It is chambered in 7.62x39mm and is most directly related to the Soviet AKMSU and AKS-74U rifles. Its shorter barrel and the folding buttstock make it ideal for vehicle-mounted soldiers, paratroopers, and others that work in tight quarters. The three cooling vents on the hand guard are a visually distinctive feature.

117 MEET THE FIRST ASSAULT RIFLE

The term "assault rifle" is bandied about carelessly by those who either don't know any better or who seek to purposely spread misinformation in order to make the civilian versions of these rifles seem more scary.

The difference between military assault rifles and the civilian look-alikes is small, but it is still significant. Military assault rifles possess the option to go fully automatic, meaning that a single press of the trigger will fire the rifle multiple times. When it is fired in this manner, an automatic rifle can empty a full 30-round magazine downrange in just a few seconds.

The civilian versions do not have this capability. Instead, they are semiautomatic rifles, which means that each press of the trigger will fire only a single bullet. Although they might look a great deal like their military cousins, these civilian sporting rifles operate just like other semiautos that are used for hunting, competition, recreation, and personal protection.

The term "assault rifle" entered the lexicon with the advent of the German Sturmgewehr 44 in World War II. This rifle was the first successful assault rifle to be employed in significant numbers. By having a look at the StG 44 in profile, it is easy to see its DNA in today's battle rifles, like the M16, M4, AK-47, AK-74, and others that are employed by military forces around the globe.

The StG 44 and its kin were game changers because they put a significant amount of firepower in the hands of individual soldiers. These rifles are easy to carry due to their light weight, are chambered in relatively mild cartridges that make them easy to control under recoil,

and, due to their excellent ergonomics and design, they are also easy for raw recruits to master.

Accuracy was not a primary concern. Advocates of the assault rifle concept recognized that most infantry combat engagements take place over short distances and that it was more important for a group of soldiers to be able to deliver withering weapons fire en masse rather than having fighters place well-aimed shots downrange one at a time.

The Soviet Union was quick to adopt this philosophy with the development of the AK-47. The United States lagged behind, mostly because of an attachment to the concept of individual marksmanship that dominated the training of our military. However, after extensive testing of small-caliber firearms throughout the 1950s, and in light of the Soviet Union's adoption of the AK-47, that attitude shifted.

118 LEARN ABOUT OTHER PROVEN BATTLE RIFLES

Assault rifles have been game-changers for armies around the world, with the Steyr AUG and the H&K G36 being the most popular—each of them is used in nations around the world, on virtually every continent (including by certain government and law enforcement divisions in the United States). Here's how they stack up.

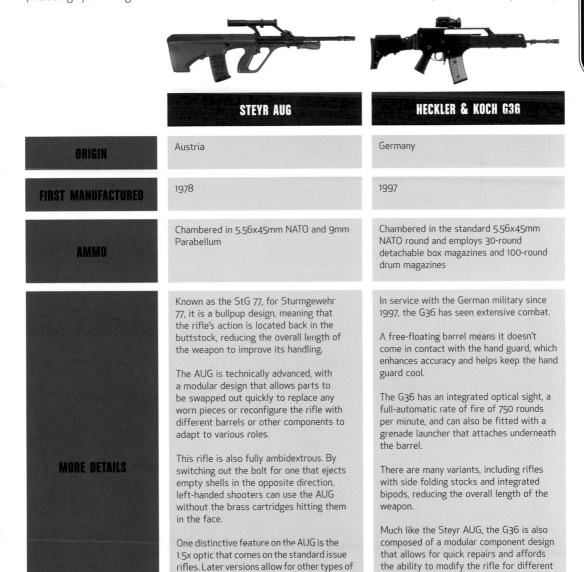

	STEYR AUG	HECKLER & KOCH G36
ORIGIN	Austria	Germany
FIRST MANUFACTURED	1978	1997
AMMO	Chambered in 5.56x45mm NATO and 9mm Parabellum	Chambered in the standard 5.56x45mm NATO round and employs 30-round detachable box magazines and 100-round drum magazines
MORE DETAILS	Known as the StG 77, for Sturmgewehr 77, it is a bullpup design, meaning that the rifle's action is located back in the buttstock, reducing the overall length of the weapon to improve its handling. The AUG is technically advanced, with a modular design that allows parts to be swapped out quickly to replace any worn pieces or reconfigure the rifle with different barrels or other components to adapt to various roles. This rifle is also fully ambidextrous. By switching out the bolt for one that ejects empty shells in the opposite direction, left-handed shooters can use the AUG without the brass cartridges hitting them in the face. One distinctive feature on the AUG is the 1.5x optic that comes on the standard issue rifles. Later versions allow for other types of scopes for different mission requirements.	In service with the German military since 1997, the G36 has seen extensive combat. A free-floating barrel means it doesn't come in contact with the hand guard, which enhances accuracy and helps keep the hand guard cool. The G36 has an integrated optical sight, a full-automatic rate of fire of 750 rounds per minute, and can also be fitted with a grenade launcher that attaches underneath the barrel. There are many variants, including rifles with side folding stocks and integrated bipods, reducing the overall length of the weapon. Much like the Steyr AUG, the G36 is also composed of a modular component design that allows for quick repairs and affords the ability to modify the rifle for different scenarios or environments.

119 TAKE A CARBINE COURSE

Good carbine courses abound around the country. Even if you're comfortable with the MSR platform, these classes are worthwhile. AR-style rifles are so versatile that a student is sure to pick up something new while training with a reputable instructor, and many schools offer specialized programs that focus on a particular facet of the platform, which is reason to keep training.

ATTEND THE ACADEMY While Gunsite Academy is best known for teaching defensive pistol skills, it offers coursework ranging from basic to advanced for all firearms. The carbine instruction here is top-notch. Plenty of time is spent covering basic drills and gun handling on a 50-yard range, but academy students will eventually engage targets out past 300 yards and get a chance to put the lessons learned to use in a series of dynamic scenarios that require shooting on the move.

GO INTERNATIONAL Gabe Suarez is one of the more forward-thinking firearms instructors in the country, and Suarez International has shown a remarkable ability to look beyond conventional thinking and innovate. Classes are taught all around the country, so chances are good that at some point Gabe will be in your neck of the woods. For rifles and carbines, his introductory rifle class focuses on training for close-range engagements and is geared for civilians, law enforcement and military alike.

ATTEND A SEMINAR Located right outside Los Angeles, International Tactical Training Seminars is run by Scott Reitz, a 30-year veteran of the LAPD. Reitz's career took him through the LAPD's SWAT unit and eventually he became the chief firearms instructor for the entire LAPD Metro division. His teaching method is grounded in real-world scenarios; in the basic carbine class, he covers the fundamentals of rifle use and has students engaging targets out to 500 yards.

GO BACK TO SCHOOL I've taken several classes at the Sig Sauer Academy in New Hampshire. The instructors are excellent and the material is well presented. The basic one-day carbine class delivers a lot for the money and is an excellent way for a shooter to become familiar with the platform. Engagement distances are mostly handled within 50 yards. The academy offers a wide variety of both firearms and armorers classes.

HANDGUN

IT IS NOT A STRETCH TO SAY THAT THE HANDGUN IS ONE OF THE GREATEST INSTRUMENTS OF PERSONAL LIBERTY EVER DEVISED.

It ranks right up there with the printing press, the Writ of Habeas Corpus, birth control pills, and convertible sports cars. The oft repeated—and often modified—statement that "God might have created man, but Samuel Colt surely made them equal" has the benefit of being not only catchy but true.

In the hands of competently trained individuals who can manage to keep their wits about them in a crisis, a handgun can dramatically improve their odds of survival. If life is a numbers game, I'll take .45 over 911 any day.

The key is "competently trained," however. Not only does one need to learn how to shoot and manipulate a handgun right the first time—or spend many hours correcting learned mistakes, also affectionately known as "training scars"—but one also needs to practice. Among all firearms disciplines, handgun skills are particularly perishable, according to many experts, including renowned pistolero Colonel Jeff Cooper, who founded Gunsite Training Academy with the express intent of helping civilians keep their shooting technique up to snuff.

Fortunately, shooting and training with handguns is not only great fun, but also readily accessible across the country. If you're looking to get started or want to take your skills to the next level, the information contained on the following pages will help make that happen. This chapter will also help with the sometimes daunting task of selecting the right type of gun for a given shooter's needs—personal protection, casual shooting, serious competition, or some blend of the three. Lastly, we point out some of the top training venues around the country. A visit to any of them is time and money well spent.

EXPAND YOUR HANDGUN HORIZONS

Handguns will always play second fiddle to rifles or shotguns when it comes down to winning a gunfight or a war, harvesting game, or hitting a distant target. Still, they remain popular for a wide range of applications. The reason for that is simple: Their compact size and weight means that the right handgun can always be at your side, and often carried discreetly. That makes them the most versatile firearms, and they can play many roles, including the following.

LAW ENFORCEMENT A holstered handgun on an officer's hip provides an immediately accessible tool to protect both him or herself and the public. Revolvers were dominant in years past, but semiautos in 9mm, .40 S&W, .357 SIG, with a few .45 ACP and .45 GAP, predominate today.

PERSONAL PROTECTION Handguns dominate the civilian personal-protection market. As the saying goes, "I carry a concealed handgun because I can't carry a cop, and a rifle is too heavy and attracts attention." This market is dominated by compact revolvers and semiautos in .380 ACP, .38 Special, .357 Magnum, 9mm, .40 S&W, and .45 ACP.

MILITARY Many military personnel have duties that preclude them from carrying a long gun. This includes pilots, medics and corpsmen, transport drivers, crewmen in tanks, and others. They are often issued a handgun for personal protection. Some Special Ops soldiers carry one as a backup and as a primary gun for some close-quarters combat missions.

HUNTING A handgun has less range than a rifle, but more than a bow. It's not easy to take game with a handgun, and many relish that challenge. There are revolvers and single-shot pistols that are capable of harvesting any game animal in North America and many African species as well. Some are equipped with scope sights and are capable of cleanly harvesting big game at more than 150 yards.

SURVIVAL A compact .22 LR revolver and a 50-round box of cartridges take up almost no room in a pack or kit bag. And if you're traveling a long way from nowhere, and things don't go quite as planned, that little gun may just supply enough small game to keep you fed until help arrives.

COMPETITIVE SHOOTING Competition is hard-wired into human genes, and handguns are an excellent choice for those who love to compete. The numerous games involving handguns are accessible to nearly everyone. They have led to some useful innovations in handgun design that benefit other users.

WOODS WALKS If you're wandering around woods that are home to bears, mountain lions, wolves, or wild boar, a big-bore handgun on the hip can be quite comforting, and comfortable to carry. You may never need it, but if you run into a big critter that decides you're lunch, it's nice to have a .44 Magnum, .45 Long Colt, .454 Casull, .460 S&W Magnum, or .500 S&W Magnum handy.

RECREATION "Plinking" is the common term used to describe shooting a handgun for the sheer enjoyment of bouncing a tin can or pine cone across the ground, or seeing how close you can come to the bull's-eye. There's no signing up for a match, no personal protection, no hunting—just make the can dance or hit the target center. It's therapeutic and fun.

121 KNOW YOUR HANDGUN'S HISTORY

The first firearms that could rightly be called "handguns" appeared in the 14th century and were nothing more than shorter, lighter versions of the muzzleloading matchlock long guns of the day. These shorter-barreled guns were awkward to use but had some significant advantages: They were easily carried on the body and immediately available for personal defense. The drawbacks were a single shot, followed by a cumbersome reloading process. Over the intervening centuries, advances in design as well as in powder and projectiles led to the versatile, powerful guns we know today.

The appearance of the earliest known "handgun," a single-shot muzzleloading tube ignited by inserting a smoldering match cord into a touch hole. Essentially, it was a small handheld cannon.

Bostonian gun inventor Elisha Collier creates the first single-action revolver, a flintlock model that primes itself with gunpowder when the hammer is cocked.

Samuel Colt designs and sells the mass-produced Paterson single-action revolver, a 5-shot model with a removable and reloadable cylinder powered by percussion caps.

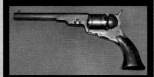

The first percussion caps are developed, consisting of tiny metal cylinders containing a small amount of explosive material. This invention enables guns to fire in any weather conditions. As a result, gunmakers eventually convert from making flintlocks to firing-pin mechanisms.

Flintlock firing mechanisms become the norm, replacing the matchlock, doglock, and wheel lock. Amazingly, this remains the state of the art for the next 200 years.

1365 — 1500s — 1600s — 1814 — 1820 — 1833 — 1836

The matchlock is developed and spreads across Europe. This innovation is adapted to firearms as far as Japan by 1600, with examples like the tanegashima pistol used by the samurai of the Edo period.

Italian Francesco Antonio Broccu invents the first percussion-cap revolver.

Benjamin Houllier invents the first self-contained metallic cartridge, removing the need to carry and load ball, powder, and percussion cap separately.

Paul Mauser introduces the "Broomhandle" semiautomatic pistol, the C96. Simultaneously, American John Browning develops the self-loading semiautos that were manufactured first by the Belgian firm Fabrique Nationale (FN) and later by Colt.

British gunsmith Robert Adams invents the first double-action revolver.

Smith & Wesson unveils the Model 29 revolver, which is chambered for the new and revolutionary .44 Magnum cartridge.

Glock introduces the first polymer-framed pistol. While the market is initially wary of a "plastic gun," it quickly becomes widely accepted and popular with law enforcement and recreational shooters.

Developments in smokeless gunpowder and detachable magazines lead to the era of semiautomatic handguns, beginning with the C-93, designed by Hugo Borchardt.

1846 · 1851 · 1877 · 1894 · 1896 · 1934 · 1956 · 1982

Colt produces the first series of truly successful centerfire double-action revolvers.

A team of developers from Smith & Wesson and Winchester join up to create the first magnum handgun cartridge, the .357, which was unsurpassed in power for over two decades.

122 UNDERSTAND SEMIAUTO ANATOMY

Semiautos dominate overall handgun sales and are available in a wide range of calibers, sizes, and styles. Regardless of the make or model, they all share a set of features common to the magazine-fed, self-loading pistol. One significant difference is in the firing mechanism that ignites the cartridge. There are two distinct types: striker fired and inertia fired.

STRIKER-FIRED ACTIONS A striker-fired pistol has its firing pin set within a channel in the rear of the slide. When the slide is cycled, the firing pin (or striker) is cocked under spring tension. Then, when the trigger is pulled, a connecting mechanism releases the firing pin and the spring drives it forward to ignite the primer. Once that is done, the slide must be cycled again to recock the firing pin.

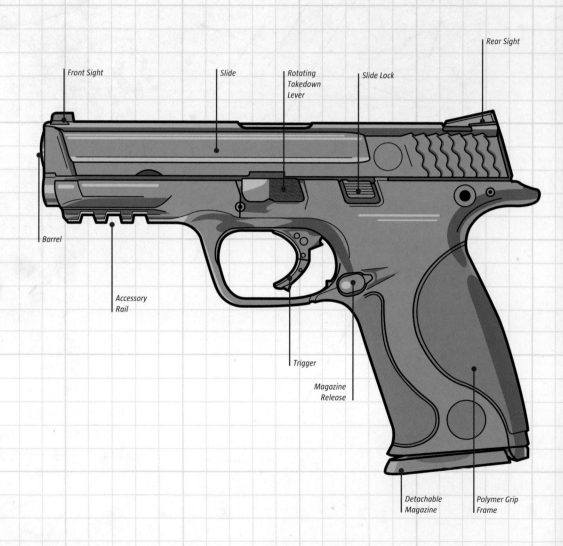

Rear Sight

Front Sight

Slide

Rotating Takedown Lever

Slide Lock

Barrel

Accessory Rail

Trigger

Magazine Release

Detachable Magazine

Polymer Grip Frame

INERTIA-FIRED ACTIONS As with the striker-fired action, this type of gun's firing pin also rides within a rear slide channel with a spring, but that's as far as the similarities go. It is not cocked under spring pressure and not released by the trigger. Instead, the trigger trips a separate hammer that hits the firing pin and slams it into the primer. The spring then returns the firing pin to its resting position.

Front Sight

Slide

Slide Lock

Manual Safety Lever

Rear Sight

External Hammer

Barrel

Trigger Guard

Trigger

Magazine Release

Detachable Magazine

123 SHOOT THE BEST SEMIAUTO

Semiauto pistols are the dominant force in today's handgun market, and there are many to choose from. Some, however, have proven themselves time and again. Here are 12 of the best.

Smith & Wesson M&P Series

Introduced less than a decade ago, this high-capacity striker-fired semiauto has earned high marks for ergonomics, reliability, and soft recoil. Available in 9mm, .40 S&W, and .45 ACP, it is a great choice for competition, law enforcement, and personal protection.

Glock G19

A 9mm compact, 15-shot, polymer-framed, striker-fired pistol, the G19 is considered to be one of the best guns Glock has ever produced. It is reliable under all conditions and is an excellent choice for personal defense.

Smith & Wesson Shield

Available in 9mm and .40 S&W, the Shield is a slenderized single-stack version of the highly acclaimed M&P. During a trip to a well-known shooting academy, this writer took a new 9mm Shield out of the box and fired over 500 rounds in two days without a single malfunction.

CZ-USA 85 Combat

A highly refined version of the classic steel frame, inertia-fired 9mm CZ 75B, this model features fully ambidextrous controls, adjustable sights, and a drop-free magazine. Whether the goal is competition or personal defense, this high-capacity 9mm is an excellent choice.

Glock G29

This striker-fired semiauto isn't much bigger than a compact 9mm, but the 10mm cartridge that it's chambered for delivers power levels approaching those of the .41 Magnum. It's a handy trail gun for those wandering through bear, wild boar, or mountain lion country.

Dan Wesson Specialist

Designed for law enforcement use, this .45 ACP 1911 is equipped with tritium night sights, 1913 accessory rail, ambidextrous thumb safety, and just about everything you could want to adapt John Browning's classic design for personal defense.

Ruger SR1911

When Ruger decided to build a 1911 .45 ACP, they kept the best of John Browning's original design and only added refinements that were necessary. The end result is an excellent stainless steel 1911 that comes at an affordable price.

Browning Buckmark

If you like shooting handguns, a .22 rimfire pistol is a lot of cheap fun, and the Browning Buckmark .22 LR is a top choice. It features a crisp trigger, adjustable sights, a target crowned barrel, and other features that make it an excellent shooter.

Ruger MK III

The classic Ruger Standard .22 LR pistol became the launching pad for one of America's greatest firearms manufacturers. The MK III is a refined version. Available in several different configurations, it will handle anything from competition to plinking to small-game hunting.

Springfield Armory XD(m)

A recent refinement of the original XD model, the XD(m) is available in 9mm, .40 S&W, and .45 ACP, and in barrel lengths of 3.8, 4.5, and 5.5-inches. The polymer-framed, striker-fired pistol is rapidly gaining favor among competitive shooters and those concerned with personal defense.

Magnum Research Micro Desert Eagle

Subcompact .380 ACP pistols have a reputation for being finicky. The Micro Desert Eagle, due to its unique gas-assist operating system, is anything but. During extensive testing, this writer could not get it to malfunction. It's an excellent choice for a small personal-defense handgun.

Colt Defender

This sub-compact 1911 features a 3-inch barrel and is available in either .45 ACP or 9mm. It comes with Novak Low Mount Carry Sight and is built from stainless steel. The frame has a tough Cerakote finish.

124 ENTER THE COMPETITIVE ARENA

A shooter who wishes to advance in his or her gun-handling skills will find action-pistol competition an excellent way to achieve that goal. For a fairly modest match entry fee (less than the cost of a case of beer in most places), a shooter will be able to draw from the holster, engage multiple targets with rapid fire, shoot on the move, master quick reloading, and execute other advanced techniques that are not allowed on a commercial indoor range.

The three most popular action-pistol organizations for semiautomatic shooters in the United States are the International Defensive Pistol Association (IDPA), the United States Practical Shooters Association (USPSA), and finally, the Steel Challenge Shooting Association (SCSA). Regardless of where you live, the chances are excellent that one or more gun clubs will be hosting these matches within a one-hour drive.

IDPA The IDPA is loosely based on actual self-defense scenarios. The target array may include buff-colored cardboard silhouette targets with embossed scoring rings or steel targets that must be knocked down. Some silhouette targets may actually be in motion when the shooter engages them, either swinging or on runners crossing the line of fire. Shooters may be required to engage these targets with a two-handed (freestyle) grip, or their weak or strong hand. There are a number of sometimes confusing penalties, but the game is otherwise simple, since shooters are told what order to shoot the targets in.

USPSA The USPSA offers similar target arrays, simpler rules, and doesn't dictate the order the targets must be shot in; many advanced shooters prefer this.

SCSA The SCSA offers a different target array, with five metal targets, each in various sizes and at various ranges. Shooters only have to "ring the steel" to score. And all shooting is done from one position.

You don't need expensive equipment to compete in any of these events, but eye and ear protection are mandatory. A strong-side holster and magazine pouches for two or more magazines are required. As for the gun, any 9mm or larger caliber can play. This writer classified as a IDPA Master using nothing more than a standard S&W 9mm M&P with aftermarket adjustable sights. Shoot what you have.

125 BUILD COMPETITION SKILLS

Action-pistol shooting is fast paced and there is a lot to think about besides pulling the trigger. Consider this: Experienced drivers don't consciously think about where their hands are on the steering wheel, the exact pressure on the accelerator, or where the brake pedal is, which allows them to focus on more important issues. A handgun should be operated the same way, and these drills can help get you there.

START RIGHT Here's a dry-fire drill you can do at home. First, clear the gun of all its ammunition. Double- and triple-check that. Then practice drawing from your normal holster, getting your sights lined up on a target, and pressing the trigger without the sights moving. Next, work the magazine release and generally become familiar with the gun. This may sound simple, but top shooters will often spend several 20-minute sessions each week doing just this.

DOUBLE TAP Most IDPA and USPSA stages require a minimum of two scoring hits per paper target. At the range, using a target appropriate for the game, practice drawing and delivering two quick rounds, at distances from 4 to 30 yards.

USE BOTH HANDS Shooters are required to perform both weak- and strong-hand shooting during some matches. Strong hand is dictated by the side on which the holster is worn. Weak hand is the other hand. The gun must be held and fired with the specified hand only. Not many casual shooters practice this, and it hurts their scores when they go to compete.

Set up two IDPA/USPSA targets 6 feet apart, then shoot at them from 7 to 10 yards. For weak-hand practice, start with the gun in a low ready position. For strong hand, begin with the gun in the holster. At the start signal, deliver two rounds to the body and one round to the head of one target, then transition to the other target and do the same. This will force you to deal with both vertical and horizontal target transitions, and it's a great skill builder for one-hand shooting.

RELOAD FAST The ability to execute a rapid reload is a critical skill and does require practice. Set up a single target at 7 yards and load all available magazines with only two rounds each. With your holster and your magazine pouches in their normal belt position, double tap the target, dump the empty magazine, let it hit the ground, and make a slide lock reload (see item 133). Repeat this, reloading as needed, for about 20 rounds per session.

These basic drills will help you prepare for a match, but you will also learn at the match itself. Try to get on a squad with Master and Expert Class shooters. Don't be intimidated by their skill. Instead, learn from them—most will be happy to share their knowledge. That knowledge can be as valuable as that gained from an expensive shooting academy—and a lot cheaper.

126 SHOOT ON THE MOVE

This drill is meant to improve your accuracy while moving and is shot at 7 and 12 yards. Set up three targets at 7-foot intervals. Your starting position, with gun holstered, is a couple of feet to the outside of the left-hand target. Draw and engage each target with two rounds while moving laterally toward the farthest right-side target. Then shift to outside of the right-hand target and move to the left side.

Next, start at 7 yards away, facing the center target. Draw and engage each target with two rounds while backing away. Move to 12 yards, then, from the same position, engage each target with two rounds while moving toward it.

You will find that dropping your hips into an exaggerated crouch and sliding your feet across the ground instead of lifting them in large steps will improve speed and accuracy in both drills. Walking fully upright with large steps causes the gun to bounce vertically each time a foot hits the ground. Do a low glide instead of a high stride.

127 DRILL FOR FOCUS

Set up a target at 5 yards and place a 1-inch black dot on it. Your goal is to chew the center from the circle by delivering five slow, aimed single shots. Take your time; accuracy, not speed, is the objective. You'll need perfect execution of stance, grip, sight alignment, sight picture, and trigger control. Start by shooting freestyle with both hands, then increase your skills by shooting with your weak and strong hand alone. Next, set up two targets spaced 6 feet apart. This drill is shot from 10 to 50 yards. On one target, fire a slow, deliberate 6-shot group. Take your time and bring the gun down between shots. The objective is to form a group at point of aim.

On the second target, draw, fire one round, holster the gun, and repeat for six rounds. The two groups should be virtually identical in size and location on the target. If you can shoot a 4-inch group slow fire, you should have no worse than a 5-inch group from the draw. If not, you may need to reposition the holster for a more consistent grip, adjust your stance, or work on the initial presentation to the target.

128 FIT YOUR TRIGGER FINGER

Action-pistol champion Julie Golob has no shortage of experience when it comes to handgunning. One of the most important lessons she has learned is about controlling recoil, which begins with the gun itself and, of course, your trigger finger.

Where you place your finger on the trigger is critical. Ideally, you want the full pad of your trigger finger on the face of the trigger. Gun fit here is key. For a larger-framed gun you need to adjust your grip to get your trigger finger in the right spot—so you will have to be flexible with your grip depending on the firearm you're using. But if you're going to shoot a handgun a lot, you want to make sure it fits you.

129 STAND AND DELIVER

Controlling a pistol is all about managing recoil. Along with trigger control and gun size, two other elements Golob has perfected are stance and grip. Here are her top tips for supreme control.

TAKE A STAND The smaller you are, the more aggressive your stance needs to be. Golob likes to stand with her feet more than shoulder-width apart, which is wider than what most shooting instructors suggest—in fact, her stance is about double that. If you're a right-handed shooter, get your right foot a bit further back than the left (reverse this if you're left-handed). Lean forward into the gun, bending at the waist, your weight on the balls of your feet. The wider stance helps get you low to the ground and you'll have less of a teeter-totter effect when shooting.

GET A GRIP Take a high grip on the gun, holding it as firmly as you can with your strong hand, but not so much that your hand shakes. Also, cant the wrist of your support hand downward so that your thumb is pointing straight downrange. Then, wrap your fingers around your strong hand, with the fingers overlapping. Get your supporting thumb under your strong-hand thumb like a puzzle piece—don't leave any gap between your hands. Squeeze your supporting hand's

fingers toward your palm. And last, use your chest muscles to compress your palms together around the back of the grip.

130 SHOOT FAST, SHOOT WELL

Another key point for rapid and skillful shooting, says Golob, is to learn the reset point of each gun's trigger—this will help you gain more speed. One thing that separates action-pistol shooters from precision-pistol shooters is that trigger control isn't a big concern, as action shooters are aiming for speed. The biggest problem for action shooters is when they anticipate the recoil and yank the gun off target during the trigger stroke. The fix is the old classic of learning how to just let the shot happen. You want to train to pull through an entire trigger stroke while watching your sights stay on the target.

131 DEAL WITH MALFUNCTIONS

Any striker-fired handgun can malfunction for a number of reasons, including problems with the gun, the ammunition, or the magazine. Semiautos are no more prone to malfunction than others, but given their widespread personal-defense use, shooters carrying one should drill to react quickly to malfunctions. Here are the three most common issues and how to correct them.

STOVEPIPE JAM When the fired case is not fully ejected and is trapped by the returning slide, it looks a bit like a little smokestack sticking out above the ejection port. This is normally caused by underpowered ammunition, a very dirty chamber, or a damaged case ejector.

THE CURE Maintain a grip with the firing hand, with the trigger finger resting along the frame, and then slap the other hand on top of the slide over the trapped casing. Sweep that hand back to clear that case and cycle the slide to chamber a new round.

DOUBLE FEED This happens when one round enters the chamber with a second round stripped out of the gun's magazine and trying to join it, with the second round jammed against the back of the first. This is most often caused by a defective magazine with worn feed lips.

THE CURE The only way to clear a double feed is to hit the magazine release, strip the magazine from the gun, and then cycle the slide several times to clear both of those rounds. Slam a new magazine in, cycle the slide to chamber a round, and you're good to go.

THE CLICK The trigger is pulled and you hear a "click" instead of a "'bang." Two causes are likely: Either your magazine was not fully inserted and the round failed to chamber or the round has a defective primer. Another, less common, cause is a broken firing pin.

THE CURE Sharply tap the base of the magazine to assure it is properly seated in the gun and then rack the slide. This seats the magazine, clears a defective round, and chambers a new one.

There is one major caveat to this technique: If you get a "pop" or a "poof" instead of a "click," the primer did ignite and that bullet may be lodged in the barrel as a squib load. Or, if you rack the slide and an empty case comes out, you have the same thing. Do not fire another round! Stop and inspect the bore for any obstruction. Firing into an obstructed bore can result in gun damage, personal injury, or both.

132 EXECUTE A STRONG-SIDE DRAW

A handgun is of little use until it gets into the hand. The ability to execute a rapid draw and accurate shot are the hallmarks of an expert. The drawing motion is quick and fluid, but it can be broken down into five easily understood steps that must be mastered. This requires practice and is best learned initially via dry fire with an empty gun. Here's how to make a perfect hit at 7 yards in less than 1¼ seconds.

STEP 1 Begin with the proper grip while the gun is still in the holster, with the trigger finger in the register position. A bobbled grip creates the real possibility of a self-inflicted wound if the gun is not under full control as it is drawn. Keep your eyes locked on the spot on the target where you want the bullet to go rather than looking at the gun.

STEP 2 Bring the gun up and out of its holster, being sure that you don't make the mistake of canting the muzzle inward toward your body.

STEP 3 While drawing the gun, as described in step 2, simultaneously move your support hand toward the center of your chest, where it will be meeting the gun. Once the gun is clear of the holster, then drop your shoulder and rotate your forearm upward to level the gun at the target. At this point, you will be in a retention position and, if there is an imminent threat, the gun can be effectively fired from this position.

STEP 4 Continue to bring the gun forward and upward to where the eyes are locked on the target. Move your support hand to meet the gun and close both hands around the grip. The two-handed grip is achieved as the gun continues forward toward the target with the sights aiming right where your eyes are looking.

STEP 5 If the draw is done properly, you can make the first shot with great accuracy as soon as your arms reach their full extension toward the target.

133 SLIDE-LOCK AND RELOAD

Sometimes called the emergency reload, this method recharges a gun that has been shot until empty with the slide locked back.

STEP 1 When you reach the point at which the slide locks back after the final shot, press the magazine release button. This can be done with the shooting-hand thumb (right-handers) or the trigger finger for southpaws. Simultaneously tilt the magazine well 45 degrees inward to the side that the new magazine will arrive from. If the gun is a drop-free magazine design, let it drop. If not, or if it instead uses a European-style release on the heel of the pistol, the support hand must linger to strip the magazine from the gun.

STEP 2 Once you have the empty magazine clear of the gun, bring the gun arm's elbow down until it contacts your torso with the gun held just below eye level. This will create a repeatable position that lets you see both the gun and your target.

STEP 3 Grasp the new magazine in the support hand with the bullets facing forward. The pointer finger is placed along the front of the magazine with the tip contacting the bullet, the remaining three fingers along the outside, and the thumb locked onto the inside. With your index finger in this position, guiding the magazine into the pistol will occur more fluidly and easily.

STEP 4 Insert the magazine into the gun and then follow it upward with the heel of the hand to forcefully seat it. This puts the thumb of the support hand into a perfect position to activate the slide release to chamber a round into the breech.

STEP 5 Activate the slide release, roll the support hand back to its shooting grip, rotate the gun to vertical and drive it toward the target. A skilled shooter makes the entire reloading process one fluid movement that can be accomplished in under 3 seconds.

134 TOP OFF YOUR PISTOL

It is sometimes desirable to fully recharge a pistol that has expended a number of its rounds, but is not completely empty. There will be a round inside the chamber with the slide forward and some rounds remaining in the magazine. This will require nothing more than getting the partial magazine out and a full magazine into the gun. There are two common ways to do that: the speed reload and the reload with retention (RWR). Both start by bringing the gun back to the slide lock reload position and grasping the new magazine (see item 133, steps 2 and 3). They differ only in what is done with the partial magazine that is in the gun.

With the speed reload, the magazine release is activated and the partial magazine is allowed to fall to the ground while a full magazine is slapped in. It's the fastest way to fully recharge a pistol, and the partial can be picked up later.

The RWR is used when there is a defined lull in the action and the shooter is in a safe position that allows the magazine to be retained for later use. The support hand catches the ejected partial magazine and slips it into a pocket before grabbing and inserting a full magazine. If the spare magazine is worn on the weak side, and the partial magazine goes into the weak-side pants pocket, the hand is then in a perfect position to grab a new magazine. The RWR uses simple movements that do not degrade under stress and can be quite fast to execute.

135 DEVELOP SKILLS—CHEAP

A handgun is the most difficult firearm to shoot well. It takes proper training to learn the basic skills and considerable practice to master them. That requires shooting a lot of rounds. Just how many is a debatable point, but many top-notch trainers consider 5,000 rounds to be the minimum to begin to develop expert skills. That can get expensive, especially if shooting factory centerfire ammunition.

For those who wish to master handgun skills, a .22 LR pistol or revolver is a smart acquisition. It requires the same mastery of grip, stance, sight alignment, sight picture, and trigger control to hit the target as a centerfire gun does, but .22 LR ammo costs a quarter (or less) than even the cheapest centerfire factory loads. A quality .22 LR pistol or revolver can cost as much as $700, but if you do the math, you'll find that after about 2,000 rounds you will have recouped that cost when compared to the price of an equivalent amount of factory ammo. Every round after that is cheap practice. And you now own a gun you can use for a lot more than just practice.

There are .22 handguns that mimic several popular centerfire models and you can probably find

one offering comparable handling characteristics to your centerfire handgun. The Ruger SP101 .22 will teach double-action revolver skills, the Browning 1911-22 is a 1911, and the S&W M&P .22 is a dead ringer for the M&P centerfire model. There are also conversion units for some semiauto handguns that replace the existing slide, barrel, and magazine with a unit capable of firing .22 LR cartridges.

136 TRY THE AIRSOFT ALTERNATIVE

Rimfire ammo is cheaper than centerfire ammo but it still requires a shooting range. Airsoft guns are even cheaper to fire and don't require a range.

Airsoft guns shoot plastic pellets, which cost almost nothing per shot—fractions of a penny. They will penetrate a cardboard target, but not much more, and are accurate enough to hit a bottle cap at 7 yards. Airsoft guns are available in a wide variety of models, from single-shots powered by a spring to midrange models that use battery power.

The most pricey, which still won't set you back more than a few hundred bucks at most, use CO_2 cartridges and are available in models that duplicate the weight,

controls, sights, and handling qualities of many popular semiautos and revolvers. They allow rapid fire and function just like the real thing.

The upper-level CO_2 guns are used by some law enforcement agencies as part of their training and by some top-ranked competitive shooters to train when the winter weather turns nasty. Airsoft guns allow you to practice working from the holster, multiple target acquisition, weak- and strong-hand shooting, and other important skills. You can put up targets in your backyard and blaze away. If you hang a swath of canvas or carpet as a backstop behind the target, you can shoot them in your living room.

137 TAKE SIRT TRAINING

SIRT, or Shot Indicating Resetting Trigger, refers to a full-size handgun in a semiauto model profile that's powered by batteries. It doesn't fire projectiles; instead, it displays a laser beam onto the target with each pull of the trigger to let you know exactly where the shot would have gone. There is no need to recock the gun after each shot. This allows rapid-fire multiple-target training.

These guns are available in several models with price tags in the few-hundred-dollar range. Some feature two lasers: One displays when the trigger is partially pulled to let you check your muzzle alignment, and a second displays when the shot is fired. Some variants only display the fired shot and are available with either red or green lasers. Both colors will show brilliantly in any indoor environment, but red disappears rapidly

outdoors. Green shows up better outside and is preferable if any outdoor training is anticipated.

The SIRT laser will show precisely where you hit a target. But you don't have to restrict yourself to boring stationary paper targets. Combine a TV with a SIRT gun and you can mimic all those expensive video-training systems used by law enforcement and the military. Both the red and green lasers will show on a TV screen with no danger of damage. Any TV show will have a number of stationary and moving targets that can appear and disappear quickly.

Hit them if you can, whether from the holster or with gun in hand. It's the type of advanced training that can cost a lot at a shooting school. But you can do it in your living room, which definitely qualifies as practice on the cheap.

138 MEET THE MAGNIFICENT 1911

Adopted by the U.S. military in 1911, the John Browning–designed 1911 semiauto handgun and the 230-grain .45 caliber cartridge it fired were the result of American combat experience in the Moro Rebellion of 1899–1913 in the Philippines.

The .45 caliber bullet traveling at 860 fps proved far more effective than the anemic .38 Long Colt, and the 1911 .45 caliber began a long, storied career as the primary handgun of the U.S. military. Although it was officially replaced in the mid-1980s by the 9mm Beretta Model 92F, it was still a popular choice of troops who had the option of selecting their own handgun.

The 1911 is effective as a combat gun because it was built with loose tolerances, allowing it to function under the dirtiest, most adverse conditions. The drawback to those loose tolerances is mediocre accuracy. That's no problem for military close-range personal-defense use, but it hardly excites civilian shooters. Fortunately, the original 1911 design is not that hard to tweak, and when properly done, can be surprisingly accurate.

139 MOD YOUR 1911

The 1911 design can be tuned to produce exceptional accuracy. This involves tightening the tolerances between the slide and frame fit, the barrel lug–to–slide lug fit, and the barrel-to-front bushing fit. Adjusting the leaf springs can tune the trigger to crisp pulls in the 2½-pound to 3-pound range.

Further refinements developed by gunsmiths included adjustable sights, extended thumb safeties, and slide release levers, more comfortable beavertail safeties, recoil-reducing compensators, fully ramped barrels that assure proper feeding with nearly any bullet shape, and other features. The 1911 platform can also be extended to cartridges beyond the .45 ACP. The most successful have been the .38 Super, such as the Les Baer seen below, the 9mm Major, and the 10mm. The 9mm Luger and .40 S&W have also been used, but with varying levels of success.

The result is a pistol that plays several roles beyond close-range personal protection, and action-pistol shooting is a major one. Many competitive associations have divisions dedicated to this versatile, popular gun.

140 GET A GOOD GUN FOR A GREAT PRICE

Those looking to purchase a 1911 can spend over $3000 for a fully tricked-out custom model, but there are good, affordable options out there. Here are two that I've tested and found to shoot well without crippling the wallet.

RUGER SR1911	PARA EXPERT
CARTRIDGE .45 ACP	**CARTRIDGE** .45 ACP
BARREL LENGTH Choice of 5 or 4¼ inches	**BARREL LENGTH** 5 inches
SIGHTS Novak windage adjustable, in a three-dot pattern	**SIGHTS** Small fixed rear and a fiber optic front; easily replaced with adjustable sights
OTHER FEATURES Single left-hand-side controls (thumb safety, slide release, magazine release) Integral plunger tube assembly Skeletonized match trigger Flared ejection port	**OTHER FEATURES** Match grade barrel 4 ½-pound trigger Flared and ported ejection port Skeletonized trigger

141 LUBE IT UP

The original military 1911 .45 ACP earned an impressive reputation for reliability, but that has changed thanks to today's crop of civilian 1911s. The tightening up of tolerances to achieve modern accuracy levels, and the use of different bullet profiles and calibers have increased the need to maintain these pistols. Some shooters didn't get the memo.

After ten years of running shooters through action-pistol stages as a Range Safety Officer I've found that if a shooter experiences a malfunction, there's about a 60 percent chance that person is using a 1911. And while some of those are due to letting the local hotshot gunsmith work on the gun, many more were a simple matter of inadequate cleaning and lubrication.

You can't run a modern, tight-tolerance 1911 without proper lubrication. They don't work when they are dry. And that lubrication needs to be of the proper type and applied to the correct spots.

A key area is the lockup between the barrel hood and slide lugs. A heavier lube or even a light grease is required. Light oil is not adequate. I have found Mobil 1 V-Twin 20w-50 synthetic oil to be a great choice. This also works well for lubricating the barrel where it passes through the barrel bushing. That solves a lot of problems. The slide-to-frame interface can be handled with light oil, but make sure that it remains lubricated.

Lube one right, and it'll purr right along. Skip the lube, and the day can go downhill quickly.

142 DROOL OVER THE 1911 TACSOL CONVERSION

The 1911 is a great gun on its own, but with a bit of modification and a few add-ons, this historic firearm becomes a high-tech plinking handgun. Here's a cool project I put together for *Outdoor Life* recently.

DOWNSIZE IT I started with a Smith & Wesson ProSeries 1911 in .45 ACP with a blue frame and matte stainless slide. The frame was stripped to bare metal and a blued .22 Tactical Solutions slide and barrel were added on.

TUNE IT UP To make the 1911 run better, the trigger was replaced and tuned to break at just under 3½ pounds. The Tactical Solutions magazines that feed the

pistol are machined from aluminum billets and are built with impressive precision. While they are billed as 10-round magazines, these both run flawlessly with 13. After the last shot from one, a tab flips out to activate the slide stop, which is an unusual—and cool—feature on a 1911 rimfire conversion. And this gun does run quite well indeed. It can digest a brick of ammo faster than any other .22 I've used. Whether you enjoy action-pistol drills, slow precision firing, or just blazing away in a joyful fit of plinking, this pistol is the very definition of pleasurable shooting—and it pleases in such a quiet and well-mannered fashion.

SEE THE SIGHTS To improve accuracy, I added an Aimpoint Micro R-1 red dot that clamps onto the Picatinny rail located in between the open sights. Lasergrips were added to the equation as well. A handy benefit of the red-dot/laser combination is that once the red dot is sighted in, it is easy to move the laser right onto target by dialing it to intersect with the red dot (or vice versa).

TURN DOWN THE VOLUME The suppressor added just over 3 ounces to the gun's weight and reduced the already minimal muzzle flip to practically nothing. It also cut down on the sound signature. Spend much time around old shooters and you're sure to see someone cup a hand behind one ear when you start to speak, a move known in some circles as the NRA salute. Hearing loss is a very serious health problem, and a real safety concern, too. Then there's the matter of noise pollution: More than one gun club has been shut down due to the noise generated by gunfire, and countless others have ended up spending lots of time and money fighting off challenges from unhappy neighbors.

KNOW THE LAW To take possession of a suppressor, you need to fill out a bit of paperwork and pay for a stamp from the ATF.

TACTICAL SOLUTIONS/S&W 1911	
Caliber	.22 LR
Capacity	13 + 1
Weight	2 lb. 13 oz.
Finish	Matte/Blue
Barrel Length	5 in.
Rate of Twist	1 in 16 in.
Overall Length	13½ in.
Trigger Pull	3 lb. 6 oz.

COMPONENTS	
.22 Conversion Kit	Tactical Solutions 2211
Sights	Aimpoint Micro R-1
Grip	Crimson Trace CustomPro
Suppressor	TacSol Cascade

143 GET TO KNOW THE REVOLVER

While revolvers don't equal semiautos in their overall popularity and sales, they are still effective for many tasks. Their caliber range includes some hard-hitting hunting loads that semiautos can't handle, and they're often more accurate with just about any caliber. Their roles include personal protection, competition, and hunting. There are two basic types to choose from: double action and single action.

DOUBLE ACTION The operating action allows a shooter to fire rounds from a hammer-down position with a longer double-action pull or by manually cocking the hammer to achieve a very light and crisp (2–3 pound) single-action trigger pull. The cylinder also swings out from the frame and allows shooters to eject, or load, all chambers simultaneously.

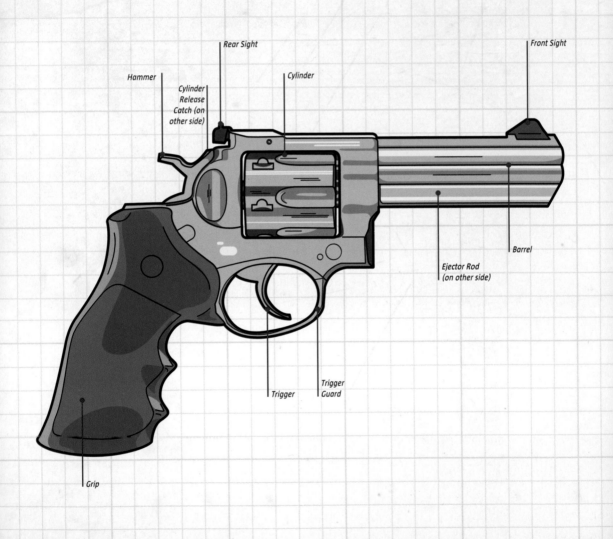

Rear Sight

Front Sight

Hammer

Cylinder

Cylinder Release Catch (on other side)

Barrel

Ejector Rod (on other side)

Trigger

Trigger Guard

Grip

SINGLE ACTION This revolver type must be manually cocked to fire each shot. In addition, the gun's cylinder does not swing out to allow ejecting or loading all rounds at once. Instead, a loading gate on the right-hand side needs to be opened and the spent rounds are then removed one at a time by pushing the ejector rod. Rounds are also loaded singly.

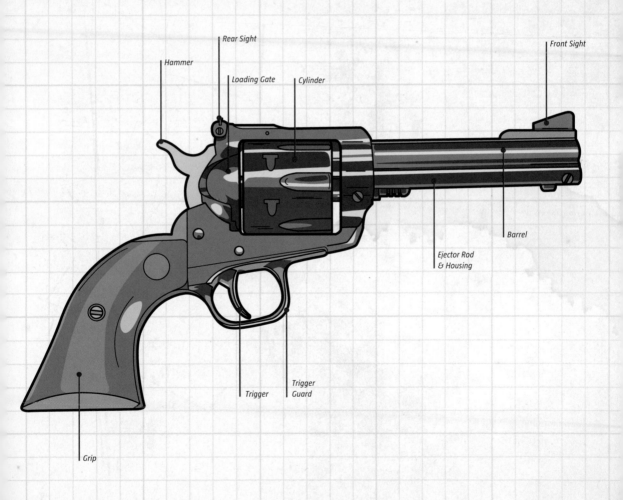

Rear Sight

Hammer

Loading Gate

Cylinder

Front Sight

Barrel

Ejector Rod
& Housing

Trigger

Trigger
Guard

Grip

144 CHECK OUT THE SHOOTING GALLERY

Revolvers lag behind semiautos in sales figures, but far exceed them in versatility. This widely varied selection of revolver models can handle most anything from harvesting the largest North American game to defending one's home to competitive shooting to fun plinking, and can slip into a pocket for personal protection. Here are 12 of the best models currently in production.

Freedom Arms Model 83 Premier Grade Adjustable Sights

Designed for hunting, this single-action revolver is built like a Swiss watch and is bank-vault tough. Highly accurate, with provisions for easily mounting a scope, it is chambered for an array of cartridges that can handle any big-game hunting chores in North America.

Ruger Single Six Convertible

This single-action rimfire handgun comes in .22 Long Rifle with an interchangeable .22 Magnum cylinder. The basic design has been a Ruger staple for over 50 years and has helped many folks learn to shoot a handgun. Available in either blued or stainless steel, the crisp single-action trigger, adjustable sights, and many barrel lengths from 4.62- to 9.5-inches make it ideal for many tasks.

Ruger GP100

This 6-shot double-action revolver is chambered for .357 Magnum. It's available in 4- and 6-inch barrel models with adjustable sights that include interchangeable front sights and a fixed-sight 3-inch model. Rugged and highly accurate, my GP100 has digested almost 30,000 rounds in heavy-duty competition use before requiring a tune-up.

Ruger Vaquero

This trim SA revolver mimics the classic feel of the original Colt Peacemaker, but with a modern design and affordable price. Chambered for .357 or .45 Long Colt, it is available with a classic or Bisley grip frame and has become a favorite with Cowboy Action competitors. It is available in blue or stainless steel.

Ruger SP101 .22

This double-action revolver is built on the compact SP101 frame with a 4.2-inch barrel. It's equipped with an adjustable rear sight with a fiber optic front sight and holds 8 rounds of .22 Long Rifle ammunition. It's an ideal kit gun, and it's also great practice for those wishing to learn double-action shooting techniques.

Ruger Super Blackhawk

This sturdy single-action handgun, chambered in .44 Magnum, has become a modern classic. Its 6-round capacity, modern lock work, heavy-duty construction, adjustable sights, affordable price, and excellent accuracy make it a top choice for today's handgun hunters.

Smith & Wesson Model 629

This double-action stainless steel revolver features adjustable sights and is available in barrel lengths from 4 to 6½ inches. Chambered for .44 Magnum, it also shoots the softer .44 Special. It has earned an excellent reputation as a big-game hunting handgun, but it is also suitable for personal defense and, with the right loads, for competition.

Smith & Wesson Model 642

Weighing 15 ounces empty, with a concealed hammer that won't snag in the pocket, this 5-shot double-action .38 Special snubby has earned an impressive reputation as a pocket pistol. The aluminum alloy frame and stainless steel cylinder and barrel are largely immune to the heat and moisture that can rust other guns in humid climates.

Smith & Wesson Model 500

This double-action 5-shot stainless steel revolver is chambered for the .500 S&W cartridge and is the most powerful revolver in the world. It is available in barrel lengths from 4 to 12 inches. In the longer barrel lengths, it's suitable for harvesting any North American game animal, and the 4-inch models make excellent personal-protection guns in big-bear country.

Smith & Wesson Pro Series Model 640

This gun takes snub-nosed revolvers to a new level. The 5-shot, stainless steel, 2¼-inch barrel gun is chambered for .357 Magnum, cut for moon clips for faster reloading, and is equipped with tritium night sights. The sights offer excellent accuracy, and in testing, we were able to achieve 15-yard groups that could be covered with a playing card.

Smith & Wesson Model 627

Revolvers are inherently more reliable than semiautos when left loaded and stored for extended periods, which is precisely the condition home-defense handguns find themselves in. The 627 is chambered for 8 rounds of .357 and makes an excellent home defense handgun. Recent USPSA rule changes have also opened the door for its use in competition.

Taurus 85VTA "View"

Introduced in 2014, this 5-shot .38 Special double-action-only revolver is built on the proven Model 85 action, but with its titanium cylinder, 1.41-inch barrel, and radically redesigned grip frame, it weighs just 9³/₁₀ ounces empty and is under 15 ounces loaded. It is the lightest, most compact multishot centerfire handgun available—and ideal for the most discreet personal-protection carry.

145 WOW THEM AT THE BBQ

The tradition of the BBQ gun started out with Texas lawmen looking to one-up each other at picnics and other social gatherings. The concept is simple: Take a nice gun adorned with a variety of trick touches (such as decorative metalwork and custom grips), be sure you have an equally fancy belt and holster to go with it, and you're in the running. Well, almost. Because there's custom, and then there's custom.

This Colt Single-Action Army revolver was built by Hamilton Bowen, one of the country's top gunsmiths, and is a difficult piece to top. It started off as a second-generation Colt with a 7½-inch barrel. After two years of work, it was transformed into what you see here. The barrel was shortened to 4 inches, a base pin and lever modeled after the famous Keith No. 5 was installed, and a Bisley-style hammer was added, among other features. The engraving was done by Dan Love, and the color case hardening was added by Doug Turnbull. The grips were carved from French walnut by Roy Fishpaw, and the holster and its belt were built by George Wathne.

One thing that didn't change during the revolver's transformation is the chambering: .45 Long Colt.

To make this revolver lightweight, metal was removed from the area around the loading gate and other sections of the frame.

Precise machining of the base pin and latch, inspired by the famous Keith No. 5, can be seen clearly in this detail shot.

146 TAKE THE HANDGUN CHALLENGE

Handguns have a greater range than bows but a shorter range than rifles. Taking game with a handgun is a challenge that requires skill sets from both bowhunting and rifle hunting, for a unique experience.

Most states allow hunting deer, elk, moose, bear, or other big game with a handgun. Regulations often stipulate minimum caliber and power levels but there are plenty of handguns that comply.

Those who enjoy calling predators, like bobcats and coyotes, will find few mandated caliber regulations. Feral hogs, which are a problem in many states, also have few restrictions on caliber and power levels. Small game like rabbits and squirrels are another enjoyable hunting experience, and the .22 Long Rifle is a favorite here.

The challenge of handgun hunting is in the ability to stalk within range and then deliver an accurate shot, which takes a higher level of skill than with a rifle. In a handful of cases, however, the handgun hasn't been chosen for the challenge. It just happens to be the ideal tool in the circumstances.

Those hunters who follow the hounds to bear, boar, mountain lions, or raccoons will spend quite a long time busting brush on the run until they reach the point where the quarry is bayed. Once there, the shooting is close and often quick. Handguns are a far easier firearm to tote than rifles and will still finish that job well.

147 PICK THE BEST HUNTING HANDGUN

The key to selecting an effective hunting handgun is to choose a caliber that has enough power to humanely harvest the intended game and then mate it with a gun that has enough accuracy to deliver the shot. There are plenty to choose from.

The Ruger line of .22 semiautos and single-action revolvers, along with the Browning Buckmark models, are excellent choices for small game and can center a rabbit or squirrel's head at 20 yards or more.

Bobcats and coyotes fall into the size range where a .357 Magnum is an excellent choice, and the Smith & Wesson Model 686, the Ruger GP-100, Ruger Blackhawk, and the Freedom Arms Model 83 single-action revolver, in the 6-inch or longer barrel lengths, have the accuracy to handle any that your call brings in.

With larger game, the .357 Magnum is a marginal performer. It can work at modest ranges, but it often takes multiple shots, and can sometimes fail with even good hits. Calibers that can humanely harvest deer-size and larger game start with the .41 Magnum, and include .44 Magnum, .454 Casull, .460 S&W Magnum, .475 Linebaugh, and the .500 S&W Magnum. Smith & Wesson offers excellent double-action revolvers in .44 Magnum, .460 S&W, and .500 S&W. The Freedom Arms 83 is available in .41 Magnum, .44 Magnum, .454 Casull, and the .475 Linebaugh. The Ruger double-action Super Redhawk comes in .44 Magnum and .454 Casull, while the Ruger Super Blackhawk single-action revolver is available in .44 Magnum.

148 TRY THE SINGLE-SHOT ALTERNATIVE

Semiauto handguns can't handle the cartridges required to harvest big game, leaving revolvers as the choice for many. There are, however, single-shot handguns chambered for rifle cartridges and, when equipped with a scope, they are essentially short rifles. While a revolver has an effective range of about 150 yards, these single shots can double that distance and, in the hands of a skilled shooter, can rival the accuracy and range of a rifle.

The Thompson/Center Encore model is the most noteworthy. A top break single-shot pistol that's been drilled and tapped for scope mounting, its 15-inch barrels are chambered for hard-hitting rifle rounds like the .30/06 Springfield, .308 Winchester, and 7mm-08.

The Thompson/Center G2 Contender is a slightly lighter version, but also drilled and tapped for scope mounting, and chambered in 6.8 Remington, 7-30 Waters, .30/30 Winchester, or .45/70 Government. When properly rigged, the Encore and the Contender are capable of handling any big-game animal in North America.

This single-shot design is inherently accurate, and these models are also chambered in popular varmint cartridges like the .204 Ruger, .223 Remington, and .22/250 Remington. On a prairie dog shoot out in South Dakota, I was hitting them regularly at 200-plus yards with a scope-equipped .223 Remington Contender.

149 PREPARE FOR BACKWOODS HAZARDS

Personal protection doesn't stop when the sidewalk ends. You may face hazards while out on a wilderness hike or when fishing your favorite trout stream. The handgun that can easily handle a street thug could be woefully inadequate if you run into a bear, mountain lion, or wolf that feels sudden hunger pangs and decides that you're its next lunch.

The only way to assuredly stop the attack of a large predatory animal is to deliver a good central nervous system (CNS) hit. This requires penetrating the skull to reach the brain or breaking the spine. A hard shot that breaks a shoulder might also redirect the animal and give you time to make the CNS hit. These will require a heavy bullet from a large caliber handgun, and the 9mm you tote around with you on the streets might not even get a big critter's attention.

Effective woods guns start off with the .45 ACP and 10mm in semiautos, and these are at the lower end of the recommended power levels. A better choice is any revolver in .45 Long Colt, .41 Magnum, .44 Magnum, .454 Casull, or .500 S&W. Concealability isn't an issue here, since open carry is commonly accepted in most wilderness areas. Bone-breaking power is the key.

150 RELOAD A REVOLVER FAST

Revolvers run out of ammo well before semiautos and need to be reloaded more frequently in a match. The ability to execute a fast reload is a key skill. The fastest and most foolproof method with either speedloaders or moon clips is the strong-hand reload.

After the last shot, the first movement (for a right-handed shooter) is for the thumb of the right hand to hit the cylinder release while simultaneously sliding the left hand under the gun to the right side (A). The two middle fingers on the left hand then push cylinder open and they follow the cylinder through the frame to hold the gun. The left hand now has full control of the gun, which frees the strong hand to grab ammo. The muzzle is then canted upwards and the thumb of the left hand hits the ejector rod to eject the empty cases, while the right hand retrieves the speedloader or moon clip from a holder located in front of the holster (B).

The gun is then tilted muzzle-down and the rounds inserted into the cylinder (C). If a speedloader is used, just drop it. You can pick it up later.

The strong hand then shifts onto the grip while the thumb of the left hand pushes the cylinder closed (D)and rotates it to the bolt stop lockup, and then resumes the shooting grip. The same procedure works just fine for left-handed shooters if they initially shift the gun to their right hand and then follow this same procedure.

Done smoothly, it takes less than three seconds to reload a revolver and get off a shot.

151 GET THE RIGHT GRIP

When shooting a double-action revolver, you need to position the web of the shooting hand as high up on the back strap as possible, and grip the gun with enough pressure to compress the web and squeeze the frame tight. This puts the axis of the bore in a direct line with the forearm.

This will reduce felt recoil and muzzle rise. The shooter shouldn't feel any of the recoil in the palm of his or her hand. Instead, it should be straight back into the wrist and arms. This helps to get the shooter back on target faster and is less fatiguing.

It also helps improve accuracy because, if the gun is gripped low, it will pivot and shift in the shooter's hand.

Since recoil begins while the bullet is still in the barrel, this can cause the bullet to wind up other than where your sights said it would. A high grip produces less felt recoil and greater accuracy.

152 MASTER THE LIVE-TRIGGER TECHNIQUE

Some shooters consider the lengthy trigger pull on a double-action revolver to be overly heavy, slow and cumbersome. Not so!

A skilled DA revolver shooter can face off against three action-pistol targets at 7 yards and—from the holster—drill two perfect hits through each in less than 3½ seconds. The elite masters can shave a second from that. Those times, however, are only possible when using the live-trigger technique.

A live trigger means that once the first shot is fired, the gun's trigger never stops moving and the cylinder never stops revolving. The trigger is either coming back to fire a round or moving forward to reset before it immediately moves rearward again. This includes while transitioning between targets. The trigger keeps moving.

This is in direct contrast to the dead-trigger technique, in which the shooter allows the trigger to go forward to reset, pauses, confirms sights on target, and begins the lengthy double-action pull all over again. The speed advantage is significant on targets inside 15 yards.

This technique requires a strong grip on the revolver, an intense focus of the front sight, and a practiced sense of timing and rhythm so that the trigger pull finishes just when the sights hit their alignment on the target. Recoil enters the picture here, too, but the act of pulling the trigger as the gun rises up in recoil helps bring the gun back down on target. The timing and rhythm will need to be learned through practice and lots of repetition.

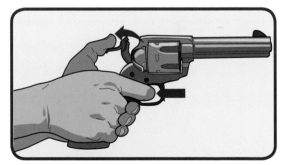

153 SLIP-FIRE A SINGLE ACTION

The classic Old West movies show the hero gripping his single-action revolver in one hand and shifting his grip on the gun to use his thumb to cock back the hammer between shots. It's slow. And, it's not the way cowboy action shooters do it today. In fact, by using a slip-gunning technique they can shoot any single-action revolver as fast as any semiauto.

The pistol is held in a firm two-handed grip. As it is brought up to the target, and before the hammer has been cocked, the shooter presses the trigger and holds it back. This retracts the cocking notch.

The supporting hand thumb then draws the hammer back and releases it. With the cocking notch retracted, it flies free and fires the gun. The faster the thumb, the faster the cylinder can be emptied. And with a firm shooting hand grip, this technique can deliver speedy, accurate fire at close to moderate ranges. This is one key to winning cowboy action matches.

154 WIELD THE ULTIMATE HUNTING HANDGUN

The Smith & Wesson Performance Center 500 can deal with every huntable animal you might encounter: It can fire loads light enough for varmints, heavy enough for thick-skinned dangerous game, or flat enough for long-distance species such as sheep or antelope. And while custom guns are never cheap, the Performance Center 500 is hand-built by master craftsmen and will put every bullet right where you point it. For under $1,500, that's pretty good. Here's what makes it so awesome.

COMPENSATOR The compensator's 360-degree design (A) throws flame like the exhaust from a Top Fuel dragster but helps to tame the .500's formidable recoil, making its 275- and 325-grain loads kick less than a .44 Magnum. It also acts as a barrel nut, suspending the barrel in the barrel shroud. In essence, it pulls the barrel between the frame and compensator, eliminating barrel stress and enhancing accuracy.

BARREL You have a choice of three barrel lengths: 6 ½, 7 ½, or 10 ½ inches. The 10 ½ pictured here (B) gives the best performance with the various loads for the 500, in both velocity and accuracy. Every Performance Center 500 barrel is made by Lothar-Walther and is precision ground at both the crown and the forcing cone, where the barrel extends through the gun frame. What you actually see is the barrel shroud. The barrel itself is contained within it, suspended in between the frame and compensator.

SCOPE Traditionally, hunting handguns have been effective to about 100 yards or so (the exception being some single-shot handguns that have been chambered for rifle cartridges). The 500's downrange energy and trajectory can increase that to 200 yards with the right scope and shooting technique. Pictured here (C) is Leupold's VX-III 2.5–8x32 extended-eye-relief scope.

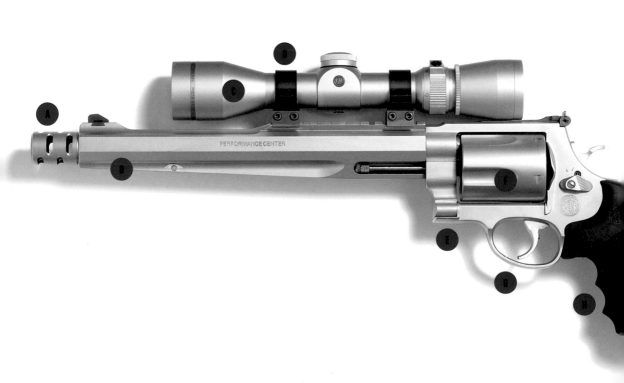

RINGS Not every scope ring withstands all of the punishing recoil generated by the 500's heaviest loads. These cross-slot-style rings (D) devised by Leupold—the company's PRWs, to be precise—offer the best grip because they have metal tabs which sit in the integral grooves machined into the top of the revolver's barrel shroud. This integral Picatinny-style rail—available only on the 10 ½-inch model—eliminates any need to use a separate scope base, thus providing another accuracy-enhancing feature.

CHIN The chin in front of the trigger guard (E) is the best spot to rest a handgun when you're using a set of sticks or any other shooting aid. Placing the barrel (or the barrel shroud in this case) on a rest can create some accuracy-destroying stress, especially when shooting at longer distances.

CYLINDER With its five charging holes (F), the 500 gives you better backup capability than most rifles. And with the exception of a double rifle, a revolver gives you the quickest follow-up shots of any repeater in the event of a misfire, a comforting advantage when you're hunting dangerous game.

TRIGGER As crisp as a mountain stream, the trigger (G) is tuned to break at 4 pounds in single-action mode. The hammer and the trigger components are forged, not metal-injected, which allows them to be matched up for a crisper let-off and better trigger pull.

GRIP Smartly designed grips (H) by Hogue feature a gel insert where the web of your hand rests to help dampen the 500's kick. Made from a special material called Sorbothane, the insert acts just like a recoil pad on a shotgun or rifle.

155 CHOOSE YOUR AMMO

You have a range of options for big-game hunting with the S&W 500. Here are our picks.

CARTRIDGE	MUZZLE VELOCITY/ENERGY	BEST FOR	NOTES
Cor-Bon 325-gr. Barnes XPB	1,800 fps/2,338 ft.-lb.	Long-range handgunning	Sighted-in 3.1 inches high at 100 yards, this spitzer-style bullet drops only 7.7 inches at 200 yards.
Hornady 350-gr. XTP Mag	1,900 fps/2,805 ft.-lb.	Deer	With .30/06-class muzzle energy, this bullet will knock any whitetail sideways. Has proven effective on bear and larger game, too.
Winchester 400-gr. Platinum	1,800 fps/2,877 ft.-lb.	Elk, bear, caribou	This bullet has the heft and construction to tackle large-bodied game animals, and works well for deer, too.
Hornady 500-gr. XTP FP	1,425 fps/2,254 ft.-lb.	Heavy and dangerous game	When your goal is to get deep penetration and a big, leaky hole, this flat-nosed sledgehammer will definitely do the trick.

156 SELECT A PERSONAL-PROTECTION HANDGUN

Both semiauto handguns and revolvers are excellent choices for personal defense, and each has advantages and disadvantages.

Semiautos offer larger ammunition capacity and the ability to reload more quickly than revolvers. Their drawback is that they are more prone to malfunction. Dependent on proper ammunition power levels and properly functioning magazines, they require regular cleaning. Revolvers are less finicky. You can clean one, load it, toss it into a drawer, and ten years later expect it to fire all rounds. That's not true for semiautos, and this can be an important factor in a home-defense handgun that may sit a long time without being shot.

Semiautos are available in a wide variety of sizes and designs. The .380 ACP caliber is considered to be the minimum effective power level for personal protection. Increasing power levels are found in the 9mm, .40 S&W, .357 SIG, .45 ACP, and 10mm. The larger the caliber, the greater the recoil. That's a factor to consider.

Double-action revolvers are available in a variety of calibers; the .38 Special and .357 Magnum are very effective and available in guns ranging from 2-inch barrel snubbies all the way through the larger-framed models with barrels in the 3- to 6-inch-plus range.

The key to selecting your handgun should hinge on four questions: Does it fit my hand? Can I operate all the controls? Can I hit anything with it? And, if it is to be carried concealed on your person: Is it comfortable enough to carry concealed all day?

The best way to answer all these questions is to try before you buy. Many gun shops with attached ranges have rental guns. Some shooting schools will provide guns. Fellow shooters at a gun club may have models you are considering and will likely let you try them if you ask politely.

A personal-defense handgun is very personal. Find the one that suits you best.

157 CONSIDER CONCEALED CARRY

The increased number of concealed-handgun carry permits available in many parts of the United States has raised a demand for concealed-carry handguns. Striker-fired, polymer-framed guns have advantages in this regard and are extremely popular and effective.

Advantages include lighter weight, greater ammunition capacity, and a lower price. For example, if a shooter wishes to carry a full-size .45 ACP, the S&W M&P .45 ACP has a 4½-inch barrel, weighs 29.6 ounces empty, and holds 11 rounds. The S&W SW1911 (a full-size .45 with specifications matching almost any steel-framed 1911) has an empty weight of 40.5 ounces and carries just 9 rounds. The difference between weight, capacity, and price exists with other caliber guns as well. It's much easier to cast a polymer frame than to machine a frame from steel or aluminum alloy so polymer designs cost less to produce.

Another advantage? Comfort. The polymer makes for smoother rounded contours and no exposed hammer to abrade the skin during daily carry. All this has made these guns the most popular choice for concealed carry semiautos.

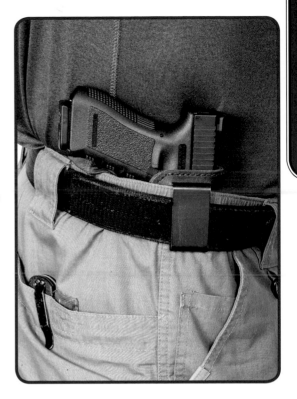

158 BE A RESPONSIBLE CONCEALED CARRIER

A permit to carry a concealed handgun is just that—a permit to carry it. It's not a permit to use it. Use of that handgun is covered by other laws dealing with self defense, and those laws would apply whether you were carrying a handgun or not. But, if you are carrying a handgun under a legally issued permit, you will be held to a higher standard of behavior and, if you have to use that gun, your every action leading up to its use will be put under a microscope.

A concealed-carry permit holder who becomes abusive, threatening, or argumentative, or whose behavior is viewed by the investigating authorities as initiating the confrontation, might be seen as the aggressor. In that case, a claim of self defense might be denied. The aggressor loses the right to be the victim in a self-defense claim in most jurisdictions. The fact that you're carrying a gun does not mean that you don't have to "take stuff" from anybody. It actually means that you have to take more "stuff" than if you were not carrying.

A gun on the hip carries with it the power of life and death. The responsible concealed carrier will comport himself with greater calm and wisdom than an unarmed man. A simple argument resulting in a fistfight when unarmed can escalate far beyond that when a gun is present.

The responsible concealed carrier will avoid any confrontations. The gun is only there as a last resort.

159 MASTER THE POCKET PISTOL

Compact handguns, whether semiauto or revolver, are among the most popular choices for concealed carry. Their modest size and light weight makes them easy to tote. Unfortunately, this also makes them among the most difficult handguns to fire quickly and accurately—the two factors that are most important in personal-defense situations. Here's how to start becoming proficient in their use.

START EMPTY Start off by facing your target at a close range—3 to 4 yards—with an empty gun secured in a carry holster. Practice drawing, dry-firing on the target, and reholstering. Repetition is key. The goal here is to do this over and over until you can perform it without conscious thought, the same way your feet and hands operate a motor vehicle.

TAKE A SHOT Once you're comfortable with dry firing, it's time to start putting holes in the target. Begin at 4 yards. The best targets to use are the ones that represent a human torso and head—IDPA or USPSA targets are good; avoid bull's-eye–style targets. Follow the same procedure as with your dry-firing drill. Draw from the holster, put a single shot in the central portion of the target, and reholster. The goal is to create a fist-size cluster of hits. Focus on being smooth, but work to build up your speed. Next, increase the distance to the target. Move from 4 yards to 7 yards. Then move back to 10 yards. Finish up at 15 yards.

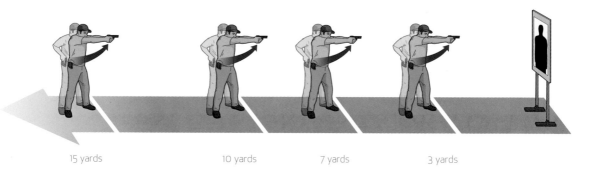

15 yards   10 yards   7 yards   3 yards

160 TAKE MULTIPLE SHOTS

Two hits are always better than one, and virtually every reputable shooting trainer out there teaches a multiple-hit technique. There are two techniques you'll want to master: the double tap (sometimes called "hammers") and the controlled pair.

KNOCK TWICE A double tap is delivered when a shooter draws and takes one sight picture on the target, but then presses the trigger twice, rapidly, from that one sight picture. This works well to deliver two hits quickly at a close range, because the recoil of the first shot will

not throw the second shot too far off. Start at 4 yards, and then see how far back you can move while making two good center mass hits. Once you reach your limit, it's time to shift to controlled pairs.

PAIR UP A controlled pair is delivered when a shooter triggers the shot on the initial sight picture, and then brings the gun down out of recoil and achieves another sight picture—or at least a good glimpse of the front sight—before triggering the second shot. It's a little slower, but allows for better accuracy at longer ranges.

161 PULL OFF EL PRESIDENTE

One of the best drills a handgunner can use to evaluate his or her skill level and make some improvements is El Presidente, a drill created in the 1970s by Jeff Cooper, as a general benchmark for handgun skills.

GET SET Three combat targets are placed side by side and 1 yard apart from each other. The shooter then stands 10 yards away with his or her back to the target. Once given the signal to start, the shooter turns to face the targets, adopts an athletic shooting stance, draws, and fires two shots on each for six total. After performing a speed reload, the shooter then fires two more shots on each target to stop the clock.

BEAT THE CLOCK Twelve center hits in 10 seconds is par for the course. But don't expect to be all that fast to begin with. Work for smoothness, especially with your reload. Practice being smooth and accurate and you will reduce your time.

STAY ON TARGET Center hits are the only thing that win pistol matches and gunfights. Spraying bullets downrange won't put you in the winner's circle and might get you in a load of trouble in the real world. Remember the saying: You can't miss fast enough to win.

162 TRIANGULATE YOUR STANCE

There are a number of two-handed shooting stance options. The most effective is the Power Isosceles. Start by facing the target squarely, with feet spread slightly more than shoulder-width apart. With your gun in both hands, raise it toward the target while leaning slightly forward. Slide your strong-side foot (the right foot for righties) about 8 inches to the rear. To engage multiple targets, pivot your body to move like a turret.

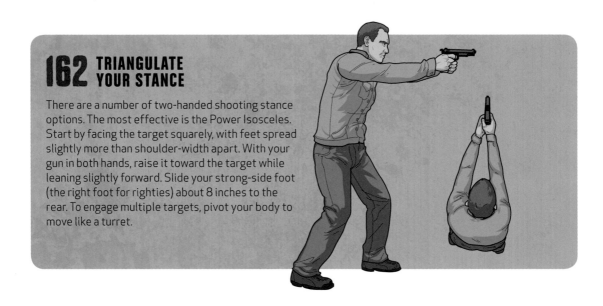

163 GET RELIABLE PERSONAL PROTECTION

When considering a personal-protection gun, a double-action revolver can be your best bet for several very good reasons.

RELIABILITY You don't want a gun to fail in a crisis, and a double-action revolver is inherently more reliable than any semiauto. The only things that cause malfunctions in a revolver are either an unexpected parts breakage or a defective round that lodges a bullet in the barrel, while semiautos can fail for many additional reasons.

LOW MAINTENANCE A revolver requires no maintenance for long-term storage. You can keep a clean, loaded gun in a drawer for 10 years and it will still fire when you need it to. Semiautos require more frequent "exercise" and maintenance. Springs can take a set and lubricants can congeal. They can't be ignored for long periods of time. This is an important consideration for home-defense guns that may end up sitting around without seeing any use.

CLOSE-UP ADVANTAGE You can jam a DA revolver against an attacker and fire all rounds, whereas a semiauto can have the slide pushed out of battery and jam. This may be the reason why the most popular revolvers today are the compact, hammerless, 2-inch snubbies that can vanish in a pocket.

Revolvers do hold fewer rounds and can be slower to reload. However, FBI statistics show that the average civilian self-defense incident is over with no more than three rounds being fired. Even the smallest compact revolver will contain five rounds, and there are larger models that hold six, seven, or even eight. As a savvy self-defense expert once remarked, "I'd rather have five that I know will fire, than a dozen I'm not sure of."

164 SHOOT WITH SUBSTITUTE CARTRIDGES

One reason to love the revolver is its versatility. A semiauto handgun requires specific pressure levels and the proper cartridge length for its ammunition to function, but a revolver is manually cycled and does not. If the round is the right caliber and fits into the chamber, it will fire. A lot of revolvers will safely, and accurately, fire rounds other than the caliber denoted on the barrel. This interchangeability allows for practice loads with less recoil, or potting small game for the table at a hunting camp. Here are some examples.

PRIMARY CARTRIDGE

Federal .327 Magnum

.357 Magnum

.454 Casull

.460 S&W Magnum

ALTERNATE CARTRIDGES

32 H&R Magnum
.32 Long
S&W .32

.38 Short Colt
.38 Long Colt
.38 Special
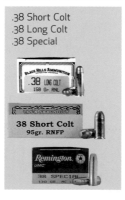

.45 Long Colt

.454 Casull
.45 Long Colt
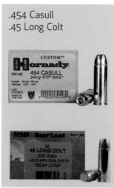

165 TRY SHOT LOADS

If you have a revolver, you have the option of using shot loads, which don't work well with semiautos.

CCI loads plastic shot capsules in .38 Special and .44 Special. The former will shred a snake at 10 feet, and the .44 will do it at 20 feet. They are popular with those wandering where venomous snakes live.

Shot loads are also available in .22 LR, and one of my shooting partners keeps his double-action revolver skills up to date by potting rats in his barn with a Ruger SP101 .22 revolver.

166 KNOW YOUR CARRY OPTIONS

If you need to bring your gun with you, here are the 10 most popular and useful holster carry options.

Ⓐ STRONG-SIDE BELT HOLSTER
Worn on the belt outside the waistband (OWB) and slightly behind the hip on the shooter's strong side, this option is very concealable. It's the first choice of many experts for carrying mid- and full-size handguns.

Ⓑ WAISTBAND HOLSTER
This slips inside the waistband of the pants and is held in place with a spring clip or leather snap loop over the pants belt. It can be positioned anywhere along the waistline and is one of the best concealment techniques.

Ⓒ SHOULDER HOLSTER
A harness positions the handgun holster beneath the weak-side armpit. These are useful in colder climates under a heavy coat that may impede access to a belt gun, but very uncomfortable in warm humid climates.

Ⓓ CROSS-DRAW HOLSTER
This OWB holster is worn on the weak side and just forward of the hip. It allows access to the gun with either hand but is a bit more difficult to conceal.

Ⓔ BRIEFCASE HOLSTER
This tactical case has an internal holster designed to conceal your gun next to your day planner and other office essentials. Also makes having your gun stolen really easy.

Ⓕ ANKLE HOLSTER
Normally worn on the inside of the weak-side ankle, some find these a convenient way to carry a small backup pistol. They are not recommended as a means to carry your only gun, since they are difficult to access.

A FANNY-PACK HOLSTER

When worn in the front, these are an excellent method of carrying a handgun when not wearing your normal attire; such as when out jogging or cycling. Some holster makers offer them with specially designed gun compartments that are quick to access.

B POCKET HOLSTER

These are designed to carry a small handgun in a jacket or coat pocket. They are very useful if your wardrobe allows it, and are a favorite backup gun-carrying method for this writer.

C BELLY BAND

These are elastic bands that wrap around the stomach above the hips with a holster pocket that can fit a small handgun. The band is easily concealed under a shirt and is a good choice for females, since the bust line helps conceal the gun when worn in front.

D BRA HOLSTER

This holster clips to the middle of the bra between the breasts and holds a small handgun. It is quite concealable, and the gun is drawn by pulling straight down.

E PURSE HOLSTER

Some holster makers offer purses with a built-in holster compartment. This makes quick access to the gun easier than when a pistol is simply dropped into a purse with all the other items, but does increase the likelihood of theft

F THIGH HOLSTER

A maximum concealment rig women can wear under a skirt, thigh holsters are also worn outside the clothing on the strong side by many LE and Military personnel to easily access a gun below bulky body armor.

167 LOOK AT LASERS

Handguns, especially the compact models popular for concealed carry, have small sights and a short sighting radius. This can make them difficult to fire accurately quickly, so adding a laser sight can be a good call.

Comprehensive studies have shown that in violent encounters, a shooter's eyes tend to focus upon the threat, not the gun's sights. With the laser on the target, the eyes can more easily control where the gun is aimed.

Lasers are not effective in bright sunlight, but even in a brightly lit building or at night, they quickly capture the eye.

Laser sights are available for many popular guns, and they are an accessory well worth having when dangerous things happen close and fast.

SNOW SAYS

My primary defensive handguns are all equipped with units that combine a laser and weapon light. These make getting hits in poor lighting and while under stress much easier. Try one out while shooting targets in dim light, and you'll see for yourself what a difference they make.

168 GET THE ESSENTIALS

A gun and ammunition are only two parts of a personal-protection system. If the gun is to be concealed, some type of holster is required, and there are many to choose from. If you select a belt holster, give some thought to the belt. The best holster in the world isn't going to be comfortable or concealable on a skimpy, floppy, dime-store belt.

Most semiautos come with a spare magazine. If yours doesn't, buy one. And purchase a magazine carrier so you can take it with you on the street. That spare magazine can be a lifesaver.

With a revolver, a speedloader or two is also a good asset. They retain extra rounds in a compact manner and allow you to reload a wheelgun quickly. These can be circular loaders (like those from Safariland or HKS) or plastic strips such as the Bianchi Speed Strip or Tuff Strips. Gun-mounted lights are another great add-on.

You will also need a cleaning kit, solvent, and oil to maintain the gun. Buying a gun without a cleaning kit is like buying a dishwasher without buying detergent. Any gun shop will have the proper equipment and can show you how to use it.

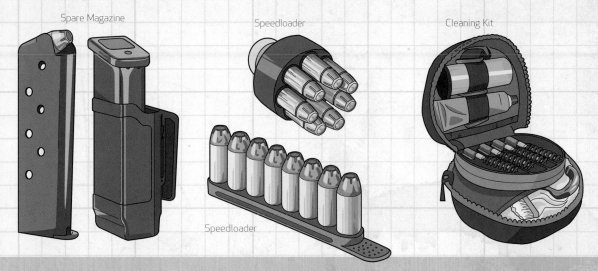

Spare Magazine

Speedloader

Cleaning Kit

Speedloader

169 PICK THE BEST AMMO

The gun's job is to launch the bullet. The bullet is what neutralizes the threat. Therefore, picking the proper projectile is key.

In an urban environment where upright two-legged predators are the threat, the best choice are premium jacketed hollowpoint bullets. They expand upon entry to increase tissue damage, while reducing the risk of over-penetration that could harm innocent bystanders. This is the reason law enforcement agencies use them. So should civilians, whether for concealed carry or home defense.

A number of trusted manufacturers offer premium hollowpoint bullets. Speer, for example, offers them in their Gold Dot line. Federal offers the HST and Hydra-Shok loads. Remington has the Golden Saber. Winchester uses the Ranger, and Hornady has their Critical Defense line. These are available in all of the popular personal-protection calibers under various personal-defense product labels.

For a walk out in the woods where the four-legged variety of predators can be a threat, the situation is reversed. This bullet needs to maintain as much of its weight and profile as possible order to punch through bone and deliver a central nervous system (CNS) hit. Semi-wadcutter designs cast from hardened lead, or softpoint bullets with a heavy copper jacket, are the most effective. All these loads will be found in the hunting product lines from the above companies.

170 JOIN THE CLUB(S)

While semiauto handguns are the more popular choice for action-pistol games and competitions, there is no shortage of alternative events for revolvers, and even a few exclusive clubs.

BE PRACTICAL The United States Practical Shooting Association (USPSA) has a revolver division, for 6-shooters in the Major Power category. The Minor Power category allows up to 9-shot revolvers—although only 8 shots are allowed before reloading.

GET DEFENSIVE Competitions in the International Defensive Pistol Association (IDPA) allow 6-shot revolvers in 4.2-inch barrel lengths or shorter in two categories. Stock Service Revolver is designed for a Power Factor of 105, and a minimum caliber of .38 Special, with speedloaders. Enhanced Service Revolver requires a Power Factor of 165, allows reloading with moon clips, and predominantly features .45 ACP and .40 S&W.

SHOW SOME STEEL The Revolver Division of the Steel Challenge allows .38 Special and higher caliber revolvers, using iron sights only (an additional Open Class allows more options like optical sights and ported barrels), and has no restrictions on the number of shots in the revolver.

GET ENTHUSIASTIC The International Confederation of Revolver Enthusiasts (ICORE) is similar to USPSA. Matches are timed to hundredths of a second, and involve various targets, such as steel targets to ring or knock

down as far as 80 yards, paper targets at 50 yards and closer (including inside 3 yards), and swinging and moving targets. Accuracy is paramount: Missing the 8-inch A Zone on a paper target incurs a 1-second penalty, missing the 12-inch B Zone loses 2 seconds, and missing the C Zone (and the whole target) is a 5-second penalty. ICORE allows virtually any revolver including .22 LR—which only needs to hit steel targets, not topple them—with a required Power Factor of 120 (excepting .22 LR), and includes Open Class (which allows optical sights, muzzle ports, and moon clips), Limited Class (moon clips only; no ammo capacity or barrel length restrictions), and Classic Division (for 6-shooters with speedloaders).

COWBOY UP Some Old West aficionados compete with modern reproductions of mid-1800s handguns, rifles, and shotguns in Cowboy Action Shooting. Single-action handguns dominate here, in .38 Special, .38/40, .44, and .45 caliber. CAS matches are often hosted by the Single Action Shooting Society, whose membership equals that of USPSA, IDPA, and ICORE combined. Competitions are electronically timed, with targets scored for additional penalty time. The biggest difference: Competitors must adopt a "Western" alias for their scoring moniker, and period costumes are encouraged—and sometimes mandatory. Single Action Shooting Society (SASS) events are as much a social and costume event as they are about shooting, with guys talking clothes and gals talking guns, and everyone having fun no matter which part they enjoy.

171 STAGE YOUR TRIGGER

Skilled double-action revolver shooters almost never cock the gun and shoot it single action. They don't have to take that extra time or shift their grip on the gun; they can stage the double-action trigger to deliver a light single-action pull.

There is a point near the end of the DA pull when the cylinder locks into the bolt stop and is now in alignment with the barrel. At this point you have a single-action trigger pull. You can feel this lock up, and the trigger is

"staged." This is best learned via dry-fire practice, and it doesn't take long to learn.

This is, of course, a departure from the live trigger technique (see item 149). But, it's a variation that can come in handy if you are faced with targets out beyond 30 yards, or with very tight shots around "no shoot" targets. It will give you time to refine your sights to a perfect sight picture while sacrificing little in the way of speed.

172 LEARN YOUR TRAJECTORY

Most revolver loads used in competition aren't traveling faster than 800 fps. When targets stretch out past 35 or so yards, those bullets will start to drop. If you use a 25-yard zero sight in, take the time to learn where your gun shoots at 35, 50, and longer distances. It can pay dividends in a match.

SHOTGUNS

MY START AS A SHOTGUNNER WAS INAUSPICIOUS TO SAY THE LEAST.

As a lefty, I naturally started shooting with the butt of the shotgun in my left shoulder, sighting down the barrel with my left eye. It never occurred to me to take lessons, and I couldn't help but wonder if my Remington 870 was to blame for my inability to hit much of anything. At times I was tempted to pinwheel it into the nearest lake. It wasn't until three years later, and who knows how many thousands of shells scattered across the sky, that I learned I was right-eyed dominant.

To make up for lost time, I taught myself to mount the gun on my right side to align the barrel with the correct eye. I also invested in lessons with some excellent instructors. Targets started breaking and more birds hit the ground.

That improvement changed my life for the better. That might sound over the top, but when I think of the time since then I've spent walking behind beloved dogs with my close friends across the uplands or calling to ducks in frozen marshes, it isn't actually an exaggeration at all. The same goes for the banter among my squad mates during rounds of sporting clays or skeet. It's good for the soul.

If you're new to shotgunning, there's a world of delight before you. The toughest decisions will be figuring out which disciplines to try first. As a versatile tool, shotguns have no peer, but the pleasure they provide the shooter is where they really stand out.

This chapter illuminates the multifaceted shotgun and demonstrates proven skills that will make anyone a better shot. I certainly wish I had known some of this the first time I took that 870 to the range.

173 MEET THE VERSATILE SHOTGUN

To get a sense of the shotgun's utility, just consider the variety of ammunition that it can use. There is standard round shot that progresses from .05-inch No. 12 up to .36-inch No. 000 buckshot. Shot materials include lead, steel, and various hybrid blends of tungsten and iron. Then there's nonround shot. And slugs, in too many shapes and sizes to list here. The shells for all these loads vary in size and length for different purposes as well. When you add it all up, there is no class of firearm that handles a similar array of ammo or as broad an array of shooting tasks.

UPLAND BIRDS The earliest true shotguns were used for bird hunting and as such were commonly known as "fowling pieces." This is still one of the most popular uses for shotguns, and an entire industry is built around the hunting of doves, pheasants, partridges, grouse, quail, and other feathery creatures. The shotguns for upland birds tend to be lighter with elegant lines and fast handling.

WATERFOWL The wet cousins of upland birds are the other major hunting quarry for shotgunners. Waterfowl shotguns are built to withstand rough weather and rough use, able to survive everything from saltwater to bouncing around in the bottom of a boat. Ducks and geese are also tough birds, requiring heavier shot and larger shells. A good duck gun must be robust, but still handle well enough to bring down fast-flying birds.

TURKEYS The gobbling of turkeys in spring sounds a wake-up call from the doldrums of winter for many hunters. As soon as the snow starts to melt (and sometimes even sooner) hunters will grab their turkey guns, which are often customized to take these large birds. Pistol grips, fixed sights (or even scopes), adjustable stocks, extra-tight chokes, 3 ½-inch chambers, and full camo are common features.

BIG GAME Hunters in many parts of the country are restricted to using shotguns for deer and other big game. Buckshot still accounts for plenty of deer, but the use of slugs has become more common. Performance has a lot to do with this. Slug gun accuracy has come a long way in the last 10 years, and specialized rigs that shoot 2- to 3-inch groups at 100 yards are not unusual. Well-made fully rifled barrels, better quality ammo, and purpose-built scopes have fuelled this trend.

PREDATORS The hunting of coyotes and predators is an obsession for many sportsmen. Depending on the terrain and conditions, a shotgun is often the favored firearm for taking on these smart critters. Camo shotguns with predator-specific loads are ideal in suburban areas and thick cover, though many open-country hunters out west will tote a shotgun in addition to a rifle for those times when the coyotes run right up to where the hunter is calling from.

MILITARY Shotguns have a rich military history and have appeared in one form or another in every major military action in U.S. history. Anywhere with fighting that was up close and personal—whether in the trenches of World War I, during the island assaults in the Pacific during World War II, in the jungles of Vietnam, or in urban combat in Iraq—shotguns have been carried into battle.

COMPETITION Shotguns are used for various forms of target games more than all other uses combined. The breaking of clay birds takes on many forms—trap, skeet, sporting clays, 5-stand, and others—and there are shotguns and loads for each application. In general, target guns are heavier than hunting models. Heavier guns will swing more smoothly, but the extra weight also allows the shooter to better handle the cumulative effect of recoil while putting dozens, and in some cases hundreds, of rounds through the guns over the course of a day.

PERSONAL PROTECTION When it comes to personal protection, shotguns are an excellent choice. They are easy to wield, pack tremendous firepower, work reliably, and are ideal for use in tight quarters. Personal-defense shotguns often have extended magazine tubes, shorter barrels, collapsible stocks, and attachment lights. Specialized ammo for self-defense minimizes recoil while retaining lethality.

LAW ENFORCEMENT Standard issue for most U.S. police departments, shotguns are used in patrol vehicles, by SWAT teams, for riot control with less-than-lethal ammunition, and are even carried by some motorcycle units. Pump-action shotguns have been a favorite platform for law enforcement personnel, though some departments also employ tactical semiautos as well.

174 LEARN SHOTGUN HISTORY

While the shotgun's history doesn't stretch back quite as far into the mists of time as that of the handgun or rifle, it's been in use in one form or another for over 200 years. And the technology has changed very little in some cases, proving rather conclusively that sometimes you don't need to improve a great machine.

Shotgun shells with a paper hull and brass base emerge to replace the expensive all-brass shells previously in use, and make shotgun shooting more affordable for all.

Rev. Alexander Forsythe, a Scottish clergyman and avid hunter, patents the percussion lock as a solution to seeing birds spooked by the flame used to ignite a flintlock.

The boxlock action is improved with a trigger block safety that is still in use today. It automatically engages when the hammers are cocked, to prevent the gun discharging when the safety is released.

Early smoothbore firearms, which are precursors to the shotgun, are popular both on the battlefield and for wingshooting, in which case they are known as "fowling pieces."

American gunsmith Sylvester Roper (pictured here) submits a patent for "choke boring," which allowed shooters to control pattern spread.

1700s **1776** **1807** **1866** **1875** **1877** **1882**

First recorded use of the term "shotgun," in Kentucky. It was noted as part of the frontier language of the West by James Fenimore Cooper.

Gunsmiths Anson and Deeley, working for the Westley-Richards company, develop the boxlock action, still essentially the state of the art in double-barreled shotguns.

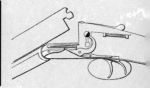

Plastic hull shotshells emerge and provide a stronger and more moisture-resistant shell. By 1980 they had become the preferred shotshell and replaced paper hulls.

While working for Winchester, John Browning (America's greatest firearms designer) creates the Model 1893, the first pump-action shotgun.

American Daniel LeFever patents the first truly automatic hammerless shotgun. The gun automatically cocks itself when the breach is closed; the design remains in use today.

John Browning patents the Browning Auto-5, an inertia-operated semiauto that was the world's first successful semiauto shotgun. It is still in production.

1883   1884   1893   1898   1900   1960

Frank Chamberlin patents the first device for automatically loading shotshells. Prior to this, all shells were loaded by hand.

William Brenneke patents the first truly modern shotgun slug, which was far more accurate than the lead balls of the day. The design is still in use today.

175 USE YOUR TARGETING COMPUTER

To watch a master wingshooter turn a speedy aerial target into a puff of smoke or a ball of feathers is to see true artistry at work. And there is also a fair amount of science involved in the task. Unlike a rifle, a shotgun is not aimed at the target. Some say it is pointed, but that's not completely correct either.

You will hit very few aerial targets by pointing the shotgun at them and pulling the trigger. That's because they won't be there when the shot charge arrives. Experts know that they have to trigger their shot at some point ahead of the target so that target and shot charge will arrive at the same spot together. Given the staggering array of speeds, angles, and distances presented by the various game bird species and the differing clay target games, there is no one correct "lead" that works for all.

In other words, a master wingshooter may look like an artist, but the computer between his or her ears is working overtime on every shot.

176 HIT YOUR TARGET THREE WAYS

No lead is right for every target, and neither is one swing technique. Here are three techniques you should master if you want to become an expert shooter; each is useful in different sporting scenarios.

SUSTAIN YOUR LEAD Mount the gun with the muzzle on the target and then move it ahead of the target to achieve the required amount of lead. Once the correct lead is established, the target speed is matched and the shot triggered without slowing the swing. This is an excellent technique for skeet, since the target speeds, distances, and required leads are known. A shooter familiar with this technique can actually be told how much lead to use on each skeet target and break a lot of them the first time he ever shoots the game!

SWING THROUGH FAST Mount the gun behind the target, accelerate the muzzle quickly through the target, and trigger the shot when you calculate the required amount of daylight between target and muzzle. Since

the gun is moving faster than the target, the leads are shorter than with sustained lead. When done in one fluid motion, the shooter is literally painting the target out of the sky. This is one of the most useful all-around techniques and deadly on the trap and sporting clays fields.

DO A PULL-AWAY Mount the gun directly onto your target, match target speed for a split second, then accelerate the muzzle rapidly ahead of the target until the required lead time is determined to trigger the shot. This was developed to reduce the amount of lead required on long-range targets.
 A duck crossing by at 40 mph and 40 yards out will need 10 feet or more of sustained lead and about half that with fast swing through. The rapid muzzle acceleration of the pull-away can cut that lead to just a few manageable feet. It's a valuable skill to have when targets are distant and also handy for sporting clays.

177 UNDERSTAND CHOKE

The choke on a shotgun is essentially like an adjustable nozzle on a garden hose. Open the nozzle up and it produces a wide spray pattern. Tighten it down and it creates a focused stream of water. By changing chokes shotgunners can do the same with their shot charges.

Choosing the right choke and load for the task at hand can go a long way toward improving your wingshooting accuracy and results.

Traditional measurement in choke determination is calculated as what percentage of the shot charge is placed within in a 30-inch circle at 40 yards. A load at 70% is considered Full choke, 60% is Modified, 50% is Improved Cylinder, and 40% is Cylinder choke. Interchangeable choke tubes are also available in Extra-Full (a favorite with turkey hunters); Improved Modified (patterning between Modified and Full);

Skeet II, which is sometimes called Light Modified; and Skeet, which was designed to produce a 30-inch pattern at 25 yards for that game.

By using the interchangeable choke tubes that dominate the current crop of smoothbores, gunners can dial in their pattern for anything from close range quail, a distant duck, or a gobbler's head at 25 yards.

While the denotation on the choke tube is a guide, there are factors that can alter the percentage patterns it produces.

The harder the shot, the tighter it will pattern. Copper, or nickel-plated shot will pattern tighter than an equivalent load of soft lead shot. Steel or tungsten/polymer shot will pattern tighter than those. Larger shot sizes normally pattern more tightly than smaller sizes of the same shot hardness.

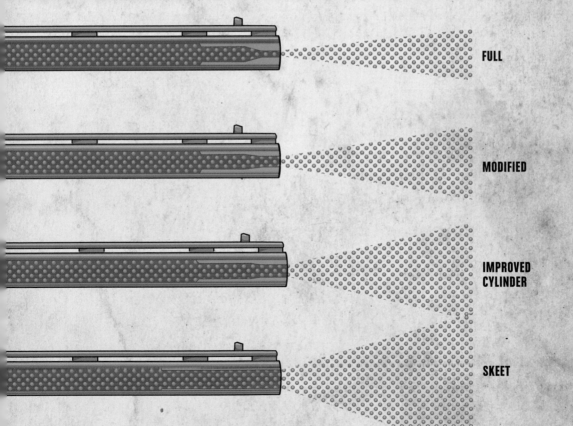

FULL

MODIFIED

IMPROVED CYLINDER

SKEET

178 CHOOSE YOUR GAME

Smoking a streaking clay target is the most popular recreational use of shotguns. While many games and variations exist, three are far and away the most popular in America today.

TRAP This is the oldest shotgun game; the first clay targets and the traps to throw them appeared around 1880. It's shot on a clear field with a single trap house, which is partially buried in the ground and throws targets that rise and move away from the shooter, much like flushing pheasant, quail, and other upland birds. The trap is set to oscillate between throws, which creates random targets that can appear at various angles to the shooter.

SKEET While trap mimics birds flushing away from the gunner, it does little to prepare you for incoming and crossing targets. So in 1900, three Massachusetts wingshooters, who got tired of missing game birds in the field, changed the target array and target thrower locations to create skeet, now played on a field with eight stations, allowing a range of angles.

SPORTING CLAYS The newest clay target game is not the rigidly programmed and predictable clay target affair we find in trap and skeet. Perfect scores are virtually unheard of. This game is normally played in the woods, and the targets the shooter will see are only limited by the imagination of the course designer. Targets zip by at speeds and angles unseen in the other two games. They may be single targets, two targets thrown at the same time, or a target thrown after the shot report of the shooter's gun addresses the first target thrown. Those targets may also be crossing, climbing straight up, falling straight down, quartering out or in, streaking high overhead coming in or going away, or even bouncing along the ground.

179 SPICE UP TRAP AND SKEET

If the standard games of trap and skeet get boring, you can try shooting the doubles version of each.

Doubles trap consists of two targets launched simultaneously from each station. This time, the trap is set to send targets on a consistent flight path of 22 degrees right and 22 degrees left. From each position, one becomes a straightaway shot and the other an extreme angle. A round of doubles is 50 shells. It's fast-paced and fun.

Doubles skeet uses only stations 1 through 7. Two targets are thrown at each station, with the shooter starting at station 1 and moving through to station 7, and then back through the stations to reach 1 again—and finally, finishing at station 2. Some of the doubles are no different than in a regular round, but the pair of targets thrown on stations 3, 5, and 7 create a new and challenging situation.

180 PICK YOUR LOAD

You don't need to turn a clay target into a puff of black smoke to score a hit. All you need to do is knock a visible piece off of the target that the scorekeeper can see. That greatly simplifies the load selection. Since all major shotshell companies make the same basic loads, we're listing them by shot size and dram equivalent instead of maker.

SPORT	GAUGE	THE BASICS	MORE INFO
SKEET	Range of gauges is used.	Any shotshell load launching No. 9 shot is best, regardless of the gauge.	A load of No. 8 shot will work, but provides no benefit given the close range of the targets.
TRAP	The 12-gauge dominates trap.	A $^1/_{18}$-ounce $2^3/_4$ dram No. 8 load works well from the 16-yard line. (A dram in an old measure of blackpowder. The dram equivalent is printed on most shotgun shell boxes giving a quick way to assess a load's downrange performance.)	Moving back to the handicap positions, which may be as far as 27 yards from the trap house, a 3 dram $^1/_{18}$-ounce No. 7 1/2 load is preferred.
SPORTING CLAYS	Any gauge, though 12 or 20 is standard.	The varied array of targets requires more than one load. The key is the break distance on the target. Inside 20 yards, use a load of No. 9. From 20–30 yards, use No. 8 1/2 or No. 8. Beyond 30 yards, 3-dram $^1/_{18}$-ounce No. 7 1/2 trap loads.	If the targets are beyond 50 yards, it can pay to tuck a few copper-plated $^1/_{14}$-ounce No. 7 1/2 loads into the cart.

181 KNOW YOUR SHOTGUN OPTIONS

Depending on your planned usage, you may wish to use one of these common variations. Or, if you're like most enthusiasts, you'll see the need to own at least one of each. Probably more.

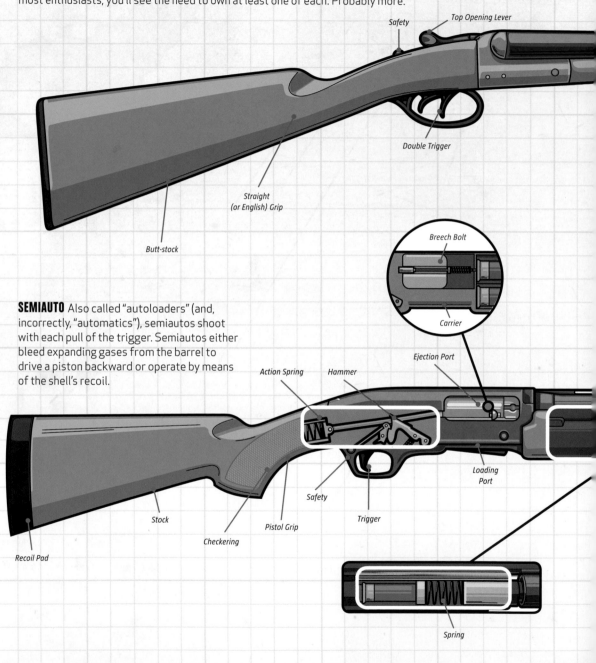

Safety

Top Opening Lever

Double Trigger

Straight
(or English) Grip

Butt-stock

Breech Bolt

Carrier

SEMIAUTO Also called "autoloaders" (and, incorrectly, "automatics"), semiautos shoot with each pull of the trigger. Semiautos either bleed expanding gases from the barrel to drive a piston backward or operate by means of the shell's recoil.

Ejection Port

Action Spring

Hammer

Loading
Port

Stock

Safety

Trigger

Pistol Grip

Checkering

Recoil Pad

Spring

DOUBLE Commonly called "side by side," the double has two barrels joined horizontally. Twin triggers, one firing each barrel, are very common on double guns.

Barrels

e-end

OVER/UNDER (O/U) The over/under has two barrels, one stacked atop the other. Most over/unders have a single trigger that can be selected to fire either the top or bottom barrel first.

Breech Chamber

Boxlock Action

Gas Ports (inside)

Middle Bead

Ventilated Rib

Front Bead

Magazine Cap

Fore-end

PUMP ACTION Also called "slide action," the pump is a manually operated repeater. Pulling the fore-end back and pushing it forward cycles the action.

Magazine

Action Bar

Fore-end

182 GET SKEET BASICS

Skeet got its start around 1900 when C.E. Davis, his son Henry, and their shooting buddy William Foster adapted trap shooting to practice hitting birds that were incoming or crossing their range.

A skeet field is laid out in a semicircle; trap houses are located at the 3 o'clock and 9 o'clock positions. On the left of the field is the high house, which launches the target from 10 feet above the ground at a slight upward angle. To the right, the low house launches targets from 3 feet above the ground at a more abrupt upward angle. The thrower

is fixed and the targets take the same path every time. Seven shooting positions are arrayed in a semicircle, with one in the middle of the field. As shooters move through them, they will see incoming, outgoing, and crossing targets. The farthest shot is about 21 yards and the closest is 4 feet. On some stations, targets are thrown simultaneously from both houses. A round of skeet is 25 shells.

Any gauge is allowed for a casual round, but in a major match, shooters will be required to shoot with 12-, 20-, and 28-gauges and the .410.

183 BREAK 25 STRAIGHT

Skeet is the only clay shooting game where the flight path of the target is fixed and known in advance—10 feet from station 8 is the 8 post; each trap is set to throw its target directly over it. Skeet is shot from a mounted gun position. With the sustained lead technique, shooters need only learn the lead for each target on each station and then find the body position (natural point of aim, or NPA) and muzzle hold point that lets them apply it consistently to break 25 straight. Here's how to get started.

STATION 1

HIGH HOUSE Take your NPA on the 8 post and elevate the muzzle 45 degrees. When the bird appears above it, swing the barrel down through the target for 6 inches of lead below it, and break it quickly.

LOW HOUSE The NPA is on the 8 post, muzzle point is 4 feet outside the house. Acquire the bird but don't hurry. Veteran shooters should break this target at the same point as during the double presentation. Ride the target to a point 45 degrees to your left. The lead is 1 foot.

Doubles Follow the same procedure: Take the high house quickly and ride the low house in.

STATION 2

HIGH HOUSE Take your NPA slightly right of the 8 post and bring the muzzle back two-thirds of the way to the house. Get on this target quickly with 2 ½ feet of lead.

LOW HOUSE The same as low house 1, but extend the lead to 20 inches.

Doubles Your strategy here should be the same as at station 1; take the high house fast and ride the low house.

STATION 3

HIGH HOUSE The NPA position is on the 8 post, with the muzzle point halfway back to the house. Lead here should be 3 feet.

LOW HOUSE Position is the same as for high house; lead is 3½ feet.

STATION 4

HIGH HOUSE These are direct crossing targets and, at 21 yards, the longest shot you'll see. NPA is on the 8 post; muzzle halfway back to the house, and 4 feet of lead for each.

LOW HOUSE Same as high house.

STATION 5

HIGH HOUSE This house becomes the incomer and gets 3½ feet of lead.

LOW HOUSE This is the quartering outgoing target; get on it quickly with 3 feet of lead.

STATION 6

HIGH HOUSE The same gentle incoming target as station 2 with 20 inches of lead.

LOW HOUSE NPA is slightly right of the 8 post with the muzzle halfway back to the house. The lead is 2½ feet.

DOUBLES The low house becomes the outgoing target in doubles. Shoot fast, the target is quick and rising.

STATION 7

HIGH HOUSE This is the easiest station. The high house is the incomer; ride it to 45 degrees on your right with 1 foot of lead.

LOW HOUSE This is the outgoing target. Take your NPA on the 8 post, elevated 30 to 45 degrees. Once you find the right elevation, you can break the low house without moving the gun—the bird will appear right on your muzzle.

DOUBLES Break the low house quickly and take your time on the high house.

STATION 8

HIGH HOUSE Forget sustained lead here. The targets here are going to be close and quick, so use the fast swing-through technique. NPA is on the trap house opening with the muzzle 4 feet outside it. Swing rapidly up and through the target, and shoot as soon as you see a hint of daylight between target and muzzle after passing through.

LOW HOUSE Take your NPA on the trap opening with the muzzle 3 feet outside the house. Swing up and through and shoot as soon as the muzzle blots out the target. You'll break this 3 feet from the muzzle.

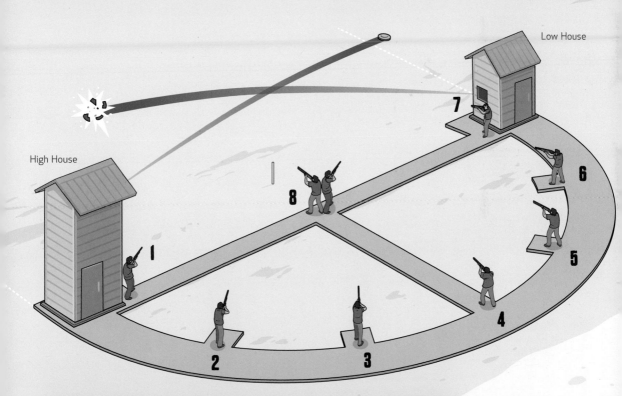

Low House

High House

A round of skeet is 25 shells. So far we've only shot 24. To get rid of that 25th, the shooter repeats the shot on the first target they miss. If you get to low house 8 with that shell still in your pocket, you'll shoot it there. If you've never run 25 straight, that second shot on low house 8 can be one of the toughest you'll ever make.

184 GET INTO TRAP

In this game, an oscillating trap throws targets at random angles somewhere between 22 degrees to the right and left of the trap house center. As a shooter moves through the five stations, the target angles that they encounter will vary greatly depending on the different station locations. Prepare for clays going hard left, hard right, straight away, and anything in between. The fast swing-through is the most effective technique here.

Mount your gun before you call for a target. That initial gun mount point is critical. Right-handed shooters have a longer swing radius to their left than to their right; the reverse is true for southpaws. The most effective spot for the initial point is at the center of the trap house where the bird will appear.

Veteran shooters often use a high hold, about 4 feet above the house, and pick the target up as it rises from under their muzzle. Newer shooters might be better served with a low hold, right on the forward edge of the trap house. You'll see the bird sooner and the target speed will encourage a faster swing.

With either hold, the shooter's foot position must be adjusted so as to allow enough swing radius to deal with extreme angles. That will vary at each of the five stations; shift your feet to adjust your natural point of aim (NPA) as needed.

STATIONS 1 & 2

A 22-degree right target will virtually be a straight-away shot. A hard left angle target requires a lot of movement. Savvy shooters (right- or left-handed) will shift their NPA to the left to give them enough swing room for hard left targets and swivel back at the hips for a center trap gun point.

STATION 3

Targets are equal spread here. NPA is at trap center to allow equal right and left swing movement.

STATIONS 4 & 5

The extreme left angle target is another straightaway. The hard-angled right target requires right-handers to shift their NPA considerably more to the right to deal with it. Southpaws have more swing radius to the right but still need to fudge their NPA a bit to the right to account for the extreme angle.

185 LEARN TRAP ETIQUETTE

A trap squad consists of five shooters, one for each of the five stations. The shooter on station 1 will shoot a target first, followed in order by the rest of the squad. Shooters are allowed only one shot per target. It is considered proper etiquette to load your gun when the shooter two stations before you call for his or her target, and not before. This shooting order continues until each shooter has fired five rounds from his or her station. The squad will then rotate to the next shooting position and repeat. When moving between stations, guns must be demonstrably unloaded: break tops with the action open and pumps and semiautos with the

action open and bolt locked back. A round of trap requires 25 shells.

Trap is a fast-paced game and experienced shooters want to fall into a quick squad rhythm. A shooter who is not ready to shoot when his or her turn comes, or is disrupting the rhythm by constantly questioning calls from the scorekeeper will not be a popular squad mate.

From the basic 16-yard line, targets will be broken at 25–30 yards. The 12-gauge dominates trap, but if you just want some practice on flushing birds, your 16-, 20-, or 28-gauge can play. You won't break them all, but you can have fun and hone some skills.

186 SELECT YOUR CLAYS GUN

Elite competitors in trap, skeet, and sporting clays often select a gun designed, tuned, and dedicated to their particular sport. However, if you just want to have fun and get in some practice, you don't need a different gun for each game. There are some that can work well for all three and won't break the bank. Here's a look at effective clay target guns from the exotic to the blue-collar.

BROWNING BT-99 This 12-gauge break-top single barrel is the classic American trap gun. It is available with barrels from 28 to 34 inches and features adjustable chokes. A number of different stock configurations are available to suit any shooter. This gun has spent a lot of time in the winner's circle and will continue to do so.

BENELLI SPORT II This inertia-operated semiauto is available in 12-gauge with 28- or 30-inch barrels, and in 20-gauge with a 28-inch barrel. It features quick-change extended choke tubes and works well for skeet and sporting clays.

BROWNING CITORI 725 TRAP This over/under 12-gauge offers many of the dedicated trap features of the BT-99, including different stock options in different model versions. The second barrel is a must for doubles trap or on the international "bunker trap" version shot in Olympic competition.

BERETTA SILVER PIGEON 1 SPORTING This is an upper level over/under chambered for 12-gauge, and it frequently shows up in the winner's circle at major international championship matches. The gun is available in 28- or 30-inch barrels with interchangeable choke tubes.

BROWNING CITORI 725 SPORTING The basic 725 over/under action is mated with a different stock, flatter rib, ported barrels, interchangeable choke tubes, and a fiber optic front bead to become an excellent choice for sporting clays or skeet. Stock options include an adjustable comb in differing models.

BERETTA A400 XCEL This semiauto 12-gauge is the latest design in the Beretta semiauto line, which has earned a sterling reputation in sporting clays. Available with a 28- or 30-inch barrel, it features interchangeable chokes, softer recoil, and faster cycling for quick pairs presentations.

CZ-USA 712 TARGET 12-30 This modestly priced, soft-shooting gas-operated 12-gauge features a 30-inch barrel with a 10mm stepped rib that is favored for rising trap targets. It uses interchangeable choke tubes and is supplied with three that will handle all trap targets.

CZ-USA 712 ALS 12-26 This is the same gas-operated 712 action as the Target 12-30, but features a 26-inch choke tube–threaded barrel (three chokes provided) and an adjustable ATI stock that allows the length of pull to be adjusted from 12 to 14 inches for smaller shooters. It's an excellent way to get young shooters into skeet and sporting clays.

RUGER RED LABEL This American-made 12-gauge over/under features a stainless steel receiver, single trigger, interchangeable choke tubes, and is available in barrel lengths of 26, 28, and 30 inches. The 30-inch model is effective at any clay target game.

PERAZZI MX 12 GAUGE This Italian-made 12-gauge over/under is a very upper-level competition gun. Designed for sporting clays and available with barrels from 29½ to 34 inches, it is also an excellent at skeet gun and works well for trap. It features a second interchangeable barrel set that can be used for the sub-gauge insert tubes popular among serious skeet shooters.

WINCHESTER SUPER X3 SPORTING W. ADJUSTABLE COMB This gas-operated 12 gauge is available in barrel lengths of 28, 30, and 32 inches. The ported barrels accept quick change interchangeable choke tubes. An adjustable comb allows shooters to fit this gun to any clay target game.

REMINGTON MODEL 1100 COMPETITION SYNTHETIC The classic Remington Model 1100 gas-operated semiauto 12-gauge action gets paired with a fully adjustable synthetic target-style stock with adjustable comb height and cast, and includes a recoil reduction system. A 30-inch barrel and interchangeable choke tubes makes this gun suitable for any clay target game. It is also available in 26- and 28-inch versions.

WINCHESTER SUPER X3 FIELD COMPACT Available in 12 and 20 gauge, with barrel lengths of 24, 26, and 28 inches, it accepts interchangeable choke tubes. The stock is shortened to a 13-inch length of pull. Although it's billed as a field gun, the 28-inch version is very effective on clay targets and a good choice for youths and smaller females who can't handle a standard length stock.

REMINGTON MODEL 1100 SPORTING SERIES Available in 12, 20, 28, and .410 (the only semiauto .410 available today) and equipped with interchangeable choke tubes, they are very popular in 4-gauge skeet competition. The 12-gauge version also makes a fine sporting clays gun.

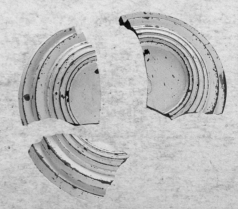

187 PLAY GOLF WITH A SHOTGUN

Sporting clays has often been called "golf with a shotgun." Unlike trap and skeet, sporting courses run through the woods and use natural terrain in their layout. Trees can be used to obscure a target, and traps are often hidden so the shooter cannot see the launch. Shooters typically start with their gun in a low, unmounted position. The puller may also delay the target anywhere up to 3 seconds after the shooter calls for it.

A squad consists of two to five shooters and is led through the course by a course guide, who will also launch the targets and score the shots. Guns are loaded only when the shooter steps into the shooting station. Each shooter will be called for his or her turn. The first shooter in the squad has the right to call for a target presentation before they shoot. This is called "the see." If that shooter forgets to call for a "see," remind them to do so. You need a look at the targets before you try to hit them.

Targets will vary greatly in distance. Some may be virtually in your face, while others may be 50 yards off or more. Changing choke tubes or loads at each new station is a common practice. Experienced shooters have found that changing loads is often as effective as changing chokes. An Improved Cylinder choke with a load of soft lead No. 9 shot will handle targets inside 20 yards. Hard lead No. 8 or No. 7½ with that choke will handle targets to 30 yards. Shift to Modified or Full choke and No. 7½ trap loads for longer shots.

188 CHECK YOUR TARGETS

The target presentations in sporting clays are limited only by the imagination of the course designers and the terrain they have to work with. Another difference is the targets: Sporting clays also employs a variety of targets:

CATCH A MIDI Also called a "quail," this is the same shape as a standard target, but with a smaller 90mm diameter. It leaves the trap faster and slows down faster. It's often thrown in pairs with a standard target and will display different flight characteristics.

SPOT THE MINI This 60mm target is an even more scaled-down version of the standard clay target. It's fast out of the trap, and sometimes requires a tighter choke because its tiny size can let it slip through a pattern unscathed. These "doves" can be thrown as two targets or mixed with standards or midis.

BREAK A BATTUE The "duck" is 110mm wide but only ⅜ inch high with a slight dome. It doesn't fly like other clays. Battues are flat when they leave the trap and then turn onto their side in flight. They're tough to hit when flat, and shooters need to wait until they make the turn to consistently break them.

GO RABBIT HUNTING Also called the "jackrabbit," this clay is similar in size to the standard target but with no raised dome, and has a reinforced rim to allow it to bounce along the ground when it is launched. Its scurrying "flight" is definitely a challenge to follow.

HOLD YOUR FIRE "Poison birds" are an additional challenge that can show up anywhere, except as true pairs. They are distinctly different and easily identifiable. A shooter who fires at one scores a miss. Refrain from shooting and it's scored a hit.

189 TAKE DIFFERENT SHOTS

Unlike in trap or skeet shooting, sporting clay targets can come flying at nearly any angle imaginable and in varying patterns. Here are some of the tougher shots you'll see.

REPORT PAIRS Experienced shooters consider the gun mount to be a part of their shot process and many find a slight dismount and remount helps on the second target. These may be incoming, outgoing, or crossing. A single target is launched, with the second target launched at the sound of the shot.

TRUE PAIRS Two targets launch simultaneously; it becomes complicated if one is a standard and the other a midi, mini, or battue. The "see" is critical here, as shooters need to plan which to hit first, or see if they can they break both with one shot.

DRIVEN SHOT Similar to skeet station 8, in a driven shot, two simultaneous incoming targets are launched low and rising above the shooter. Right-handed shooters often break the right target and swing left, while the reverse is the case for southpaws.

FUR AND FEATHERS This crossing shot, which presents the shooter with a ground bouncing rabbit target and a low-flying clay, can be accomplished with true, report, or following pairs. Many shooters prefer to take the rabbit as quickly as they can, since this keeps the flying clay within their field of vision. If you shoot the clay first, you can lose sight of the rabbit.

TOWER SHOT The trap is located in an elevated tower as tall as 70 feet, and targets may come from behind the shooter as dropping outgoing birds or come toward the shooter. Outgoing birds need to be taken quickly with a lead below the bird. Incomers are best taken just before they come over the shooter.

SPRINGING TEAL In this challenging presentation, the target rises straight up as high as 70 feet, and does it quickly, too. The shooter may encounter either a single or a true pair in this pattern. Lead on the rise is difficult since the muzzle blots out the bird. Many seasoned sportsmen find it best to delay their mount until the target has almost reached its apex and shoot as it hangs before dropping.

190 PICK THE RIGHT SHOT

When on a hunt, you need to pick not only the right type of shot, but the best size as well. And keep in mind, some hunting requires nontoxic pellets. This handy chart will help you determine what you should be shooting with.

	SHELL	GAUGE	LOAD
PHEASANTS	2¾ inch	12 gauge	1¼ ounces of No. 6 shot (lead), 1,300 fps
			1⅛ ounces of No. 3 shot (steel), 1,500 fps
DUCKS 	3 inch	12 gauge	1¼ ounces of No. 2 shot (steel), 1,450 fps
GEESE 	3 inch	12 gauge	1½ ounces of No. 4 HEVI-Shot (tungsten-iron), 1,400 fps
TURKEYS	3 inch	12 gauge	1¾ ounces of No. 6 HEVI-Shot (tungsten-iron)
	3 inch	20 gauge	1¼–1½ ounces of No. 6 Heavyweight or HEVI-Shot (tungsten-iron), 1,100 fps
DOVES	2¾ inch	12 gauge	1 ounce of No. 7 shot (steel), 1,300 fps
	2¾ inch	12 gauge	1⅛ ounces of No. 7½ or No. 8 shot (lead), 1,180 fps
	2¾ inch	20 gauge	⅞ ounce of No. 8 shot (lead), 1,200 fps
QUAIL 	2¾ inch	20 gauge	⅞ ounce of No. 8 shot (lead), 1,200 fps
RUFFED GROUSE 	2¾ inch	20 gauge	⅞ ounce of No. 7½ shot (lead), 1,200 fps
WOODCOCK 	2¾ -inch	28 gauge	¾ ounce of No. 8 shot (lead), 1,200 fps
DEER (RIFLED BARREL) 	2¾ inch	20 gauge	Sabot slug with premium bullet, 1,500–1,600 fps
DEER (SMOOTHBORE) 	2¾ inch	12 gauge	1-ounce slug, wad attached, 1,600 fps
PRACTICE	2¾ inch	12 gauge reloads	⅞ ounce of No. 8½ shot (lead), 1,200 fps

191 KNOW YOUR OPTIONS FOR WINGSHOOTING

There are a variety of game birds for wingshooters to pursue, and the sport encompasses a wide range of conditions, each of which calls for differing ranges and shot-size requirements. It's hard to make one shotgun and load do it all.

The quick-handling gun that's so effective for upland birds like quail, woodcock, grouse, snipe, and others is a poor choice for a duck or goose blind, where magnum loads of steel or tungsten/polymer nontoxic shot are not only the most effective, but are required by game laws.

Much like golfers, a shooter needs a few different "clubs" in his or her bag. Here are some effective choices for different applications.

WATERFOWL

CZ-USA 612 Wildfowl Magnum

This inexpensive 12-gauge pump features a synthetic stock with a camouflaged finish, interchangeable choke tubes, a 26-inch barrel, and weighs in at a quick-handling 6⁴/₅ pounds. Chambered for 3½-inch shells, it's rated for all nontoxic waterfowl loads.

Remington Versa Max Waterfowl

This gas-operated semiauto is Remington's newest, and handles 12-gauge shells from 2¾- to 3½-inch lengths. The stock is easy to fit to a shooter's dimensions. The waterfowl version comes with four extended choke tubes for its 28-inch barrel, and a synthetic stock with a camo finish.

Mossberg 835 Ultra-Mag Waterfowl

This 12-gauge pump has a 28-inch barrel, a full range of interchangeable choke tubes and barrels, is rated for all nontoxic shot, and is chambered for 3½-inch shells. It tips the scales at 7¾ pounds and the barrel is ported to reduce muzzle rise.

Winchester Super X3 Waterfowl Hunter

Available in 12 gauge (with 3- or 3½-inch chamber) and 20 gauge (3-inch chamber), this gas-operated semiauto features a camouflaged synthetic stock with textured gripping surfaces, barrels in 26 or 28 inches, and accepts various interchangeable choke tubes.

UPLAND GAME BIRDS

Benelli M2 20 Gauge Left Hand

A perfect field gun for southpaws, this inertia-operated 20-gauge is a true left-hand gun. Chambered for 3-inch shells, it has five interchangeable choke tubes, and includes a shim kit to adjust drop at comb and cast. At $5\frac{4}{5}$ pounds, it carries easily afield.

CZ-USA Bobwhite

This modestly priced side-by-side double is available in 12 and 20 gauge with 26-inch barrels and a traditional double-trigger system. It features five interchangeable choke tubes, straight English buttstock, and is chambered for 3-inch shells. It can handle any upland chores.

CZ-USA Wingshooter

This over/under is available in 12 or 20 gauge with 28-inch barrels and five interchangeable choke tubes. Chambered for 3-inch shells, it's a stylish upland O/U that won't break the bank.

Mossberg SA-20

This gas-operated 20-gauge comes with a 28-inch barrel (with a set of 5 choke tubes included) and a synthetic black stock and is chambered for 3-inch shells. Weighing 6 pounds, it's light to carry and quick to handle but has the power to handle all upland game birds.

Weatherby SA-08 28 Gauge Deluxe

This gas-operated semiauto 28 gauge weighs in at $5\frac{1}{2}$ pounds and is available with a 26- or 28-inch barrel that includes three interchangeable choke tubes (IC, Mod, Full). A joy to carry afield, it's ideal for smaller upland species like quail, woodcock, or ruffed grouse.

VERSATILE CHOICES

Benelli Ethos

An inertia-operated 12-gauge semiauto chambered for 3-inch shells and also handles 2¾-inch loads as light as ⅞ ounce; 5 interchangeable choke tubes, inter-changeable fiber optic front beads, and an advanced recoil reduction system make this $6\frac{1}{2}$-pound gun capable of virtually anything.

Browning BPS Hunter

This pump-action shotgun is available in 12, 16, 20, and 28 gauge, as well as .410. The 16 and 28 gauges feature a 2¾-inch chamber, while the others take 3-inch shells. All have interchangeable choke tubes and can be tuned for just about any wingshooting task.

Remington 11-87 Sportsman Series

This gas-operated semiauto is available in 12 or 20 gauge. It features a black synthetic stock and 26- or 28-inch barrels, with some accessory interchangeable barrels available. Threaded for interchangeable choke tubes, it can handle anything from waterfowl to quail.

Weatherby SA-08 Synthetic

This gas-operated semiauto is available in 12 or 20 gauge with either 26- or 28-inch barrels. Both are chambered for 3-inch shells and are supplied with interchangeable choke tubes in IC, Mod, and Full.

Winchester SXP 12 Gauge 3" Field Compact

This 12-gauge pump is built with a shorter (13-inch) length of pull to properly fit younger and smaller-framed shooters. Available in barrel lengths of 24, 26, or 28 inches, it can handle 2¾-inch and 3-inch loads. The interchangeable choke tube system makes it a versatile and affordable wingshooting tool.

192 GET THE RIGHT HOME-DEFENSE SHOTGUN

A shotgun delivers massive close-range stopping power and can be a very effective home-defense tool, but only if you choose the right one. The two most important keys to an effective home-defense shotgun are maneuverability and reliability.

A 10-gauge goose gun with a 32-inch barrel can deliver all the power needed to stop a home invasion. But if you're awoken at 2 AM by the sound of your front door breaking in, how handy is that gun? How easy is it to maneuver room to room? What happens if an assailant is on the other side of the door and grabs that long barrel when it pokes through? A home-defense shotgun needs to be short, lightweight, and easy to navigate in tight quarters. Barrels in the 18½- to 20-inch range are preferred. If it's light enough to fire with one hand, that's a plus.

A home-defense shotgun is often loaded, tucked away, and never shot. But, if after a couple of years of sitting in a closet, it is suddenly needed, will it work? Firearms, in general, do not fare well in long-term storage. Lubricants congeal and springs can take a set. It's advisable to fire, clean, and lubricate any firearm on at least a semiannual basis. With that said, a pump-action shotgun (properly prepared) is the one most likely to work in this case. An exposed-hammer side-by-side double-barrel would likely be second. An inertia-operated semiauto ranks third.

193 CHOOSE YOUR LOAD CAREFULLY

Choosing a load for home defense requires balancing stopping power and safety. You need to think about penetration, whether from a missed shot or actually through the attacker. This is a serious concern in tight living quarters where your shot may penetrate an apartment or room wall to kill or injure an innocent. The heavy buckshot loads (000, 00, and even 0) can penetrate excessively. Slugs can zip through the attacker and several walls beyond. Reduce the shot size and stopping power remains, but with a greatly reduced risk of over penetration.

Home-defense situations seldom involve ranges beyond 40 feet. At this range, No. 4 buckshot (available in 12 and 20 gauge) is very effective. So too is No. 3 buckshot (the standard 20-gauge load). These provide more than adequate stopping power, but their smaller pellet size greatly reduces the risk of over-penetration.

194 TRY A 20-GAUGE FOR PROTECTION

Those looking for an effective home-defense shotgun are often directed toward one of the 12-gauge law enforcement tactical models. That's not always the best choice. The 20-gauge is much easier to shoot than the 12-gauge, produces significantly less recoil, and is lighter and more maneuverable. It's a shotgun virtually any member of the family can master, and at the ranges encountered in home-defense situations, it is just as effective as a 12-gauge.

The average 12-gauge tactical shotgun weighs between 7 ½ and 8 ½ pounds. The average 20-gauge tactical model with the same barrel length tips the scales at between 5 ½ and 6 ½ pounds.

Home-defense situations are normally close, quick, and fluid. The lighter gun has an edge in quick handling,

especially in any case where a smaller-framed family member has to wield it. The 20-gauge also has plenty of stopping power.

The 12-gauge load most often recommended for in-home defense is the standard 2 ¾-inch No. 4 buckshot load holding 27 pellets, launched at 1100–1200 fps. Each pellet is .24 caliber, weighing approximately 20 grains. It's a very effective close-range load.

The standard 2 ¾-inch 20-gauge buckshot load is 20 No. 3 buckshot pellets, launched at 1100–1200 fps. These are .25 caliber and weigh slightly more than No. 4 buck. This load is every bit as effective at home-defense ranges, and from a cylinder-choked gun, will normally deliver an 11- to 12-inch pattern at 30 feet. Inside the home the 20 is plenty.

195 PREPARE YOUR HOME-DEFENSE SHOTGUN

Home-defense shotguns spend a lot of time sitting around doing nothing, but when they're needed they're needed quickly. How those shotguns are prepared can play a major role in whether or not they work.

Pumps and semiautos should not be stored with a round chambered and the safety on. This places the firing-system springs at their maximum compression and, over time, can cause them to weaken or set. I once violated this rule and left a semiauto "cocked and locked" for a year before firing it. Flipping the safety off and pulling the trigger produced nothing. Cycling the action reset things and it fired, but I'm glad I found that out on the range instead of in a crisis situation where a delay like that could mean the difference between life and death.

Pumps and semiautos with tubular magazines should not have the magazine completely filled for long-term storage. This creates the possibility of the fully compressed magazine spring deforming a plastic shotshell and creating a feed failure.

The best way to prepare a home-defense pump or auto—starting with an unloaded gun—is to send the bolt forward on an empty chamber, flip the safety off and leave it off, pull the trigger to decock the gun, then load the magazine one or two shells below capacity. When needed, you have only to cycle the action to chamber a round and it's ready to fire. This is called "cruiser carry" and it's the way law enforcement and military shotguns are carried.

If a side-by-side double barrel is chosen, those models with internal hammers are not suited to long-term storage. The hammers are cocked when the action is closed, and the springs compressed. A better bet is an exposed-hammer double barrel. These can be left loaded and uncocked, and require nothing more than cocking the hammers when the gun is employed.

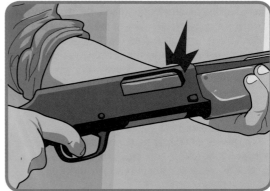

196 MASTER THE SHOTGUN LOW READY

The proper shotgun firing stance is with the gun fully mounted into the shoulder pocket, the head down on the comb, and the eyes aligned with the rib. This is a poor way to investigate a bump in the night because it funnels the eyes and causes the loss of much-needed peripheral vision. In these cases, the low ready is a better bet.

Assume this stance by bringing the gun butt up and into the shoulder pocket, but with your arms holding the gun about 4 inches below the full gun mount, and the head fully erect. The muzzle will be pointing where your eyes are looking, and this position can deliver accurate fire at close range while providing you with full peripheral vision. If a longer shot is needed, it takes only a fraction of a second to raise the arms, drop the cheek to the comb, and assume the traditional firing stance.

This stance requires practice. That can be done with light target loads at 4 or 5 yards. Set up several targets and use the upper body as a turret to pivot between them. You might be surprised by how accurately shots can be delivered from this stance.

197 TRY THESE USEFUL ACCESSORIES

There are accessory items that can improve the effectiveness of your home-defense shotgun. Here are three of the most useful.

LIGHTS A light is needed in the dark, but a hand-held flashlight is tough to use with a shotgun. Getting a weapon-mounted light is the way to go. Some light units also have a laser sight, which is an even better bet. The light illuminates the target, the laser beam aims the shot charge, and even at 30-plus yards, one can deliver accurate fire from the shotgun low ready position. There are a number of these units and mounting systems on the market, and most shotguns can be fitted with one. The best mounting position is where your non-firing hand naturally contacts the forearm in a shooting stance.

SHELL CARRIERS Gun-mounted carriers hold four to six shotshells and attach to the gun. Some are elastic cuffs that fit over the gun butt, and some are metal units affixed to the receiver. Grabbing the gun now gives you enough extra shells for a reload.

EXTENDED MAGAZINE TUBES These replace the existing magazine cap on a number of pump and semiauto models and increase the magazine capacity by three or more rounds. They not only allow you to carry a few extra shells in the gun, but add forward weight that helps reduce muzzle rise.

There is no shortage of shotguns out there that are particularly well suited to self defense. Here are some of the best ones to consider.

MOSSBERG SA-20 TACTICAL This gas-operated 20-gauge features a 20-inch cylinder choke barrel chambered for 3-inch shells, a ghost ring rear sight with a fiber optic front sight, a receiver rail to allow other sights be mounted, a 5-round magazine, and a manageable weight of 6 pounds.

BENELLI M2 TACTICAL This inertia-operated 12-gauge comes with an 18½-inch barrel, extended magazine, and adjustable ghost ring sights. The black matte synthetic stock is available in three configurations, including a full pistol grip model. The average weight is 6.7 pounds. It is used by some U.S. military units.

MOSSBERG 510 MINI ALL-PURPOSE 20-GAUGE This affordable 20-gauge pump has an 18½-inch barrel chambered for 3-inch shells, interchangeable choke tubes, camo finish, and stock spacers to allow the butt stock to be adjusted from a 10½- to 11½-inch length of pull. It's advertised as a field gun for smaller shooters, but its compact size and 5-pound weight make it a very maneuverable and effective home-defense shotgun.

FNH FN P-12 The 12-gauge pump (3-inch chamber) has a black synthetic stock and features an 18-inch barrel, a 5-round magazine, and a flip-up rear rifle sight with a fiber optic front sight. The barrel is topped with a Weaver-base cantilever extending over the receiver for optics mounting and is threaded for interchangeable choke tubes.

MOSSBERG SPECIAL PURPOSE 20-GAUGE This pump-action Model 500 has a 20-inch 20-gauge (3-inch chamber) with a cylinder choke and an 8-round magazine. Its black synthetic stock has a shortened 13-inch length of pull. A ghost ring sight and a fiber optic front complete this 6-pound package.

FNH FN SLP TACTICAL This 12-gauge gas-operated (3-inch chamber) shotgun sports a black synthetic stock with a full pistol grip, an 18-inch barrel threaded for interchangeable choke tubes, interchangeable cheek pieces for a custom fit, high-profile adjustable sights with a Weaver rail for optics mounting, and forward rails for lights and/or laser.

MOSSBERG 500 CENTER MASS LASER This 12-gauge pump is chambered for 3-inch shells with a cylinder bore choke. It holds 8 rounds and has a 20-inch barrel in a synthetic black stock. It is equipped with a LaserLyte laser sight that displays a circular ring of laser dots at the point of impact, which expands as range increases to show the pattern spread.

MOSSBERG 500 TACTICAL TRI-RAIL This 12-gauge, 3-inch chambered pump holds 6 rounds, has a cylinder choke, weighs 6.75 pounds, and provides three 1913 rails for mounting lights and laser sights. It includes a synthetic butt stock adjustable for length of pull and a full pistol grip.

REMINGTON VERSA MAX TACTICAL This tactical model of the gas-operated Versa Max 12-gauge features an extended 8-round magazine, forward barrel clamp with Picatinny side rails for light/laser, and a receiver rail for sight mounting. It is threaded for interchangeable choke tubes.

REMINGTON MODEL 870 EXPRESS TACTICAL MAGPUL This 12-gauge, 3-inch chambered, pump has an 18 ½-inch barrel threaded for tactical choke tubes. The Magpul SGA stock incorporates spacers to allow length-of-pull adjustments and interchangeable cheek pads for use with optical sights. Folding rifle sights mount on a Weaver rail that allows the use of optics.

WEATHERBY SA-459 TREAT RESPONSE This gas-operated semiauto is available in 12 and 20 gauge and features an 18 ½-inch barrel threaded for tactical ported choke tubes. The black synthetic stock has a full pistol grip. Adjustable ghost ring sights ride on a receiver rail that can accept optical sights.

WEATHERBY PA-459 THREAT RESPONSE This is the pump-action version of the SA-459 Threat Response, and it is virtually identical in specifications, chokes, and sights. It is also available in 12 and 20 gauge; the latter weighs only 5.75 pounds.

WINCHESTER SXP EXTREME DEFENDER This 12-gauge, 3-inch chambered pump-action comes with an 18-inch barrel that is threaded for external ported choke tubes, a ghost ring rear sight on a Picatinny rail that allows optics, forward mounted rails for lights/lasers, and an ATI pistol grip stock with an adjustable cheek piece.

WINCHESTER SXP ULTIMATE MARINE DEFENDER This 12-gauge pump is built on the same action as the Extreme Defender, with the same barrel, choke tube, sight arrangement, and accessory rails. It differs in its straight stock and matte chrome finish on barrel and magazine tube for marine environment use.

199 POINT, DON'T AIM

One of the biggest challenges shooters in 3-gun face is adapting to the shotgun, according to Mark Hanish, who works for gunmaker FN Herstal and is a member of their pro shooting team.

"Many 3-gunners come from pistol backgrounds and they pick up the rifle pretty well but struggle with shotgun," he says.

His top suggestion for aspiring 3-gun shooters is for them to take their action shotguns to the nearest sporting clays or skeet facility. "Go shoot skeet, go shoot trap, go shoot sporting clays," he says. "Do that and take a lesson."

With the exception of slug targets, where the shotgun is aimed as a rifle, the shotgun needs to be pointed and swung and shot with correct lead on targets that either move or need to be taken down in quick succession.

200 CALCULATE THE LOAD

When setting up a shotgun for a stage, shooters will load with shells that correspond to their strategy for the targets. To make sure the shotgun is loaded correctly, Hanish lays the shells out lined up in the order he wants them in the tube.

"If you're loading slugs and birdshot in the tube at the same time when you're starting a stage, you want to lay out the ammo in the reverse order that you're going to need it," Hanish says, meaning that the last shell you put in will be the first shot out of the gun.

201 HAVE A CONTINGENCY PLAN

Smart shooters pick specific spots to recharge the shotgun over the course of a stage to have an efficient run, but mistakes happen. And when a target is missed or something else unexpected happens, the shooter needs to have a backup plan that gets him back on track, Hanish says.

In the event that a target is dropped and requires and extra shell, be ready to throw an fresh shell in the shotgun right away, he says. "You might need to load one right then to get back into your pattern so that you pay for that miss just once, rather than pay for it several times over the course of the stage by running dry at your remaining loading breaks," he says.

202 COUNT 'EM ALL

Of all the guns in 3-gun, most competitors find shotgun to be the most mentally demanding because the shooter needs to keep track of exactly how many shots have been fired. "You have to count your shots so you know where you're at," Hanish says. "Ammo management with a shotgun is critical because it's limited."

203 LEARN TO 'LOAD TWO'

Among the firearms used in 3-gun, the shotgun is the toughest to master. Not because the targets are more difficult, but because in order to do well with a shotgun, the competitor needs to be able to load it fast. Shooters have come up with techniques over the years that allow them to stuff shotguns with shells quickly. These methods involve grabbing multiple shells at once with either the strong (trigger) hand or the weak (lead) hand.

At this writing, the "load two" technique has quite a following. The shells are placed in rows stacked two deep, with the shells in the top and bottom contacting each other. The rounds are positioned so that the brass is facing up. They are grabbed two at a time, with the thumb placed on the brass of the top shell, though some can grab four shells at once. With the shotgun rolled over so that the loading port is facing up, the shooter loads two shells, grabs two more, and repeats. If grabbing four rounds at once, the shooter loads the first pair, then the second pair, and then grabs more shells.

One key is to hold the shotgun so that the loading port is close to the shell carrier to minimize the amount of motion it takes to get the rounds into the gun. With practice, a shooter can load 10 rounds in 8 seconds or less.

204 SHOOT THE TEXAS STAR

The Texas Star is one of the most popular targets in 3-gun. It can be intimidating for beginners, but the star is really quite easy to shoot and shoot quickly—provided the shooter doesn't miss.

Take the plate closest to the top of the star first. As soon as it is knocked away, the star becomes unbalanced and begins to rotate. The target doesn't move quickly at first, so the key is to move down to the next plate quickly and take it before the star gathers speed.

With two plates down, the star will begin to spin fast. Move your barrel to the third plate, shoot it, and then hold the gun in place. The last two plates will spin around to where your muzzle is pointed. Shoot them each as they come into view. You should look to run a Texas Star in about 3 seconds or so.

205 KNOW WHAT SHOT TO USE

Light target loads work fine on the majority of shotgun targets in 3-gun, but it can pay to step to a larger shot size in some cases. Assuming the match allows them, bring along some high-velocity No. 5's for knock-down targets that are either placed far away from the shooter or that are particularly heavy. The additional recoil from these rounds is more than made up for by their ability to knock over tough targets with one shot when compared to light target loads.

206 ADD ON SIGHTS

Most shotguns, even those that are configured for 3-gun, don't come with proper sights. A plain rib with a front bead is too coarse to place slugs on distant targets reliably. A clamp-on rear sight is an unobtrusive way to improve the gun's ability to aim. Of course, the gun still needs to be sighted in with whatever type of rifled slug you plan to use. If the shotgun can hit an 8-inch square at 50 yards or more, while shooting from field positions, it will be good to go.

207 SHOOT THE SPINNER

Timing and precision: Those are the two things needed to successfully engage the spinner with a shotgun. The goal is to make the spinner flip all the way over on its axis, which isn't easy since the bottom plate is much heavier than the top one. Because of the shotgun's limited capacity, every shot counts.

Start by hitting the bottom plate to get the spinner moving. If the target is close enough, and if you're confident in your shooting, put your second shot on the top plate as it rocks back to the high point. If not, wait for the bottom plate to swing forward and then put your second shot on it as it swings back. Either way, you only want to shoot the plates as they are moving away from you and hit them when they are perpendicular to the ground in order to take advantage of the target's momentum.

A third or fourth solid hit is often enough to get the spinner to flip all the way over.

If disaster strikes and the gun runs dry before you flip the target, take the time to reload the gun with at least eight shells. You don't want to just load a couple and find yourself with an empty gun again before the spinner has flipped over.

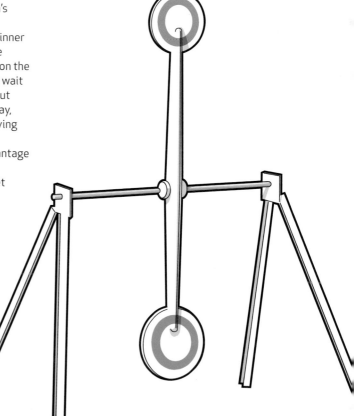

208 SLUG IT OUT

The shotgun earned its name by firing a charge of shot, but it was always also able to launch a single large projectile—and it frequently did, although when a round ball was launched from a smoothbore barrel it was anyone's guess as to where it would go.

The first modern conical lead shotgun slug that could be fired accurately was invented by Wilhelm Brenneke in 1898 and is still in use today. In 1931, Karl Foster invented a solid soft lead slug with a hollow base, rifling grooves on the sides, and a weight-forward round nose. This design formed the basis for the most popular lead slugs in use today. In the early 1960s, Ballistic Research Industries created the first sabot slug—a smaller-than-bore projectile encased in a two-piece plastic sleeve that guided the slug down the bore, then split to fall away when it left the muzzle.

Slugs were popular in many parts of the world, but in the early 1960s, they finally gained a large following in America. Many states east of the Mississippi River began mandating that shotguns be used on some, or all, of their public hunting lands for deer. The reasoning was that shotgun projectiles had less range than a rifle—an important factor in populated areas. That impacted a lot of hunters and, given the minimal effective range of buckshot, prompted a serious interest in slug guns.

Current slug guns are available in both smoothbore and rifled barrels. The latter can rival the accuracy of a rifle and can be had in single shot, bolt action, pump action, and semiauto models. Pumps and semiautos feature a cantilever scope mount on the barrel itself that allows the barrel to be removed without changing the point of impact.

209 CHOOSE YOUR SLUG SYSTEM

Obtaining a slug gun is easy: You can buy a complete gun or, if you own a popular pump or semiauto, there might be an accessory barrel available for your model at a lower price. But there are significant differences between smoothbore and rifled slug guns.

With a smoothbore gun (many are equipped with adjustable iron sights) firing Brenneke or Foster slugs at 100 yards are typical. When sighted in 2 inches high at 50 yards, they will be several inches low at 100 yards and then drop like a rock to about 10 inches low at 125 yards. Their effective deer hunting range is 100 yards at best.

These slugs can be fired in rifled barrels, but they will quickly foul the barrel with lead and destroy accuracy. They are best used in smoothbore guns.

However, those 1-ounce, .70 caliber slugs, launched at 1,300–1,400 feet per second, make an effective close-range personal-protection gun in big bear country, and are widely used in that role by outdoorsmen and many wildlife biologists.

A sabot slug in a rifled barrel changes things considerably. For example, the Federal Vital Shok 12-gauge 3-inch Magnum Sabot Slug launches a 300-grain jacketed softpoint projectile at about 2,000 fps and, given that the rifling engages the sabot and applies spin stabilization to the projectile, is capable of 2-inch groups at 100 yards. When sighted in 3 inches high at 100 yards, it will be about on at 150 yards and around 7 inches low at 200 yards, with the power to harvest deer at 200 yards.

210   UPGRADE YOUR SLUG GUN

Hunting big game with a rifle is not permitted in many parts of the country, which means that all too often, hunters are left toting shotguns that are usually better suited for grouse at close quarters than venison at longer range. A modern saboted shotgun load is perfectly capable of delivering lethal performance at distances well beyond 100 yards. But can you put that projectile where it needs to go? According to Dave Klotz of Da Mar Gunsmiths in Weedsport, NY, with just a few modifications to your shotgun, you sure can.

PIN THE BARREL Shotguns are not rifles. Barrels are easily removed and tolerances aren't tight where it slides into the receiver. If the barrel moves and vibrates, it won't deliver consistent accuracy. To fix this, Klotz drills a hole through the side of the receiver and through the shank of the barrel, then inserts an Allen head screw to about five threads deep. The result is a barrel that doesn't wiggle.

IMPROVE THE BORE "Shotgun barrels usually don't leave the factory in a condition that leads to really accurate shooting," says Klotz. "We lap the bore, lengthen the forcing cone, and crown the barrel." The high polish in the bore after lapping helps minimize plastic buildup from sabots, which can degrade accuracy. Extending the forcing cone gives the slug a better transition into the rifling.

FIX THE TRIGGER It's nearly impossible to shoot well with the creepy 8-pound triggers typical of most production shotguns. "You can't shoot accurately with a trigger like that," Klotz says. His shop used to be a Remington Service Center, and he refitted my model 870 with a trigger that breaks crisply at 2 ¾ pounds.

USE A BETTER SCOPE MOUNT Klotz doesn't believe in barrels with cantilever scope mounts. "On a shotgun, you need a mount that does not shoot loose and will not bend or break. There wasn't one available, so we designed our own," he says. The Da Mar mount uses six screws (three per side), and each screw is located on the sides of the receiver where the metal is thickest. It features a Weaver-style rail and rings

REDUCE RECOIL To take the sting out of my slug gun, Klotz did some bonus work and installed a Remington SuperCell recoil pad and put a steel plug in the stock to increase its weight. Slug guns are never a pleasure to shoot, but these alterations made a big difference and were no doubt part of the reason my groups improved.

211 BECOME A SHOOTING SCIENTIST

Skilled wingshooters consistently crush aerial targets by applying fundamentals in a smooth and fluid manner developed through repetition. To do this, practice is important, but until the proper foundational techniques are learned, practice is of little use. Indeed, practicing the wrong techniques is worse than no practice at all.

These fundamentals not only include using the proper mount position for the gun, but also hand and foot position, natural point of aim, right and left swing arc, and the swing style appropriate for the target (sustained lead, fast swing-through, or pull-away). In addition, you need to ask yourself these questions:

Does your gun fit your body, and is it looking at the same spot you are when shouldered? Or, are your eyes looking where you think they are?

It's not all that common, but 6 to 10 percent of the population is cross-dominant, which means they are right-handed and have a dominant left eye, or vice versa. Until this situation is discovered and addressed, hitting an aerial target can be more luck than skill.

A competent instructor can address all of these questions and get a shooter started on the path to becoming an expert. And there are a lot of places to get that training.

212 GO BACK TO SCHOOL

A large number of shotgun schools can be found across the United States. The curriculum at some may lean more towards field shooting or specific clay target games, but the shotgun handling skills will transfer. There are even a few schools that offer tactical training courses in personal protection. All have websites that will explain what they teach. Attending may require travel and can be expensive. Another, more affordable option, is to look closer to home.

Virtually every clay target range will have someone who provides instruction. It may be a staff member or just one of the upper-level club shooters who earns a little "shell money" on the side. Just because they're local doesn't mean they're bottom drawer. Some are state champions. In fact, at one central Florida range some years back, one of the instructors was a former member of the U.S. International Shooting Team, a three-time National Ladies Sporting Clays Champion, and the captain of the National Sporting Clays Association Ladies All-America Team.

Her hourly rates were about the same as a couple rounds of skeet. You could call that a bargain.

INDEX

ABOUT THE AUTHORS

JOHN B. SNOW is one of the country's leading firearms authorities. He is the shooting editor for *Outdoor Life* magazine, only the fifth person to hold that prestigious title since the magazine's founding in 1898. Snow is an accomplished competitive shooter, firearms instructor, worldwide hunter and award-winning journalist. He lives in Bozeman, Montana, with his family.

ABOUT OUTDOOR LIFE

Ever since it was founded in 1898, *Outdoor Life* magazine has provided survival tips, wilderness skills, gear reports, and other essential information for hands-on outdoor enthusiasts. Each issue of the magazine delivers the best advice in sportsmanship as well as thrilling true-life tales, detailed gear reviews, insider hunting, shooting, and fishing hints, and much more to nearly 1 million readers.

CHRIS CHRISTIAN is an award-winning outdoor writer who has published over 2,600 magazine and newspaper articles. This is his fifth book. A former military firearms instructor and Navy Rifle & Pistol Team member, he continues to do some teaching, and is a well-known Action Pistol competitor in his home state of Florida.

All text in the Rifle and AR chapters was written by John B. Snow.

The Handgun and Shotgun chapters were written by Chris Christian, with the exception of the following items, which were written by John B. Snow:

chapter introductions, items 128–130, 142, 15–149, 154,159–161, and 199–207

Item 190 was written by Phil Bourjaily.

ACKNOWLEDGMENTS

JOHN B. SNOW: This book is for my family, especially Ava and Jack. I couldn't imagine better companions for life's adventures.

CHRIS CHRISTIAN: My thanks to Matt Rice at Blue Heron Communications, Tim Brandt and JJ Reich at ATK Sporting, and Ken Jorgensen at Ruger for their product knowledge and assistance. A special thanks to my good friend and shooting buddy, Massad Ayoob, for the wisdom he has imparted to me over the years.

PHOTOGRAPHY COURTESY OF: *Shutterstock Images*, except where otherwise noted; *Accuracy International:* 16 (AX308), *Ambush Firearms:* 109 (300 Blackout); *Ashbury Precision Ordnance:* 16 (ASW 338LM); *Barrett Firearms Manufacturing:* 16 (M107A1); *Benelli USA:* 186 (Sport II), 191 (Ethos), 198 (M2 Tactical); *Beretta USA:* 186 (A400 Xcel, Silver Pigeon 1 Sporting); *Eddie Berman:* 142, 145, 154; *Black Hills Ammunition:* 98 (77-grain OTM); *Bowen Classic Arms:* 145; *Browning:* 123 (Buckmark), 186 (BT-99, Citori 725 Sporting & Trap), 191 (BPS Hunter); *Bill Buckley:* 175, 211; *Burris Optics:* 102; *Bushmaster Firearms Int'l:* 109 (450 Bushmaster); *Bushnell:* 37 (LRHS 3–12x44); *Colt's Mfg. LLC:* 75 (logo), 106 (AR15 A4), 109 (Competition Pro CRP-18), 123 (Colt Defender); *Jed Conklin:* AR Intro (shooter); *Rab Cummings:* A Note from the Editor, A Note from the Author, 48, 51, 90; *CZ-USA:* 26 (455 Varmint Precision Trainer), 35 (557 Sporter), 123 (85 Combat, Dan Wesson Specialist), 186 (712 ALS 12-28 & Target 12-30), 191 (612 Wildfowl Magnum, Bobwhite, Wingshooter); *Daniel Defense:* 106 (M4 ISR-300 Blackout); *DPMS, Inc.:* 109 (GII Hunter), *Cpl William J. Faffler:* 25; *Nick Ferrari/thelicensingproject.com:* 60; *Federal Premium:* 164 (.327 Magnum, .460 S&W); *FNH USA:* 198 (P-12, SLP Tactical); *Freedom Arms:* 144 (Model 83 Premier Grade Adjustable Sights); *FTW Outfitters:* 29; *Gaetano Images Inc./Alamy:* 30; *Frank Galli:* 3; *Andrew Geiger:* 139; *Glock USA:* 123 (G19, G29); *John Giammatteo:* 33 (Marlin 308MXLR); *Gorman & Gorman:* Contents (slug), 208; *John Hafner:* 24 (hunter), 210; *Heckler & Koch USA:* 118 (G36); *High Impact Photography:* Shotgun intro (splash page); *Hornady USA:* 98 (NTX .22LR); *Hulton Archive:* 174 (James Fenimoore Cooper); *Spencer Jones:* 99; *JP Enterprises:* 106 (GMR-13); *Lauer Custom Weaponry:* 74 (AR); *Leupold Optics:* 37 (VX-3 2.5–8x36); *Magnum Research:* 123 (Micro Desert Eagle); *MidwayUSA:* 164 (.32 H&R Mag., .32 Long, .32 S&W, .357 Mag., .38 Short Colt, .38 Long Colt, .38 Spl., .45 Long Colt, .454 Casull); *Mr. Quigley Photography:* 170; *Montana Rifle Company:* 35 (M1999); *O.F. Mossberg & Sons:* 191 (SA-20), 198 (500 Center Mass Laser & Tactical Tri-Rail, 510 Mini All-Purpose 20-Gauge, Special Purpose 20-Gauge, SA-20 Tactical); *JO2 Charles Neff, USN:* 75 (Navy SEAL); *Nemo Arms:* 106 (Omen Match 2.0); *Nikon Sport Optics:* 37 (Monarch BDC 2.5–10x42); *Luke Nilsson:* 65; *Nosler:* 98 (Varmageddon .223), 106 (Varmageddon AR); *Noveske:* 111 (Shooting Team Rifle); *Para Ordnance:* 140 (Para Expert); *Perazzi:* 186 (MX 12 Gauge); *Dean Powell:* 155; *Primary Weapons Systems:* 106 (MK107 Diablo), back cover (MK107 Diablo); *Proof Research:* 02, 16 (Tac II); *Erik Rank:* 39; *Travis Rathbone:* Credits, *Remington Arms:* 16 (MSR), 33 (Model 750 & 7600), 35 (M700), 58 (Model 700 Ultimate Muzzleloader), 186 (Model 1100 Competition Synthetic & Sporting Series), 191 (11-87 Sportsman Series, Versa Max Waterfowl Mossy Oak Duck Blind), 198 (Model 870 Express Tactical Magpul); *Sako Finland:* 35 (Sako 85); *Savage Arms Company:* 35 (M12); *J. Scott Photography:* Shotgun intro (shooter); *Seekins Precision:* 111 (SPR03G); *Sig Sauer:* 16 (SSG 3000), 18; *Dusan Smetana:* 146; *Smith & Wesson:* 123 (M&P Series, Shield), 144 (Model 500, Model 627, Model 629, Model 642, Pro Series Model 640); *John Snow:* 100; *Vincent Soyez:* Rifles intro (shooter), 10, 64; *Springfield Armory:* 123 (XD(m)); *Stag Arms LLC:* 109 (Model 7 Hunter 6.8 SPC), 111 (Model 3G); *Steyr Mannlicher US:* 62 (Scout), 118 (AUG); *Sturm, Ruger, & Co.:* 33 (No.1 Sporter), 35 (American), 62 (Gunsite Scout); 123 (SR1911, Mk III) 140 (SR1911), 144 (GP100, Single Six Convertible, SP101 .22, Super Blackhawk, Vaquero), 163 (GP100), 186 (Red Label); *Will Styer:* 178; *Suarez International:* 119; *Yamil Sued:* Contents (shooter), The Challenge of 3-Gun, Rifles intro (splash page), 12, 18–19, 22, 28, 31, 43–46, AR intro (AR), 83–84, 92, 103, 106 (Alexander Arms G6.5 Grendel GDMR), 107–108, Handgun intro, 124, 127–130, 135, 152, 156–157, 187, 199, 202–203, About the Authors (shooter), back cover (shotshells); *Superstock:* 115; *Surefire:* 204; *Swarovski Optik:* 37 (Z6I 1–6x24 EE); *Tactical Solutions LLC:* 89; *Taurus USA:* (85VTA); *Thompson/Center Arms:* 33 (Encore Pro Hunter Predator); *Traditions Firearms:* 58 (Vortek); *United States Army Heritage and Education Center:* 75 (Viet Nam soldier); *Vortex Optics:* 37 (Viper PST 4–16x50 FFP); *Weatherby:* 35 (Vanguard Series 2), 191 (SA-08 28 Gauge Deluxe, SA-08 Synthetic), 194 (SA-459 TR), 198 (PA-459 TR, SA-459 TR); *Nathaniel Welch:* Title spread, Backmatter (rifles spread); *Westley, Richards, & Co.:* 36 (Model 98 Takedown); *Wikimedia Commons:* A Brief History of Firearms (M1 Garand, Mauser M98, precision guided firearm, Steyr AUG, wheellock pistol), 97, 114 (Konflikty.pl), 117, 121 (Chinese gun, percussion pistol, Colt revolver, Adams revolver, S&W Model 29), 174 (James Cooper, John Browning, Sylvester Roper); *Wikipedia:* A Brief History of Firearms (Colt revolver), 121 (flintlock, Glock 17), 174 (boxlock action, shotgun); *Jeff Wilson:* Front cover photo, 182; *Winchester Repeating Arms:* 186 (Super X3 Field Compact & Sporting w/ Adjustable Comb), 191 (Super X3 Waterfowl Hunter, SXP 12 Gauge 3" Field Compact), 198 (SXP Extreme Defender & Ultimate Marine Defender); *Windham Weaponry:* 106 (Varmint Exterminator); *Windigo Images / Mitch Kezar:* 52, 55, 57; *Lucas Zarebinski:* 190, closing image, back cover (shotshells); *Carl Zeiss Sports Optics:* 37 (Conquest HD 5–25x50)

ILLUSTRATIONS COURTESY OF: *Conor Buckley:* Front cover icons, 7, 8, 32, 60, 70, 112, 159, 177, 181, 207, back cover (revolver); *Hayden Foell:* 59, 72, 116; *Liberum Donum:* 15, 17, 20, 21, 38, 42, 66, 68, 78–81, 83, 85, 86, 94, 125, 126, 131–133, 137, 150, 151, 153, 161, 162, 166, 183–185, 195, 196, back cover (prone position, suppressor);

Samuel A. Minick: 77, *Shutterstock:* 1, 74, 120, 173, 190; *Stephanie Tang:* Chapter Icons; *Lauren Towner:* 76, 87, 93, 104, 122, 143, 168, 197

weldon**owen**

President, CEO Terry Newell
VP, Publisher Roger Shaw
Director of Finance Philip Paulick
Associate Publisher Mariah Bear
Project Editor Ian Cannon
Creative Director Kelly Booth
Art Director William Mack
Designer Stephanie Tang
Illustration Coordinator Conor Buckley
Production Director Chris Hemesath
Associate Production Director Michelle Duggan
Senior Production Designer Rachel Lopez Metzger

Weldon Owen would also like to thank Jan Hughes,
Katharine Moore, and Bill Schuch for editorial and
production assistance and Kevin Broccoli for the index.

Library of Congress Control Number
on file with the publisher
ISBN 978-1-68188-653-4
10 9 8 7 6 5 4 3 2
2024 2023 2022
Printed in China

OUTDOORLIFE

Executive Vice President Eric Zinczenko
Publisher Gregory D. Gatto
Editorial Director Anthony Licata
Editor-in-Chief Andrew McKean
Executive Editor John Taranto
Managing Editor Jean McKenna
Senior Deputy Editor John B. Snow
Deputy Editor Gerry Bethge
Assistant Managing Editor Margaret M. Nussey
Assistant Editor Natalie Krebs
Senior Administrative Assistant Maribel Martin
Design Director Sean Johnston
Deputy Art Director Pete Sucheski
Senior Associate Art Director Russ Smith
Associate Art Director James A. Walsh
Photography Director John Toolan
Photo Editor Justin Appenzeller
Production Manager Judith Weber
Digital Director Nate Matthews
Online Content Editor Alex Robinson
Online Producer Kurt Schulitz

2 Park Avenue
New York, NY 10016
www.outdoorlife.com